BOOZE, BRAWLS AND BAWDS

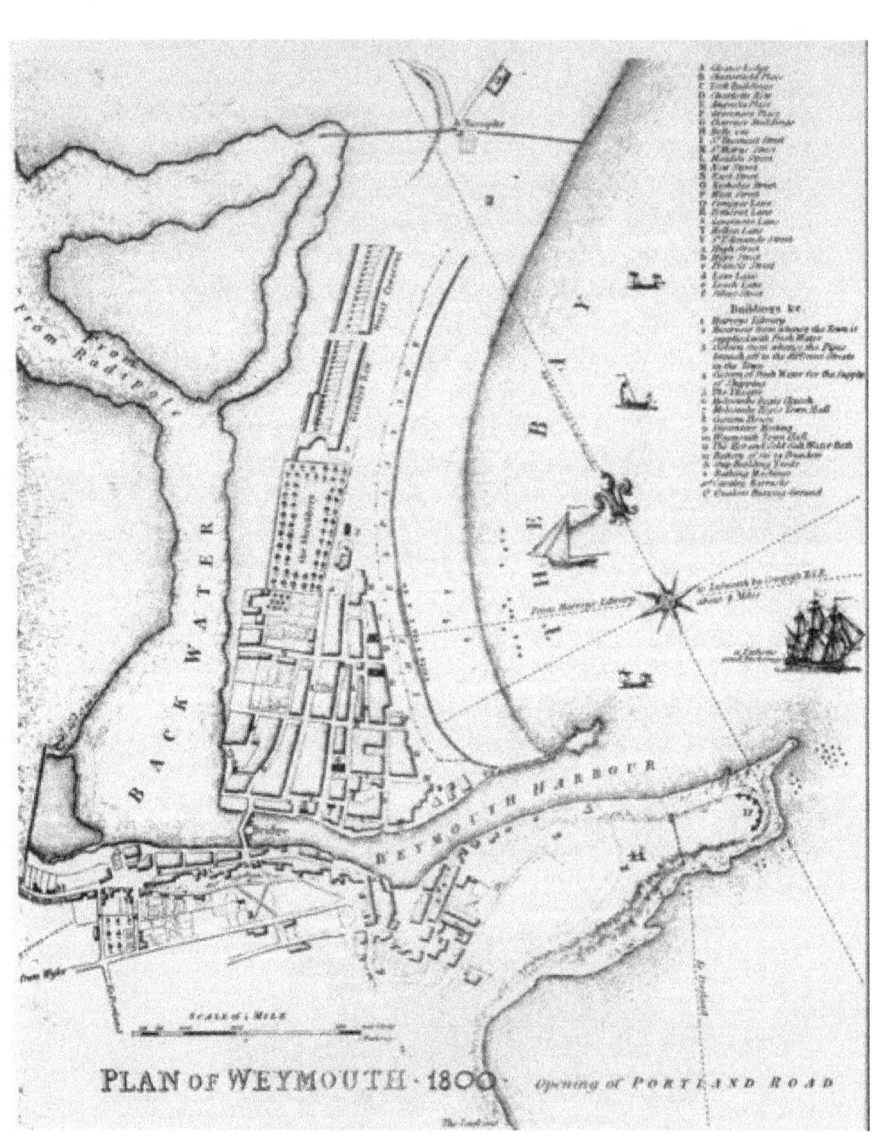

BOOZE, BRAWLS and BAWDS

A Social History of Weymouth Inns
ca. 1700 – 1939

MICK DAVIS

THE HOBNOB PRESS

First published in the United Kingdom in 2025
by The Hobnob Press,
8 Lock Warehouse, Severn Road, Gloucester GL1 2GA
www.hobnobpress.co.uk

© Mick Davis 2025

The Author hereby asserts his moral rights to be identified as the Author of the Work.

All rights reserved. No part of this publication may be reproduced, stored in a retrieval system, or transmitted in any form or by any means, electronic, mechanical, photocopying, recording or otherwise, without the prior permission of the publisher and copyright holder.

British Library Cataloguing in Publication Data
A catalogue record for this book is available from the British Library

ISBN 978-1-914407-97-0

Typeset in Adobe Garamond Pro, 11/14 pt
Typesetting and origination by John Chandler

CONTENTS

Acknowledgements
Introduction

Albert Hotel, King Street, Melcombe Regis	1-3
Albion Inn, Commercial Road, Melcombe Regis	6-9
Albion Inn, Franchise Street, Weymouth	9-11
Albion Inn, St Thomas Street, Melcombe Regis	4-6
Anchor Beer House, St Mary Street, Melcombe Regis	12-15
Antelope Inn, St Mary Street, Melcombe Regis	15-17
Baltic Inn, Park Street, Melcombe Regis	17-19
Bear Hotel, St Mary Street, Melcombe Regis	20-23
Belvedere Inn, High West Street, Weymouth	23-25
Bird in Hand, St Nicholas Street, Melcombe Regis	25-28
Black Dog, St Mary Street, Melcombe Regis	28-33
Boot Inn, High Street, Weymouth	34-38
Bridge Inn, St Thomas Street, Melcombe Regis	38-40
Bridport Arms, *see* Duke of Edinburgh.	
Brig Inn, High Street, Weymouth	40-42
British Queen, *see* The Forester's Arms.	
Brownlow Tavern, Ranelagh Road, Melcombe Regis 42-44	
Burdon Hotel Tap, Victoria Street, Melcombe Regis	46-48
Burdon Hotel, Victoria Terrace, Melcombe Regis	44-46
Butchers Arms, West Street, Melcombe Regis	48-49
Cambridge Arms, St Mary Street, Melcombe Regis	49-52
Canteen *see* The Nothe.	
Castle Inn, Horsford Street, Weymouth	51-53
Chapelhay Tavern, Franchise Street, Weymouth	53-55
Chelmsford House, Hardwick Street, Melcombe Regis	55-56
Clifton Hotel, Queen Street, Melcombe Regis	56-59
Coal Hole, South Parade, Quay, Melcombe Regis	59-60
Cooper's Arms, Maiden Street, Melcombe Regis	60-63

Cornopean Inn, St Leonard's Road, Weymouth	63-64
Cove Inn, Cove Row, Weymouth	64-66
Cross Keys, *see* Jersey Tavern.	
Crown Hotel, St Thomas Street, Melcombe Regis	66-71
Crown Tap, *see* Bird in Hand.	
Cutter Inn, St Alban's Street, Melcombe Regis	71-74
Dolphin Inn, Park Street, Melcombe Regis	74-76
Duke of Albany, Park Street, Melcombe Regis	76-78
Duke of Cornwall, St Edmund Street, Melcombe Regis	78-82
Duke of Cumberland, *see* Duke of Cornwall.	
Duke of Edinburgh, St Thomas Street, Melcombe Regis	82-82
Eagle Tavern, Lower Bond Street, Melcombe Regis	84-86
Edward Hotel, *see* Marine Hotel.	
Finns *see* Prince Albert.	
Fisherman's Arms, High Street, Weymouth	87-90
Forester's Arms, Great George Street, Melcombe Regis	90-91
Forester's Retreat, St Thomas Street, Melcombe Regis	91-92
Fountain Hotel, King Street, Melcombe Regis	93-96
Fox, St Nicholas Street, Melcombe Regis	96-99
Freemason's Arms, High Street, Weymouth	99-102
Friendship Inn, Park Street, Weymouth	102-103
Gardener's Arms, *see* The Castle Inn.	
General Gordon, Franchise Street, Weymouth	103-105
George Inn, Custom House Quay, Melcombe Regis	105-108
Globe Inn, East Street, Melcombe Regis	108-111
Gloucester Hotel, Gloucester Row, Melcombe Regis	111-115
Golden Eagle, *see* Eagle Tavern Melcombe Regis.	
Golden Lion, St Edmund Street, Melcombe Regis	115-118
Greyhound, St Nicholas Street, Melcombe Regis	119-120
Half Moon, King Street, Melcombe Regis	120-122
High West Street Tavern, High Street West, Weymouth	123-124
Hope Tavern, Hope Street, Weymouth	124-126
Jersey Hotel, St Thomas Street, Melcombe Regis	126-128
Jolly Sailor, *see* Friendship Inn.	
King's Arms, Trinity Road, Weymouth	129-130
King's Head Hotel, Maiden Street, Melcombe Regis	133-136
King's Head Inn, East Street, Melcombe Regis	130-133
Lamb & Flag, Lower Bond Street, Melcombe Regis	136-138
London Hotel, Upper Bond Street, Melcombe Regis	138-141

Luce's Hotel, *see* Victoria Hotel Melcombe Regis:
Mabb's Hotel, *see* Albion, Franchise Street, Weymouth:
Marine Hotel, Bank Buildings, Esplanade, Melcombe Regis — 141-144
Market House Inn, St Edmund Street, Melcombe Regis — 144-146
Market House Tavern, Maiden Street, Melcombe Regis — 146-148
Mason's Arms, St Alban's Row, Melcombe Regis — 148-150
Military Arms, Barrack Lane, Weymouth — 150-152
Milton Arms, St Alban's Row, Melcombe Regis — 152-155
Nag's Head, New Street, Melcombe Regis — 155-156
Nelson Inn, North Quay, Weymouth — 156-158
Netherbury Arms, *see* Belvedere.
New Arrival Inn, *see* Duke of Albany.
New Bridge Hotel, Little George Street, Melcombe Regis — 158-160
New Cooper's Arms, Maiden Street, Melcombe Regis — 160-161
New Inn, High Street, Weymouth — 162-163
New Music Hall Tavern, St Nicholas Street, Melcombe Regis — 163-164
New Rooms Inn, Cove Row, Weymouth — 164-166
Nothe Inn, Barrack Lane, Weymouth — 166-169
Old Bridge Inn, *see* Bridge Inn.
Old Rooms Inn, Cove Row, Weymouth — 169-173
Park Estate Inn, Lennox Street, Melcombe Regis — 173-175
Park Hotel, Grange Road, Melcombe Regis — 175-177
Phoenix Hotel, Great George Street, Melcombe Regis — 177-178
Plume of Feathers, Little George Street, Melcombe Regis — 178-180
Porters' Arms, St Mary Street, Melcombe Regis — 180-183
Portland Arms, Maiden Street, Melcombe Regis — 183-185
Portland Railway Hotel, Commercial Road, Melcombe Regis — 186-187
Prince Albert, Great Little George Street, Melcombe Regis — 187-189
Prince of Wales Tavern, Park Street Melcombe Regis — 189-190
Queen's Hotel, King Street, Melcombe Regis — 190-193
Railway Dock Hotel, Rodwell Avenue, Weymouth — 193-195
Railway Hotel, Park Street, Melcombe Regis — 195-196
Railway Tavern, Commercial Road, Melcombe Regis — 196-198
Ranelagh Hotel, Ranelagh Road, Melcombe Regis — 198-200
Red Lion, Hope Street, Weymouth — 200-201
Red White & Blue, *see* Yacht Inn.
Rest & Welcome, Boot Lane, Weymouth — 201-202
Rising Sun Inn, Prospect Place, Chapelhay, Weymouth — 202-203
Rodwell Hotel, Rodwell Road, Weymouth — 204-205

Rose & Crown, Crescent Street, Melcombe Regis	205-206
Royal Canteen, *see* Nothe Tavern.	
Royal Engineer, Inn Prospect Place, Chapelhay, Weymouth	206-208
Royal Hotel, Gloucester Row, Esplanade, Melcombe Regis	208-212
Royal Hotel Tap, Gloucester Row Mews, Melcombe Regis	212-213
Royal Oak, East Street, Melcombe Regis	214-216
Sailor's Home Inn, Chapelhay Street, Weymouth	216-218
Sailor's Return, St Nicholas Street, Melcombe Regis	218-220
Ship Inn, Maiden Street, Melcombe Regis	220-222
Shipwright's Arms, Salem Place, Weymouth	222-224
Somerset Hotel, King Street, Melcombe Regis	224-225
Stacie's Hotel, *see* Royal Hotel.	
Stag Inn, Lennox Street, Melcombe Regis	225-227
Star & Garter Hotel, Crescent Street, Melcombe Regis	227-228
Star Inn, Hartford Terrace, Park Street, Melcombe Regis	228-230
Steam Packet Inn, Custom House Quay, Melcombe Regis	230-232
Sun Inn, King Street, Melcombe Regis	232-234
Swan Inn, St Thomas Street, Melcombe Regis	234-235
Terminus, Queen Street, Melcombe Regis	236-238
Three Tuns, Maiden Street, Melcombe Regis	238-240
Tivoli Gardens Inn, Franchise Street, Weymouth	240-242
Turk's Head, East Street, Melcombe Regis	242-244
Union Arms Inn, St Leonard's Road, Weymouth	244-247
Victoria Hotel, Augusta Place, Esplanade, Melcombe Regis	247-250
Victoria Tap, New Street, Melcombe Regis	251-252
Waterloo Stores, William Street, Melcombe Regis	252-254
Welcome Home, St Nicholas Street, Melcombe Regis	254-255
Wellington Arms, St Alban Street, Melcombe Regis	255-257
Weymouth Arms, High Street, Weymouth	257-259
White Hart, High Street, Weymouth	259-260
White Hart Tavern, Lower Bond Street, Melcombe Regis	260-262
White Horse Hotel, St Mary Street, Melcombe Regis	262-264
Yacht Inn, Governor's Lane, Melcombe Regis	264-266
Books	266
Useful Contacts	267
Index of People, Places and Pubs	268

ACKNOWLEDGEMENTS

Firstly, all credit must be given to my wife Lorraine who has provided invaluable support and assistance through long train journeys, photographic sessions, pub lunches and a diet of crab sandwiches and cider without complaint. I am extremely grateful to Richard Samways and Maureen Attwooll at Weymouth Museum who took the trouble to seek out relevant documents and read through the text for me even though their museum is packed up in boxes and stored in a warehouse. The research and voluminous files of historian Margaret Morris have also proved invaluable. Thanks, are also due to David Parsons and to Lyn Mackenzie of the Black Dog for their help in the initial stages and Dr Pat Smith for her help. I am very grateful to John and Louise at Hobnob Press for their guidance and early enthusiasm for the project.

I have taken as many recent photographs as I can myself but some have been downloaded from the internet, newspapers, and books and it has not always proved possible to give credit where it is due. If anybody feels that their graphics have been misused please let me know and I'll try to put it to rights. This is perhaps the place to apologise for the quality of the graphics, there are very few old photographs of the local pubs and the ones that do exist are often in very poor condition often being photographs of photographs, but poor as they are they are often all that remains and worth including for that reason.

Mick Davis September 2025

INTRODUCTION

This is not a pub guide. You will not find recommendations of where to go for lunch or insightful comments on craft beers. Nor is it an academic study, that would take a huge amount of time and many volumes. It is primarily an exercise in local and social history as seen through the activities of the many hostelries dotted throughout the town of Weymouth past and present. It is aimed to be a rather gossipy and entertaining slice of largely Victorian life through a delightful seaside town and hopefully it is as entertaining as it is factual. It is sad for many of my generation to see beer and skittles replaced by lager and football but tastes and customs change and it seems a worthwhile project to record what is known of the old inns before they go.

Historically, there have probably been pubs or their equivalent in the town for as long as there have been people, most lost to history and surviving in name only, any of these would be worthy of research in their own right and a fair few are mentioned in Maureen Attwooll's excellent two volume *Bumper Book of Weymouth* but for now their story remains unexplored, labelled with 'location unknown' and would provide fertile ground for future research. In the early days many of the town's trades would have been concerned with food and drink not only for the land-based population but for the victualling of the many ships that passed through and the soldiers stationed at the barracks.

Ale of various strengths was particularly important in an age with little or no tea or coffee, wine and spirits were expensive and heavily taxed with water in many cases undrinkable making the humble beer house even more important as a place of sustenance as well as entertainment. For present purposes lines have to be drawn and I have concentrated on the town beginning with its Georgian period as the health resort of George III and his social circle and continuing on through the town's rediscovery which ushered in its golden age, the Victorian era. The introduction of the Beer Act of 1830 enabled anyone to brew and sell beer on payment of a license costing two guineas. The result was the opening of hundreds of new beerhouses, public houses and breweries throughout the country. It was hoped that by increasing the sale of beer, and thus lowering its price, the population might be weaned off stronger alcoholic drinks such as gin.

Research has been assisted immensely by the ten-year census returns which began in 1841 providing a huge amount of genealogical information and a great expansion in local newspapers following the abolition of stamp duty in 1855. Local and national news became accessible to working people and those that survive contain a treasure trove of material detailing the lives of publicans and their customers throughout the town in far more detail than would be reported today. The opening of the railway station in 1857 was another huge influence making the seaside easily available and cheap fares led to people being able to afford a trip to the coast with the accompanying need for accommodation and refreshment. Bank holidays started in 1871 giving more leisure time, photography was in the early stages of its popularity bringing with it the picture postcard recording many of the town's buildings and streetscapes for the first time, street maps too experienced their finest hour with Ordnance Survey charts from the 1860s naming buildings and features with details not attempted since that era and regular pleasure trips on steamers to the Channel Islands followed on after the opening of the railway. All of these factors and more, led to large numbers of visitors who needed somewhere to stay or just to sit and have a drink increasing the number of pubs needed to fulfil the demand. In the run up to the Second World War which brought so much destruction to so many historic streets interesting reportage of the ups and downs of pub life slowly declined to be replaced by sports fixtures making it a fitting place to stop, the census returns as well give progressively less information after the First World War making research difficult.

As with many towns during this period local authorities seem to have taken great delight in renumbering and renaming streets as though they had placed all the house numbers in a Scrabble bag, shaken it up and then handed them out randomly. This being the case house numbers have been used sparingly as they can become counter-productive and confusing. They are given only when they can be followed through with some certainty making the precise location of some buildings quite challenging; 1872 was a particularly bad year.

The area of interest had to be defined geographically as well has historically and this has been done by ending at the A354 Rodwell Road on the Weymouth side and Cassiobury Road on the Melcombe Regis side, the sea of course accounts for a more obvious boundary. This area covers the historic heart of Weymouth and Melcombe Regis with over 120 pubs which is quite enough for one book and all of which should be accessible on foot from the railway station. Portland is of course deserving of a book of its own.

As has been said a large percentage of the information contained here comes from census returns and local newspapers and in case it is thought that this paints a very dismal picture of town life in the 19th century please remember that it is only the bad things that come to court or appear in the press and that the English country inn has provided much joy and company to many communities for centuries making its present decline very sad.

Inevitably, this study is incomplete, some things will be missed out, misdescribed or just plain wrong and for that I apologise but I have made start on a subject that fascinates me having produced a similar study on my town of Frome some years ago. Any comments or criticisms can be sent to the publishers and will eventually find their way to me.

THE HISTORIC INNS OF WEYMOUTH

THE ALBERT HOTEL
corner of King Street and Park Street, Melcombe Regis

Named after Prince Albert, Queen Victoria's consort, the first mention comes from the census of 1851 when it was described as situated at the 'northern end of Park Street' on the corner of King Street. The landlord then was George Hewlett from Essex aged 27, inn keeper, and his wife Elizabeth 37. They had moved on by 1853 when John Jefferies applied for a licence to sell spirits based on its proximity to the railway terminus – despite the fact that the latter was not to be finished until 1857. His argument was that the licence would bring in many more customers flocking to the resort once the station was completed. Referring to the house across the road, the Half Moon, Jefferies stated that a 'Full Moon' would be required to service the increased demand but despite his attempt at humour his application was refused. Two years later he tried again on the rather strange grounds that the windows of his house would overlook the railway when the station was completed and would be a very convenient spot for intending passengers to see the arrival of the trains. A similar application had just been refused for the Dolphin a little further down the road and he attempted to justify his application over that one by describing it as a, 'little pokey place' whereas the Albert was large and commodious.

In opposition it was stated that during the previous year Jefferies had been fined 40/- for selling beer on a Sunday during divine service and with regard to arrivals at the railway, it was perhaps not wise to 'reckon one's chickens until they have hatched as that period had not yet arrived'. A testimonial in favour of the licence being granted was produced supposedly containing the names of local worthies but upon examination it was discovered that one was living with his father at the Belvedere Inn and would hardly be in need of the Albert

The Albert Hotel renamed the Queen's 1862

for a drink and another was merely, 'a bird of passage' from Lyme who would soon be off somewhere else and will not be in great need of the Albert and yet another had to go and away with the militia very soon. Setting these aside the police reports alone were quite sufficient grounds for disqualification and he was advised to reapply when the railway was in operation. The licence was granted the following year.

In 1860 Jefferies was up before the magistrates when at 12.40 am Superintendent Lidbury found several persons drinking at the bar after the legally enforceable closing time. In his defence he said that the south-western trains did not reach Weymouth until after 12.00 and those found drinking in his establishment were new arrivals all connected to the railway. He cited an old legal case to show that he had done nothing wrong, which the magistrate's clerk found to be totally irrelevant and he was fined 5/-.

Trouble of a different sort broke out later in the year when the body of William Wright, a man of 'independent means' from Jersey, was found at the hotel with his throat cut and a bag containing a pistol and two bottles of poison was discovered in his room, a verdict of suicide due to temporary insanity was brought in by the coroner.

John Jefferies was also Brother Jefferies of the Ancient Order of Foresters, King George III Lodge no. 3425 and during May of 1861 he put on a dinner for 300 brethren and friends to great acclaim and the following April, presumably in an attempt to drum up some trade he placed an advert in the local paper, informing the gentlemen of the Dorchester Yeomanry Cavalry that he had accommodation for eight horses and masters at his hotel and that an 'ordinary' or sitting of a simple communal meal would be provided each day during their stay.

That September there was a rather unpleasant altercation with PC Powell resulting in Jefferies being charged once more with having his house open for the sale of beer on a Sunday morning, it then being about 12:30 pm, a very common offence at the time. The constable observed a number of men at the door and saw landlady Mary Jefferies supply them with bread, cheese and beer but noted that no money changed hands and they did not enter the premises. The men were engineers, stokers and guards from the railway who had arrived late on a goods train but who did not reside in Weymouth and who had had no refreshment for several hours. Mrs Jefferies believed that she could do as she liked with her own goods but the magistrates took a contrary view and a fine of 20/-plus costs was imposed. The situation was made much worse by Mr Jefferies who, it was claimed, was drunk and used foul and abusive language to the constable resulting in another 5/- fine with costs. In August of 1862 Jefferies had his licence suspended because of the 'irregular' way in which he ran his house and by October his tenure was over and owners Eldridge, Mason and Co advertised for a new tenant in the local papers. The Albert was to be no more but reopened soon after as the Queen's Hotel, the subject of a following entry.

THE ALBION INN
St Thomas Street, Melcombe Regis

THE ST THOMAS Street Albion, one of three of that name in the town, opened its doors in 1879 as the Albion Dining & Supper Rooms run by James Whittle and his wife Hester, formerly suppliers of provisions; 'a good English dinner' could be had for 9d and hot joints were served daily from 12.00 till 2.00.

In August Whittle announced that he intended to apply for a licence to sell beer, cider, perry, wine and other intoxicating liquors, but this may have been unsuccessful as in the census for 1881 he is still shown as a refreshment house keeper now aged 35. Nothing more is heard of the place until 1891 when it is listed as licensed refreshment rooms run by Fredrick Smedley and his wife Matilda. In 1895 they were hauled up before the bench for refusing to admit a constable who had come looking for after-hours drinkers. In their defence they claimed that they had been there for seven years without any trouble and had great respect for the law, so much so that Frederick kept a book on licensing laws which contained the clause

The Albion Inn 2017

'under the present laws no constable has the right to enter the private room of a landlord without warrant' which he believed gave him the right to refuse anybody after hours including the police. A public bar of course was not a private room but this mistaken notion received the sympathy of the bench and he got away with just paying their costs. Former owner James Whittle died in 1893 and by 1901 the premises were being run by James Warland, 38, a licensed victualler, and his wife Annie, described in the census as a pub before reverting once more to 'refreshment and dining rooms' in 1911. In the summer of 1915 the following ad appeared in the local paper,

OPENING OF THE ALBION DINING AND SUPPER ROOMS,
36, St. Thomas-street, Weymouth.

JAMES WHITTLE,

IN returning his best and sincere thanks to his numerous Friends and Patrons in Weymouth, Dorchester, Portland, and the County generally for the kind support which he has received in the Ham, Beef, and Confectionery Business for the last seven years, most respectfully begs to announce that he has OPENED the above

SUPPER AND DINING ROOMS,

And he hopes with superior accommodation, prompt attention, with Cleanliness and strictly Moderate Charges, to still merit a continuance of their kind Patronage which has hitherto been so liberally bestowed upon him.

Where to get a Good English Dinner for 9d.—The Albion Dining Rooms.
Hot Joints Daily from Twelve till Two o'clock.
Grilled Chops, Grilled Steaks, Hot Sausages and Mashed Potatoes, at the Albion Luncheon and Supper Rooms.
Tea, Coffee, and Refreshments—Coffee, 1d. ; Tea, Cocoa, or Chocolate, 2d. per Cup.
Private Rooms.   Tea Parties Accommodated.
All Charges are strictly Moderate.
A large Stock of Home-Cured Hams, ready dressed for Picnic Parties, &c.
Roast Chicken, superior Ox Tongues, ready dressed, 2s. 6d. and 3s. each.
Chicken, Ham and Tongue, and German Sausages.
Saveloys.
Spiced Beef and Brawn.
Sausage Rolls, &c.
Beef and Pork Sausages Fresh Twice Daily by Steam Power.
Specially-appointed Agent for Evans' celebrated Melton Mowbray Pies.   Fresh Delivery Daily.
A large and choice Assortment of the Purest Confectionery.

Take Note—
THE ALBION DINING AND SUPPER ROOMS,
36, St. Thomas-street, Weymouth
(Opposite Mr. G. Russell's Outfitting Establishment),
JAMES WHITTLE, Proprietor.
Steam Sausage Manufactory : Lower St. Alban-street.

Sausages by Steam Power 1879

For Disposal, Licensed Restaurant in the best position of naval seaside town doing good public bar trade. Furnished, everything as a genuine concern. The management of the place being too much for the health of the proprietress. £325 including furnishings. No Agents.

Perhaps the description implying that it was hard work had put off potential buyers as it was still up for sale a year later this time boasting a beer and wine licence but still citing ill-health as the reason for the sale. It was back on its feet by 1921 under the care of Charles Harding, innkeeper, and his wife Edith, who had presumably bought it from the harassed lady owner. In June 1932 Thomas White the licensee who had been there for seven years was arrested for, 'committing a serious offence' and despite his denials he was found guilty of gross indecency and sentenced to 12 months' imprisonment. Despite its prominent position, this little house never seemed to be sure of its purpose, ranging from coffee house to supper rooms to refreshment house, dining rooms and inn. It was listed as a building of historic interest in 1974 and in recent years as it has been The Cider House, Cider Press, Orange Bar, Babylon Bar, The Bar on the Corner, and finally the Batida Bar. In February of 2025 an application was made to convert the Albion into two flats.

The Albion in the 1970s

THE ALBION INN
Commercial Road & Bath Street, Melcombe Regis

THIS INN OPERATED from the corner of Commercial Road and Bath Street, but nothing has been found before details of the funeral procession of its landlord William Dunn Taylor in August of 1859 at only 21 years of age. It seems probable that the property was owned by the family, a George Taylor in particular. William had been a member of the Ancient Order of Foresters 'Plume of Feathers Court' no.3152, which had been founded at the Albion. Local branches were termed 'courts', rather than 'lodges' like other friendly societies because they were named after the ancient law courts of the royal forests. The order was formed in 1834, when over 300 branches of the Royal Foresters Society (established in the 18th century) created the new Ancient Order of Foresters and it was they that organised William's funeral. His widow Margaret, shopkeeper and beer retailer, made a successful application for a spirits licence that same year.

In 1860 the landlord was Joseph Blackburn, a 56-year-old engine driver and inn keeper from Durham with his wife Mary. He was possibly just a temporary stand-in as shortly after the census of 1861 in May another landlord named William Taylor was summoned by his wife for assaulting her, but as she did not appear to give evidence the case was dismissed. By February of 1864 things became much worse when Taylor flew into a drunken rage attacking both his wife and mother-in-law, who lived next door, threatening to kill them both. He smashed six panes of glass in her house, jammed her against the door and once evicted, tried to smash his way back in through the back door, saying that his mother-in-law will be dead before the night was over. He was arrested and taken to court but when giving her evidence Margaret senior collapsed and had to be carried out of court. His wife said in evidence that he had threatened her so many times that she had been compelled to leave the house on several occasions believing her life to be in danger when he was in his drunken fits. This time he had grabbed her by the throat and bashed her head against a partition. He had been drinking rum and milk all day. Despite this awful catalogue of violent events they said that they did not want him punished, just bound over to keep the peace. In his defence Taylor said that the situation arose over a dispute about money. He normally gave his wife money but on this occasion, she had accused him of holding some back, thrusting her hands in his pocket to look for more, which so aggravated him that he had got drunk and did not know what he did afterwards, but he did not think that he had assaulted his wife. He gave evidence to say that he had been a teetotaller for some time past and once this affair was over he would sign the pledge once more despite keeping a public house. Unimpressed by this defence and

The Albion Inn 2024

describing the events as a most cowardly assault on two women, he was sent to jail for one month's hard labour and bound over to keep the peace for six months himself in the sum of £20 and two sureties of £10 each. Maybe there was something good in him when sober, as a short time later he dived into the Backwater to rescue a small child who had fallen in, and upon finding two sets of soldier's clothing also in the Backwater he was at pains to make sure that they were returned to the proper authorities. The clothing had belonged to two deserters who had disappeared.

Shortly before this the Foresters had decided to hold their meetings at the local literary institution as the Albion was 'too small for their increasing numbers', but as the pub was beset with drunkenness and violence it can be assumed that this was not the only reason for the move. A few months later Margaret took one of her neighbours to court for using insulting language towards her in the street but the magistrates persuaded them both to play nicely in future and the case was dismissed.

A landlord makes a pub for good or ill and this was a situation which could not be allowed to continue, and the Taylors were out by the middle of 1865. It seems that things settled down as there are no reports of any further disturbances. By the 1871 census the pub was being run by 50-year-old bricklayer and innkeeper John Clark and his wife Elizabeth – it was not uncommon for the wife to run the pub while the husband continued in his previous trade bringing in the extra money. William Gillingham was next, and apart from a rap on the knuckles – a 10/- fine plus costs with no endorsement on his licence over a misunderstanding about closing time on a Sunday – the pub was run well without incident. Outside of the pub Gillingham was hauled up for shooting two partridges on somebody else's land without a licence. In one priceless exchange an eye-witness describing the field deposed that it was square and had four corners, but he could not say if it had any more than that.

Gillingham, full of outrage was convicted and fined £1 for killing the partridges, £1 for shooting without a licence, 5/- for trespass and £1/7/- – £3/12/- in total or 70 days imprisonment. He said he would not pay. Unfortunately the report ends there but presumably he saw sense and paid his fine. He continued at the pub but was summoned again for keeping his house open on a Sunday when three men were seen drinking at the bar at 2.55. This time he pleaded guilty, laying all the blame on his clock which he claimed had stopped at 2.40. He was fined £1 including costs with Police Superintendent Vickery saying that the house was generally well conducted.

Next up was William Symonds aged 35 from Crewkerne in Somerset with wife Alice who took over in January 1881. At a licensing hearing in

1910 the premises were described as having a kitchen with a one bar parlour on the ground floor, one good size double sitting room, one bedroom and three bedrooms on the second floor. There was also a public bar and a jug and bottle. The turnover was about £41 per month and Mr Symonds was a very respectable landlord who had been there for 29 years. Landlords Devenish said that there was absolutely nothing known against the house which was thoroughly well conducted and that Mr Symonds was a very good tenant in every way, business was increasing and the licence was granted. William Symonds died at the Albion in 1913 at the age of 77 and the licence was taken up by his widow Alice, followed with remarkable continuity by her daughter Annie into the early 1950s. The pub closed for good in 1977.

THE ALBION INN / THE BEEHIVE
Franchise Street, Weymouth

The Albion Inn Chapelhay

THE INDICATIONS ARE that the Chapelhay Albion had its origins in the marriage of William Russell Mabb, a mariner, to his Scottish sweetheart Elizabeth McDougall in 1850 and that they acquired the house at 1 Salem Place on the corner of Franchise Street and Queen's Place sometime during 1851, before which it had been occupied by a tinsmith. They called it Mabb's Hotel and over the next ten years produced four children, before Elizabeth was widowed in 1860 when William was killed at sea and she had to struggle on alone. Remarkably, the magistrates had granted William a highly prized and hard to obtain spirits licence in August of 1859 despite objections that he had signed his name Wm. rather than William.

By the census of 1861 Elizabeth is shown as a licensed victualler aged 32 and by May of 1863 the pub had been renamed the Beehive in a newspaper report. This tells the story of a drunken soldier who banged on the door after the pub closed saying that he was the police and demanding entry or he would break every window in the place. He managed to smash two and crack another before Mrs Mabb bravely rushed out to confront him. They had a struggle during which he struck her. The police arrived and he proceeded to fight with them. In court the prisoner claimed that he was not capable of looking after himself and was fined £5 which he could not pay and was sent to Dorchester Gaol for one month.

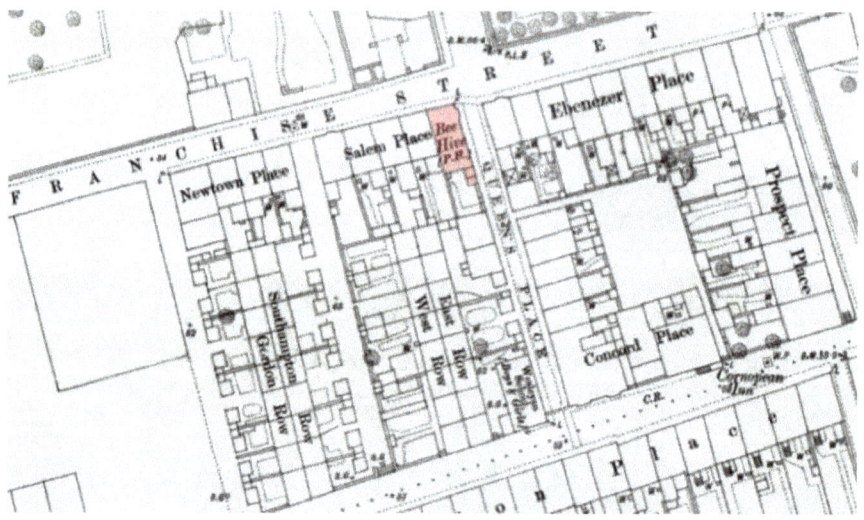

The Beehive on the O/S map of 1864

Mrs Mabb was replaced by George Pope a 43-year-old cooper and innkeeper who changed the pub's name from the Beehive to the Albion, which meant that the town now had three pubs with the same name although widely spaced. Pope advertised his new situation in the local papers, but he was gone within a couple of years and the Albion Tavern was put up for rent by the owners the brewing firm, Eldridge Pope and Co. of Dorchester.

From 1865 the local papers record a new arrival almost next door at 4–5 Salem Place, the Shipwright's Arms. Landlord Thomas Vallance applied for a spirits licence in 1865 and again the following year, both of which were refused.

George Pope, Cooper & Innkeeper

The Denning family from the Milton Arms were in charge by 1879 with Charles operating as a greengrocer and fruiterer, a business which he ran from the pub. He died in 1906 and the licence passed to his widow Sophia who fell foul of the 1902 Licensing Act which had changed the onus of proof from the prosecution to the defence whereby licence holders had to satisfy the bench that they had taken all reasonable steps to prevent drunkenness on the premises. In October of 1906 two women began drinking at the pub between 7.00 and 8.00 am, 'most probably on empty stomachs due to the early hour' and were, 'supplied with a larger quantity of drink than was discreet'. The ladies became incapably drunk and were arrested in a helpless condition outside the house.

There was some sympathy from the bench as the house had been conducted very satisfactorily by her husband for a great many years and the case was dismissed with a warning. Sophia continued to run the Albion until her death in 1924.

In September 1940 the licence passed from Walter Northam to Francis Sterling, not that he had much time to enjoy it as the whole Chapelhay area was devastated by German bombing in December and the Albion along with many others was no more.

THE ANCHOR BEER HOUSE
St Mary Street, Melcombe Regis

The Anchor was first mentioned in the 1851 census when it was kept by 42-year-old Harriet Parker, beer house keeper, and widow of Edward Parker, a currier or leather worker from Hampshire; she was aided by her son George. Within a few years, in December 1854, landlord Robert Carter, son in law to Harriet and husband to her daughter Sophia, had moved from the Porters' Arms to the Anchor and it wasn't long before he was accused of keeping a disorderly house. A crowd of soldiers, sailors, navvies and prostitutes had assembled in front of the house and created a disturbance. Superintendent Morris entered the premises and saw 19 prostitutes, 15 navvies and 30 soldiers and sailors making a great noise in two of the rooms. Giving evidence in defence of the landlord Corporal John Mackay of the 58th Regiment, who was in the house at the time, stated that he had called for the assistance of the police in removing a female who was endeavouring to prevent him from enlisting a recruit, and a crowd had collected whilst he was engaged with the woman, but there was no noise during the time he was there, between five until eight in the evening. The mayor informed Carter that he had rendered himself liable to a penalty of £5 but in consideration of this being his first offence they would mitigate the fine to 40/- There was another summons against Carter which was

Prostitutes in a Victorian beer house

not proceeded with in the hope that his conviction of the present charge would act as a caution. It didn't, as we shall see.

In September of 1858 Carter applied for a licence to sell spirits on the grounds that he had been there for several years and had a very roomy house which could take many guests who often requested spirits. An application the previous year had been disallowed on the grounds that his house was badly run and a 'harbour for prostitutes'. He was advised to wait another 12 months which, given the constant complaints against the way his house was being conducted, seems a lot more encouraging than the advice given to many other applicants.

Despite his previous conviction and many complaints, it seems that Mr Carter was not one to respond to criticism. In January 1860 Superintendent Lidbury had him summoned before the magistrates once more for, 'permitting persons of notoriously bad character to assemble and meet together in his house'. His defence responded immediately arguing that the word, 'knowingly' was omitted from the summons and that it was invalid, but the case was allowed to proceed and Lidbury gave his evidence. He and a constable had visited the house shortly before 8 o'clock one evening to find six prostitutes in company with some marines and sailors. When Mrs Carter saw him she told her servant to turn the girls out. He returned at 10 pm and finding five prostitutes standing in the bar, said to Mrs Carter, 'You are aware that these are prostitutes', to which she replied, 'I suppose I had better bar my door up'. The prosecution asked about the general character of the house, a question strongly objected to on the grounds that it would not have been allowed in any court in the country. The question was allowed and Lidbury replied that prostitutes were in the habit of using the house and he had seen as many as 20 at one time. The magistrate asked if any of the women occupied rooms there but Lidbury did not think this was the case and Mrs Carter said that she did not let beds to anyone. It was argued that the women were standing and waiting to be served with a glass of beer which was apparently allowable under the act but sitting down was most definitely not. It was denied that there was a sentry at the door to warn of approaching constables and Mrs Carter said that due to the constant police surveillance she had lost a lot of her customers.

Inexplicably, the bench decided to dismiss the summons once more despite agreeing that the house was the worst in the town 'next to Coopers'. It was asked on behalf of the publicans of the area if characters known to be common prostitutes could be served with a glass of beer, as the general impression was that they had no right to refuse them. The answer was that there could not be much impropriety in such a case, but it was a different matter when six characters known to be prostitutes frequented a house. It was a very different thing from having a glass of beer now and then. They evidently go there to meet men and the consequences are a great increase in the divorce rate and immorality. The bench would be glad if Mrs Carter would pledge herself not to harbour these characters in future. It was not uncommon during the Victorian period for women of dubious character to be found frequenting public houses, though their presence was often met with unease by both proprietors and patrons. While the law did not expressly forbid prostitutes from entering such establishments, publicans were under increasing pressure from licensing magistrates to maintain a respectable house. A woman may be served a glass of beer at the bar – that much was grudgingly tolerated – but should she take a seat within the premises, particularly in the company of men, it was seen as a sure sign that she intended to linger and possibly solicit custom. In such cases, it was not the woman who faced censure, but the landlord, whose licence might be endangered for 'harbouring improper persons.' As one magistrate in the town observed, 'It is one thing to take a drink; it is another to sit and trade upon it.' Thus, many publicans found themselves in the unenviable position of serving but not seating, tolerating but not condoning. This fine line between commerce and condemnation shaped much of the uneasy relationship between the Victorian innkeeper and the more shadowy elements of society. By the census of 1861 the couple were still running the pub but all was far from well. Within a month of their marriage in 1850 Sophia claimed that Carter had started beating her regularly, cut her with a knife and thrown her down the stairs. In mid-December 1861 he 'took on' the Antelope pub nearby and started to move furniture out but then returned still threatening to kill her. The final straw came in early December 1863 when he took up with Maria Bascombe, who had been barmaid at the pub for 15 months before leaving in 1860, and they were now living together. Sophia started divorce proceedings later in the month on the grounds of cruelty and adultery which were finalised in November 1864. Finally free she moved to the New Inn on North Quay which was run by her brother George Parker, and when he died in 1868 she took over the licence; her story continues under that entry.

Carter moved to the Antelope and the new landlord was George Rashleigh, who in 1867 was summoned for having in his possession one quart cup, two pint cups and a half pint cup of deficient measure. The quart was deficient of half a gill and the other cups quarter of a gill each. The defendant claimed that he had bought the cups off Mr Warry the inspector of weights and measures who, he said, was not fit for his business. Rashleigh's wife entered the witness box and asked Warry if he would swear that she did not purchase the cups off him. He said that she had not, even though he sometimes supplied cups for different parties and gets a trifle for his trouble; he would be an idiot to supply cups under measure. Rashleigh was fined 10/- including costs. and it seems that the Anchor closed soon after.

THE ANTELOPE INN
St Mary Street, Melcombe Regis

Mentions of an Antelope Inn on St Mary Street go back to the 1760s when it was run by a J. Newman. James Sansom and his wife Sarah are recorded as being there from around 1823 until his death in October 1829 in his 51st year after a long illness. His obituary describes 'The relative duties of husband, father, and neighbour, he discharged most faithfully. He held the offices of town constable ten years and Sergeant at Mace 15 years with the diligence and fidelity which ensured him the approbation of his superiors'. His widow Sarah took over and was still there at the age of 60 in the census of 1841 after which builder John Parsons from Chapelhay assumes control. The inn appears to have been small and well run in these early days as there are no reports in the press of any misbehaviour or wrongdoing.

In November of 1862 landlord Robert Carter who had taken over in 1861 and whose career can be traced via the Porters' Arms and the Anchor was taken to court by his gas supplier over an unpaid bill of £9/3/10d. This

The site of the Antelope Inn 2024

was to cover the previous seven months, a quantity that he said was impossible for him to have consumed. When at the Anchor he claimed that he had one more burner than at the Antelope and his bill averaged only £12 for a whole year. In what must be considered a rather strange judgement the magistrate asked if the supplier could prove that the gas had been delivered to which he replied that it was metered and that the meter had been tested and proved correct. Magistrate Ayling judged this to be insufficient proof and dismissed the claim. In a bizarre twist sometime later in June of 1864 Carter's successor at the Anchor, George Rashleigh was charged with damaging the gas meter so that it did not register fully the amount used, by soldering a wire inside the box. This meter was installed after Carter left but perhaps the previous one had been treated in a similar way, giving rise to Carter's confusion as to why he had to pay so much in his new house! In December of 1862 Robert Carter 'licensed victualler, dealer in potatoes and herrings' of 48 St Mary Street was declared bankrupt. Presumably he could not continue running the pub but he could still occupy the property if his lease was still valid, and indications are that he continued there as a greengrocer. Sophia Carter obtained a divorce from him in December 1863, the details of which are discussed in the Anchor entry. Now aged 38 Carter's career had consisted of mismanaging three public houses, bankruptcy and finally a divorce; what became of him after that is still to be discovered.

On annual licensing day during August of 1865 the magistrates refused to renew the licence requested by the incoming landlord, a Mr Cox, due to objections from the police, who stated in evidence that the house was being kept in a disgraceful manner and they had received a petition 'most numerously signed' to that effect. Superintendent Lidbury gave the house a bad name as it had had eight or nine different landlords in the past two years, and every change had been for the worst. The house was managed in an appalling way and a petition signed by the respectable people of the neighbourhood had also been sent to him. For the owners, Mr Howard the solicitor, said that the house was

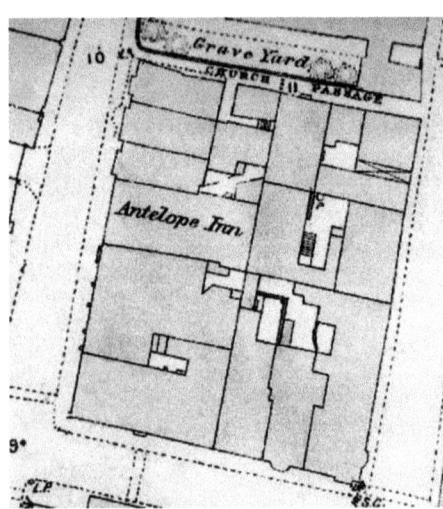

The Antelope Inn from the 1864 O/S Map

about to change hands but this was not enough to convince the bench and the Antelope closed shortly after.

THE BALTIC INN
4/5 West Parade now Park Street, Melcombe Regis

The Site of the Former Baltic in 2024

THE BALTIC ONCE stood on the east side of Park Street then known as West Parade almost opposite Wooperton Street. Its unusual name derives from the cargoes of timber brought into the port from that region and used for shipbuilding. The inn was close to the timber yards and ponds along the Backwater shore where timber was unloaded into the river from ships arriving from Canada, New Brunswick, Prussia or Russia. The timber was then formed into rafts and moved to one of the ponds for storage and seasoning. Posts driven down into the riverbeds held the floating timber in place, but by 1914 the arrival of pre-cut timber and steel construction meant that few of the ponds remained in use.

The first recorded landlord was journeyman carpenter George Seaman aged 39, first shown as living in George Street on the census return of 1841 with wife Sarah and two children. He is not recorded as a publican at this date and ten years later he is still following his trade as a carpenter, but is now listed as a beer retailer in West Parade, although no pub is named.

In August of 1854 his son Charles Seaman was up in court charged with assaulting John Clapp, a regular at the pub who was asked to pay off his slate but, when told that it amounted to 10/-, refused to accept it saying, 'If I owe ten shillings, I must have drunk 25 quarts of beer in a fortnight! – 'And so you have', replied Seaman 'and if you don't walk out of the house I will kick you out,' upon which the complainant left. The two men both worked for a builder and Seaman is alleged to have attacked Clapp in the yard soon after, and so badly that he was unable to work for three days. The defence made him out to be a very heavy drinker, which he did not deny, but rejected the accusation that he was off work through drink and that the medical man who had attended him had told him as much. As there were no witnesses to either event the bench decided to rely on the medical certificate – but that was not in court and so the case was adjourned, but the outcome has not been traced.

By the 1861 census George was aged 60, and gave his profession as innkeeper, now presumably retired from the building trade. Son Charles has done well and at the age of 26 was still living at the pub but now a builder employing 30 men. The family moved on and the pub name appears in print for the first time in April 1866 with a new landlord, Joseph Bridgeman, who was summoned for refusing to admit the police into his house on a Sunday morning to search for furtive drinkers. The bench admonished him and he was ordered to pay costs. There was more trouble in 1873 when an argument over who should pay for a quart of beer coupled with a reluctance to leave at closing time resulted in the landlord Benjamin Darley and his wife being seriously assaulted and two months later the brewery advertised the pub to let with immediate possession.

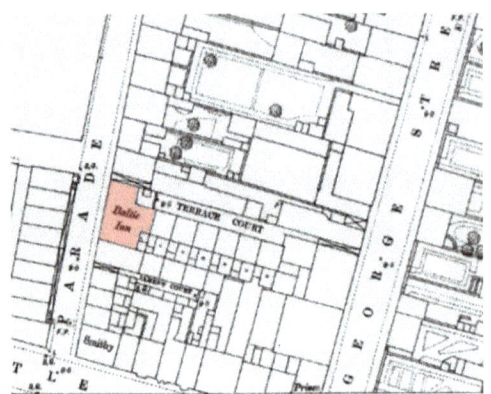

The Baltic Inn from the 1864 O/S Map

Questions were asked in October 1882 when landlord Henry Curtis was taken to court but, instead of being tried in the usual way, the hearing was held in a separate room with the press being excluded. Despite enquiries no explanation was forthcoming as to the charge, which prompted letters to the local papers. Whatever it was it could not have been too serious as upon pleading guilty to the unknown offence he was fined £1 plus costs of 2/6d.

"SEQUAH" IN WEYMOUTH

A great sensation which is likely to increase during the next week or two has been created in Weymouth by the visit of a gentleman who has adopted the above North American Indian name and professes to relieve and cure liver complaints, rheumatism and numerous ailments by means of, 'Sequah's Prairie Flower and 'Sequah's Oil'. He first appeared on Friday when a young fish hawker who had been confined to bed for five weeks with rheumatism and was quite crippled submitted himself to the treatment. After being rubbed with the oil for a quarter of an hour or so a wonderful change was affected in his limbs and he could walk with ease. In the evening the immense hall was crowded and Mr Curtis landlord of the Baltic Inn who is well known as having been a great sufferer for many years from rheumatism and who wasn't able to stand when brought into the hall experienced such a relief that he was able to walk with comparative ease.

There was a bizarre report in the local paper for January 1890 - Sequah's real name was Ernest Osmonde.

At the licensing hearing during March of 1903 the Baltic was listed amongst seven public houses to be closed. It was described as rented for £18 per year with no stabling but had six bedrooms for public use with a jug and bottle entrance used mainly as a ticket office. There were three entrances, with a back entrance on to George Street. It was occupied by Albert and Ada Lawrence who had no family and had moved in during November 1894, having paid £50/18/6d entrance. The house had been well conducted without a complaint against it. There was a slate club where women came to pay subscriptions to save together for a particular purpose such as Christmas. Lawrence had paid over £300 to improve the premises, mainly on furniture. He stated that if the magistrates took his licence away he should lose £350. He estimated his monthly takings to be around £50 which showed that his house was necessary. If he lost his licence there was no agreement with the brewers to pay him anything in the way of compensation and if he sold his furniture and utensils he would not get a quarter of their value, as some of the fittings would be unsaleable except to an incoming tenant.

Earnest appeals were made on behalf of the Baltic and the other six, the Shipwrights Arms, the Steam Packet Inn, the Three Tuns, the Yacht, the Porters' Arms and the Royal Hotel Tap, that they should be allowed to trade until their licences expired in October. The bench agreed that they would grant this concession with the exception of the Yacht Inn and the Royal Hotel Tap, which would be closed forthwith.

THE BEAR HOTEL
St Mary Street through to St Thomas Street, Melcombe Regis

IN ITS TIME the Bear was one of the largest and most important inns in the town. The earliest known mention takes us back to the 1600s when there are references to an inn called the Bear described as 'newly built'. Town minutes from 1681 refer to a pub of the same name when Matt Sweetman accused the mayor Thomas Hide of being 'a rogue', but there are no further details. In 1700 there is another mention when the town constables came across some important people gambling and arguing at the pub, landlord Richard Arnold showed them in but no action seems to have been taken despite the law having been broken. In July 1705 Daniel Defoe, later to become author of *Robinson Crusoe*, but then a government spy was involved with Arnold in uncovering some letters containing seditious remarks about Queen Anne, but again nothing seems to have come of the matter. Richard Arnold 'innholder' of Melcombe Regis made his will in 1726 leaving his property to his wife Margaret.

In the 1730s an Edward Beard is shown as possessing a brandy and beer licence for his house in St Mary Street, the owner is named as Susanna Bond. In

The Bear Hotel St Mary Street entrance 1905

June of 1780 the house is advertised for sale or rent and described as 'Situated in the Marketplace with a large yard, coach houses and stabling for 40 horses, a good brewhouse and cellars with good water. Any part of the stock or goods may be taken at a fair appraisement, as the present tenant who has lived on it for 22 years is going to leave off the public business. Enquire of William Tizard at Weymouth'. In June of 1786 two poulterers, Charles Hemmings of Bath and Jonathan Wildey of Cheltenham, decided to establish a, 'caravan between Bath, Gloucester and Cheltenham as a clean, safe and expeditious conveyance of passengers and parcels'. After Dorchester the waggons went to the 'Bear Inn at Weymouth' before making the return trip 'all delivered with care, punctuality and reasonable prices'. Not only that but Mr Hemmings was able to furnish the 'nobility and gentry of Bath with pigeons at more reasonable prices than have ever been supplied in the Bath market'.

In 1807 the Bear is put up for auction once more at the nearby King's Head. The 'extensive, commodious, and old-established inn' was to be sold with the remainder of the term of 99 years, situated partly in Thomas Street and partly in St Mary Street, comprising six good sitting rooms, 15 good bed chambers with closets, garrets, a kitchen, bar, brewhouse, cellars, and other convenient offices together with stabling for 70 horses and a yard that will contain 100 market horses'.

Two years later it was reported that on 20 May 'a serious fire broke out at the Bear Inn St Thomas Street Weymouth. As soon as the alarm was given, the drums of the 2nd Somerset beat to arms, and Colonel Cooper with his officers and men immediately repaired to the spot. Such were their exertions and activity, that, in the course of two hours they put a stop to a calamity that threatened the destruction of several valuable and extensive premises'.

The Land Tax Returns for 1813 show the property as owned by William Bower and occupied by James Hatton, a relationship which continued until around 1824 with Bower still having ownership in 1827 along with a number of other pubs in the town. A notice in the local paper during 1825 complains that somebody swapped an old nag for a light bay mare pony in the stables – possibly by mistake, the notice continues, optimistically, but offers a reward of three guineas for the detention of the offender. A short time later a man calling himself Anderson went one better and hired a gig and horse from the landlord John Caddee for 24 hours; he was traced as far as Bridport but still missing a week later. All reasonable expenses would be paid once the man was in one of his majesty's jails.

Other than a man from Guernsey committing suicide by throwing himself out of the attic window things were quite quiet until 20 October 1829 when William Bower died. He owned the Fordington Brewery in Dorchester and was a local landowner, former mayor, alderman and Lieutenant-Colonel of the Dorset volunteers. His death on 27 March 1829 at the age of 83 caused the auction of 16 public houses. Apart from the brewery buildings themselves the Weymouth sale comprised two lots: Lot 1 The Bear, The Old Rooms Tavern, The Boot, The White Horse, The Globe, The Three Tuns, The White Hart, The Duke of Cumberland, and The Royal Oak. Part of this lot was freehold and the reminder leasehold upon lives and at 'very trifling quit-rents'. A further lot consisted of the Crown Hotel, described as commanding a first rate trade divided into several suites of rooms with 25 beds, an assembly or ballroom, capricious cellarage, an attached Tap, stabling, lock up coach houses, and all the usual appurtenances which are generally attached to a tavern of a first rate description. This is in the occupation of Mrs Cass at an annual rent of 100 guineas. There were a number of other properties in and around Dorchester and Portland. The auction was described as crowded to excess and unusually spirited. The Weymouth pubs along with the Dorchester brewery buildings sold for a total of £10,800, well over £1m today, with the Crown Hotel held on three lives aged 10, 40 and 55 realising £1,404.

Getting back to the Bear, John Caundle was landlord by 1837 until moving to the Ship on the Quay in around 1844. In the census of 1841 he is aged 40 with his wife Elizabeth aged 25 who was to cause a lot of problems as we shall see in the Ship entry. They were followed by William Stote who was there with his family, having moved up from the Victoria Tap by the census of 1851. He soon became noted for his catering skills and initiated alterations and repairs to the premises shortly after taking charge. In early 1854 Stote became the leading light behind the formation of the Weymouth Cricket Club and, despite scores with the bat of 9 and 7 in two innings at a Melcombe Regis v Weymouth match in August, he did take 11 wickets for Melcombe Regis to win by 88 runs. The formation of a club was well overdue and meetings of the tradesmen of the town were held at the pub to form a committee and get the ball rolling, as it were. A little later he hosted a magnificent dinner to celebrate the marriage of brewer and pub freeholder Henry Devenish, which included all employees and their wives, who sat down to roast beef and plum pudding with an ample quantity of beer. Stote was apparently noted for his 'comic wit and song' and once celebrated the Queen's birthday with a 21lb turkey.

The increasing popularity of the house brought its own problems. In December the police summoned various tradesmen and others for leaving their carts blocking the road outside. Mr Stote said that these were the property of his customers and as his yard was very small if somebody wanted to move theirs from the back, all the others had to be pulled out into the street which occupied a considerable time. Mr Stote said that he would pay all the costs of the defendants himself rather than have them, 'imposed upon', a phrase which annoyed the magistrates as they were only doing their duty. The matter was resolved with fines totalling 9/- which Mr Stote paid immediately. Stote left the pub in May of 1857 in favour of a Mr Hatchard who dropped dead while having supper with his family in May of 1859 leaving his widow Mary to carry on, which she did for a few years. The Bear was mentioned at a council meeting in 1867 when the problem of housing cattle before their visit to the slaughterhouse was discussed. Most of the slaughterhouses lay on the Weymouth side but the Melcombe Regis site took the Alderney cattle, which were normally herded into yards attached to the Fox or the Bear. Records show that Devenish carried out repairs, including a repair to the roof and the whitening of three bedroom ceilings in 1895.

In a sad tale from 1907 James Williams stationed at Portland was besotted with Annie Holloway, a barmaid of 'decidedly prepossessing appearance', despite her being engaged to another. He kept pestering her and one day stole the engagement ring from her finger which he refused to give back despite several promises to do so. She eventually found it in a pawnshop and paid 10/- for its return. Williams threatened to shoot her if she didn't stop ignoring him and began writing letters, and so she went to the police. At his trial he made the ridiculous claim that she had given him the ring but the magistrates accepted that he had stolen it. Not wanting to send him to prison because of his clean army record he was fined 50/- and the barmaid's money refunded.

Well-known local architects Crickmay & Son prepared plans for some alterations and rebuilding in 1915 particularly to the stables and hotel tap at the rear. In 1926 the Bear was marked for closure when Devenish & Co. had the licence transferred to their new hotel at Rodwell, the Old Castle, and sold the extensive site. The Bear closed in 1929. Its last landlord, Thomas Russell, moved to the Sun but died shortly after and the site was redeveloped by Montague Burton the tailors before being split into two shops in 1967.

THE BELVEDERE INN
High West Street, Weymouth

THE BELVEDERE FIRST opened as the Netherbury Arms sometime before the census of 1851 when 39-year-old Jeremiah Hibbs occupied the premises. Although the pub is not named at this time it must have been

The Belvedere Inn 2017

trading, as in 1856 he was listed as a 'grocer, baker and publican'. A spirits licence for the 'Netherby Arms' was granted in 1859 and renewed the following year, indicating that he had some track record and respectability. Hibbs was an interesting character and seems to have started out as a joiner before adopting his usual occupation as a baker. In 1860 he was described as 'late overseer of the poor' and was summoned before the magistrates for not paying an arrears of the poor rate amounting to £1/8/1d. The overseers were responsible for the administration of poor relief such as apportioning money, food and clothing. Two were appointed every Easter, the position was unpaid and supervised by the magistrates. According to Hibbs the dispute arose because an original rating for his property of £30 had been increased to £40 when the position was taken over by a political rival; despite his protests he was ordered to pay what he owed. Hibbs was gone within the year in favour of George Bazzell, baker, grocer and inn keeper, of whom little has been discovered except that by 1871 he had become a milkman and moved out to Wyke. The inn is quite clearly marked on the Ordnance Survey map of 1864 as the Netherbury Arms, and the first mention of its appearance as the Belvedere Inn occurs in that same year when an inquest was held into the accidental death of a young lad on a farm at Chickerell.

In 1868 the Belvedere was kept by Joseph Curtis whose licence was objected to by the police because he kept it open at irregular hours. The magistrate remarked that landlords sometimes stood in a kind of fear of men who had been drinking elsewhere and got into a noisy state, so that they would often draw them a little beer to get rid of them, just as a person might give a sturdy beggar a coin. Giving a man beer was strange way to get rid of someone intent upon causing trouble, remarked those opposing the application.

Some years later in 1874 the licence had passed to the Binns family and landlord John stood on the election committee for Charles Hambro and Sir Frederick Johnstone of the Conservative Party during the general election of that year which was won by the Liberal candidate Henry Edwards. Johnstone was a prominent businessman and property owner which included the Belvedere.

Landlady Elizabeth Binns was involved in an unpleasant case of child cruelty the following year when she was asked to help in the case of a neighbour's child. Six-year-old Caroline Ford was beaten with a heavy belt by her father who described his daughter as very naughty, and the press pitched in with her being, 'rather simple and heavy looking'. This is perhaps not surprising, as one of her father's allegations was that she would eat up all the provisions as soon as they were brought home, which on the last occasion was a half-pound of butter. Mrs Binns took her in and looked after her. Father Francis had tried to get the Union to take Caroline and his other children but they refused as it was thought that it was within his means to hire someone to look after them – which he had. A Mrs Ozzard used to take care of them, but, continues the report, 'she was sent to prison'. Ford was remanded to the higher court but unfortunately there is no record of the outcome. John Binns died in 1876 and the licence passed to his widow until 1879 when John Wells from Blandford and his wife Elizabeth took over. This family were there until 1909 when George Harry Russell from Sheffield, an elected member of the 'South Dorset Licence Holders Trade and Protection Association and Benevolent Fund', became landlord and ran the place until 1912. The Belvedere is still open today serving the locals with a variety of beers and good hospitality.

THE BIRD IN HAND/ CROWN TAP
St Nicholas Street, Melcombe Regis

Until the mid 1860s the Crown Tap was a small drinking establishment in St Nicholas Street attached to the rear of the Crown Hotel, where non-residents could obtain a drink without going through the main entrance of the hotel in St Thomas Street. Little early detail is known but they would have been in the same ownership but catering for a different class of person. The original Crown Inn on the St Thomas Street side was a going concern before 1765 when a Mrs Stanway held a property auction there. The first mention of the Tap by name as a separate establishment occurs in the census of 1851 when it was being run by Catherine Whetton a widow of 55 and licensed victualler. By 1854 it was home to John Jeanes and his wife Harriet, who according to the census return was deaf. During that year and in common with most licensed premises Jeanes was summoned for selling on a Sunday, after a woman was seen leaving the building with something under her apron which, upon examination, proved to be a jug containing a pint and a half of beer. As this was his first offence Jeanes was fined 5/- plus costs and warned against any recurrence. Putting forward what he thought was an excellent case for being granted a licence to sell spirits in 1864 he applied on the grounds that the old Methodist Congregational Chapel from 1804 was now disused and would shortly be converted into a theatre. This was refused but two years later his case was a lot stronger as the New Concert Hall

The Bird in Hand 2017

or Theatre Royal was now open with Captain Cozens running its theatrical performances. There was a large piece of land adjoining which was used for all sorts of amusements and to which large numbers of people resorted nightly. If the licence was granted, Devenish Brewery, the owners would improve the house which Jeanes had occupied for the past 12 years. Despite this convincing argument the bench adopted its default position and refused. It was when the main hotel was rebuilt that the Tap took on a life of its own and became the Bird in Hand.

John Jeanes gave up and moved to the New Inn over the river in 1870 but the licensing situation had not improved when the new landlady, Elizabeth Smith, reapplied in her husband's name while he was away. Until recently, she said, the house had been part of the Crown Hotel but when that was rebuilt in 1868 the licence was lost. Objections were that the house was very small but Mrs Smith said there were six bedrooms and four other rooms. She admitted that husband Joseph had been fined recently for keeping his house open on a Sunday. Superintendent Vickery said that he believed there was a need for the house to be licensed but did not believe that the present landlord or landlady were suitable as the premises were the haunt of prostitutes; and even a night or two ago a person complained of being robbed there, and the application was again refused. During May of 1876 owners Devenish advertised the house to let due to the illness of the tenant, the premises being described as 'a newly erected beerhouse'.

Things took a sad turn in the autumn of 1878 when a, 'heartless case of seduction and robbery' was heard at the Dorset Quarter Sessions. George Hargreaves, a soldier stationed at Portland, convinced Edith Cox a young serving girl of 19 that he was about to leave the army and wanted to marry her, which induced her to stay with him at the Bird in Hand where he seduced her and persuaded her to go home and collect all £11 of her life savings, upon receiving which he decamped. The poor maid was now penniless and homeless because her brother with whom she had been living and working for would not receive her into his house again. The chairman of the bench said that this was a brutal and heartless case, only £5/5/4d was found on Hargreaves when he was arrested and he received a sentence of two years imprisonment with hard labour.

In February 1884 the Bird was subject to a raid by an inspector looking for illegal weights and measures, during which many unstamped cups were taken away and landlord John Downing appeared in court along with nine others. In the end they were all dismissed with a caution and a more complete account is included in the Royal Oak entry.

The owners Devenish advertised the premises to let in 1894 and again in 1898, perhaps showing that it was not the most profitable of establishments. This probably had a lot to do with the Theatre Royal having closed in 1893 before being converted into a foundry.

By March 1907 William Charles Goodwin had held the pub for five years and the whole question of its continuance was discussed by the licensing magistrates, who enjoyed nothing more than being able to deny a spirits licence or close a pub down. As usual the police report began with measuring the distance between the Bird and nearby hostelries of which there were a large number in close proximity – a mere 49 paces to the Sailors Return for instance, which was a fully licensed house. Other matters were considered. The house was described as being old but in good repair, for which a rent of £10 per annum was paid. There were two bedrooms, one of them having three double beds available and two in the smaller room when the fleet was in, but the house could accommodate eight or nine men and provide them with meals. Considering the large number of sailors and visitors the incidence of drunkenness was extremely small, despite custom increasing greatly during the last four years. The matter of its continuance was referred to the quarter sessions and it was allowed to remain open. Sixteen years later in 1923 another attempt was made to close the pub along with five others by local temperance movements, fronted by the wife of a Baptist minister claiming that they were unnecessary. Landlord Goff, an ex-serviceman, had held the pub for 14 years and was now approaching 70 years of age. It had been described as one of the best conducted houses in the area and its closure would not reduce the amount of drinking, it was claimed, people would just squeeze into the remaining houses. The licence was renewed and continued until 1931 when the landlord was a Richard Joseph Sutton and the Bird finally closed

THE BLACK DOG
St Mary Street, Melcombe Regis

It seems generally accepted that the oldest pub still surviving in Melcombe Regis is the Black Dog, formally known as the Dove. Its precise date is unknown but there is a date of 1621 above a ground floor window and the building is considered to have its origins even earlier, being traced back to a lease of land from 1603. During the construction of the Marks & Spencer's building at the rear of the pub in 1970 a gabled end facing on to New Street was revealed and appears in the photograph below. This interesting feature is

The Black Dog in 2017

now completely obscured, but the pub can still be entered from a passageway in New Street.

Such an ancient and popular pub is bound to attract more than its fair share of myths and legends, and it is quite possible that some of them are true. These are some of the more interesting and outrageous claims.

In February 1645 during the civil war, Royalist sympathisers in the town plotted to overthrow the Parliamentary garrison commanded by Colonel William Sydenham, and it is said that 500 people died in one night during what became known as the Siege of Melcombe Regis. A report in the *Southern Times* for 5 March 1910 tells the following tale.

> There is a well-known public passage which leads into New Street on the south side of the pawnbrokers shop to St Mary Street. This passage was known until recently as Blockhouse Lane because it led to a square stone-built Elizabethan fort facing the bay known as the 'Blockhouse'. On the site of the pawnbrokers shop during the Civil War was what is described in an old record as a 'house of entertainment', meaning of course a public house, which was kept by a man called John Chiles. The house was described as being for the most part full of people day and night. A few days after the siege a middle-aged trader with flaxen hair and a yellow beard named William Courtney from Taunton Dene

The 17c gable end facing New Street uncovered in 1970 (Weymouth Museum)

in Somerset, was lodging at the pub and sleeping on the floor. He had with him £288 in gold and £12 in silver. A fabulous sum. At about midnight Chiles talked his wife into agreeing to murder him for the money and he was battered over the head with a hammer by the landlord as he slept. Margaret, his wife, gave evidence against her husband who she claimed had said that there was no better time to kill someone, as it was a time of war and one more corpse would not be noticed. They stripped the body and, in the darkness, carried it out to a nearby jetty and threw it into the sea. Sometime later Margaret Chiles confessed to their crime which Chiles denied. Some reports say that the body was not recovered, and conflicting evidence was given to show that Courtney was still alive; the wife's statement caused great puzzlement to the justices who spent four months considering the case before Chiles was committed to the Dorset Assizes for trial.

Unfortunately, that is where the story ends as there seems to be no surviving record of the outcome.

Another story is that Daniel Defoe met former desert island castaway Andrew Selkirk in the pub, thus forming the basis for his story, *Robinson Crusoe*, first published in 1719. The problems with this tale are that it was never confirmed that the two ever met, and if they did it was probably at the Star Inn or Llandoger Trow in Bristol. However, it is true that Selkirk died from a tropical disease off the coast of West Africa on HMS *Weymouth* which may have given rise to the legend.

It is claimed that the change of name from Dove to Black Dog came about when Weymouth won the contract to trade with Britain's first colonies of Newfoundland and Labrador, claimed by Sir Humphrey Gilbert in 1583. The story goes that the landlord purchased one of the first Newfoundland dogs from the master of a ship, and so many people came to see this unusual dog that the landlord renamed the pub in its honour. It is always a pity to spoil a good story but it is not thought that there were any black Labrador dogs there during that time and genome research suggests that they are descended from the Irish Water Spaniel, taken over from Europe only returning to England in the late 18th century, brought back on board ships carrying dried and salted cod. Fortunately, this fact does not mean that the lovely story of the Black Dog's name is necessarily wrong, just that it may have happened 200 years later than proposed. In fact, records show that the pub was still known as The Dove Alehouse in 1749 and that the name only changed between then and about 1800, consistent with the arrival of the first black St John's dogs from Newfoundland. A recent survey counted 14 pubs still open with the name Black Dog which is often associated with spectral or daemonic animals and not confined to pubs. And now from one shaggy dog story to another.

Another well known tale is that in 1758 a Richard Hawkins was whipped and beaten to death by members of a notorious gang of smugglers known as the Hawkhurst Gang, named after their base in Sussex. Those charged with the murder were John Mills, known as 'smoker' and John Reynolds; others managed to escape, at least one of them moving to France. The gang had smuggled in 12 bags of tea which they had hidden in a barn under some straw. When Mills came to pick up the contraband two bags were missing and it was decided that Hawkins, a farm labourer who was thrashing the corn, must have stolen them. The smugglers were a vicious breed of men who would not hesitate to commit murder should they think it necessary. They grabbed Hawkins and subjected him to a 'smugglers court'. Accused of the theft he was beaten and whipped in front of the inn fireplace until, at the point of death and in desperation, he named his father-in-law and brother-in-law as the culprits. Leaving Hawkins at the inn the smugglers posse went off to capture the two men, both named Cockrel. Returning to the inn with their prey they discovered that Hawkins had died. Taking fright at this they released the prisoners, having sworn them to secrecy and dumped Hawkins's body into a pond. There it lay for nine months until the facts of the events emerged and Mills and Reynolds were arrested and charged with murder. At their trial Mills was convicted and Reynolds acquitted. Mills was executed and his body hanged in chains.

Richard Hawkins beaten to death

A fascinating story and all perfectly true except that it had absolutely nothing to do with the Black Dog or Weymouth. The murder took place at the Dog and Partridge pub on Slindon Common, 100 miles away in Sussex and ten years previously, in 1748; it was all well recorded at the time. How and when the tale was moved to Weymouth is a mystery in itself, as is the reason for a painting of a contemporary depiction of the murder scene appearing on the wall of the Sailor's Return. Never let the truth get in the way of a good story, as they say.

During more recent times the land tax returns of 1802 show that the property was owned by John Arbuthnot Esq, one time Alderman, and mayor during 1798/99. His tenant was Thomas Mitchell, who died in around 1813 leaving his widow Jane to run the pub. This she did for about a year before marrying Job Sargeant, late of the 13th Regiment of the Light Dragoons, This was a cavalry regiment which fought in the Napoleonic wars, culminating in victory at Waterloo on 18 June 1815. They married on 12 October 1814, possibly he had just been discharged and retired. She died in 1818, upon which he married another Jane before dying himself in 1825. The inn passed to the Munden family and during 1833 the landlady called the constable when, 'several young men drinking and smoking' fell into a dispute concerning a young lady. They stripped to the waist determined to settle the affair by 'pugilistic arbitration', causing considerable uproar, during which it was alleged that Constable White was assaulted. In court enough of the company denied that such an assault had taken place and the jury brought in a verdict of not guilty.

From about 1835 Hubert Willis and family from Corfe Mullen were in control. Willis was born in 1787 and had run the Crown Inn at Winfrith Newburgh before coming to Weymouth. He appears in the census of 1841 with his first wife Jane and in 1851 with his second wife Elizabeth. The Black Dog was put up for auction in September 1850 along with much farmland, houses, shops and property, including the King's Arms, being part of the estate of the late Taver Penny of Boot Lane Weymouth. He was son of a former mayor and commander of the *Marlborough* at the Battle of Ushant, and the Willis family remained as tenants after the sale. Hubert died of heart failure in 1855 at the age of 68 and his widow Elizabeth took over until 1867, after which the pub is described as having been completely remodelled and refitted, with new landlord John Longman, whose family were licensees until 1894. The ancient inn passed without incident throughout most of the 19th century with long term landlords and nothing to trouble the press or the courts, indicating a well run and popular pub.

Things became a bit more exciting during July 1923 when the landlady Eva Victoria Dominy was accused of permitting eight children under the age of 14 to be on her licensed premises. She argued that they were in the passage leading from St Mary Street to the sea front, which was not covered by the licence, despite that area having shelves with glasses containing liquor. It seems that the outcome of this case went unreported so presumably it was not proceeded with. There was more trouble in store for the Dominy family when in July 1925 Vere suffered a serious assault as he was closing the pub. Two stokers from HMS *Revenge* objected to being asked to leave. One of them smashed a window and struck a very violent blow with a bottle to the right of his jaw fracturing the bone in three places, which he was told would result in a slight disfigurement. When the two men came to court in October charged with maliciously causing grievous bodily harm it was judged impossible to prove who had struck the blow and so the two were acquitted. Dominy died in 1930 at the age of 44. Eve remarried and ran the pub as Eve Richards throughout the war years until she retired in 1943. The Black Dog became part of the Greene King chain in 2017.

The Boot Inn 2017

THE BOOT INN
High (West) Street, Weymouth

THE BOOT IS undoubtedly the oldest surviving pub on the Weymouth side of the town and is thought to date from around 1600. Architecturally, it has been described as having 'hooded stone mullion windows which are late Tudor and being built on a slope, the road falls away to the level of the old boat ramp, one door is at lower level. The bare boarded floor carries on up into the main room, which opens out to the full width of the house. A waist high skirting board follows round the room and the black beams are certainly original.' How the pub got its name will always remain a mystery, one theory being that in Elizabethan times the River Wey was closer to the back of the building with a public slipway running down the side. The Melcombe Regis ferry operated from here and Boat Inn could have been corrupted to Boot Inn, but the name is not as unusual as might be thought and occurs throughout the country similarly without explanation. It was probably just an easily recognisable symbol in a largely illiterate age.

During the civil war battles were fought around the Boot and along the old High Street and many Royalist and Parliamentary soldiers lost their lives in these skirmishes. In 1645 Colonel William Sydenham and his Commonwealth troops formed a defensive line at the top of High Street near the Boot and the Roundheads set up cannon on the raised pavement by the Town Hall. It is said that they pounded King Charles's men, leading to a major massacre of 500 Royalists outside the pub and along the quayside.

One story in the town records states that on 3 July 1728, 'Thomas Parker a customs officer went to the Boot ale house to see if he could seize any 'runned' or smuggled goods, whereupon Lawrence Soaley and William Farr seized Officer Parker, called him a rogue, shook him up and threw him to the ground in such a way that he hurt his head.' In the 1790s the pub was owned by Simon Jenkins who in his will of 1793 left to his 'two daughters Mary Newton and Elizabeth Fowler, to be equally divided between them, the Boot public house.' He also owned a number of properties in Love Lane. The name R. Fowler is mentioned as being at the Boot in a directory of 1816, quite possibly the same family.

In 1829 the Boot was auctioned as part of a collection of local pubs and property owned by the Fordington Brewery, which was part of the estate of the late William Bower containing a large portfolio of public houses throughout the county, (see The Bear entry for more details.)

In 1840 the inn was taken over by George Gulliver and his wife Ann, both aged 35 and seemingly childless. It was the beginning of a reign that was to last for the next 30 years, and their long occupancy was not entirely uneventful. He was of course summoned for selling beer out of hours on a Sunday, as was every other pub in town over the years. In 1863 PC Mitchell was passing the pub at 4 pm on a Sunday afternoon when he saw six men in the kitchen with pints of beer in front of them. Gulliver said that he thought this was okay as the ban on sales was only applicable during divine service, which had finished at Trinity Church. At this time the permitted trading hours on a Sunday were 12.30–2.30 and 6.00–10.00. He rather spoilt this attempt at naivety by saying that he had run the same house for 25 years and had never been 'pulled up afore'. Gulliver was fined 1/-plus costs and treated to a free copy of a paper explaining the governing of the closing of houses of refreshment on Sundays. Mrs Gulliver was taken to court in November 1865 charged with unlawfully detaining three lanterns in lieu of payment for lodgings, which the owner had insisted was paid but she had forgotten. The matter was referred to the County Court.

Opposite the Boot stands the ancient town hall building in the undercroft of which Gulliver kept chickens. One morning in 1865 he noticed that three were missing and the following day, three more; he valued the six at 10/- It emerged that these had been stolen by three local lads who had taken them a few hundred yards down the road to the Chapelhay Tavern and sold them to Robert Parkman the landlord. A lad named Symes was arrested and named his two companions who tried to deny all knowledge. 'You me and Bretty done it,' he insisted, 'Your mother was there when we shared the money! 'Did anyone see the three of us together?' Asked one conspirator, and apparently a young lad had and said that one of them had something underneath his slops which he insisted was his handkerchief but was more the size of a loaf, claimed the witness. Each was committed for two months' hard labour with a warning that if they came before the court again they would be sent to a higher court with the probability of being sent into penal servitude for many years.

Gulliver was in trouble himself not long after. He accepted the pledge of a watch worth £5/16/- for 26/- from a soldier but when the owner came to reclaim it the watch was not forthcoming. Mrs Gulliver said that it had been given to two of his comrades who said they had been authorised to receive it. The court report says that the case occupied a considerable time behind

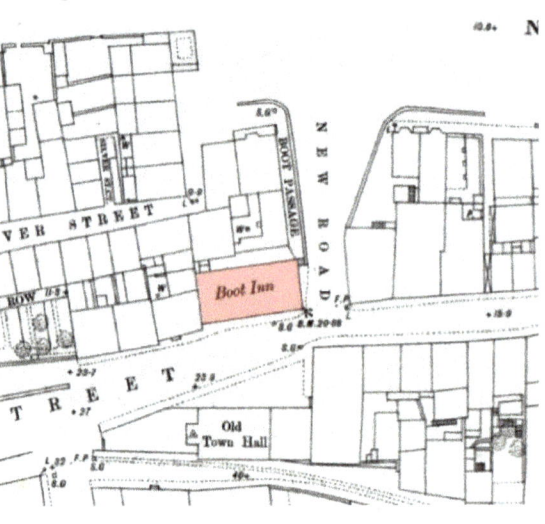

The Boot from the 1864 O/S map

closed doors with the result that Gulliver was ordered either to pay £4 or to give up the watch and pay costs in either case. Gulliver was out by 1871 and replaced by Robert Francis Bugler, cab proprietor, an occupation pursued by a number of landlords in the town, while his wife Elizabeth run the pub.

In 1893 Charles Rex was the landlord when he was attacked by two drunks who beat him about the head and continued to do so until a constable arrived. The men were fined £5 for the assault and Rex made the interesting comment to the court that he was unable to continue his usual occupation of gardener.

In 1909 the very existence of the Boot was called into question when objections were raised to the continuance of its licence as there were six other licensed houses in the vicinity. It was described as a fully licensed ale house belonging to Devenish & Co., with Sydney Stokes as landlord who sometimes operated as a cabdriver. The rent was £25 with a turnover about £75 per month. The property was described as a stone and cement building with a slated roof, and consisted of three cellars, two rooms, two bars on ground floor, four rooms on the first floor, and a garret. One cellar is used as a kitchen, one as a beer cellar and one a wood cellar. There is a private room, smoking room, one public bar and one private bar with a jug and a bottle entrance. There are three entrances, one private to the cellar or kitchen and two public, one into the public bar at the front of the house, and the other at the end of the house into a private bar or jug and bottle entrance. These bars were inline and divided with wooden partitions and doors.

The measurements were given as, private bar 16'10" x 6' and 8' 11" high: public bar 13' x 7'8" and 7' high: smoking room 13'4" x 19'7" and 6'11" high. The sanitary accommodation is nearly new and a short passage leads from the public bar to the same. The upstairs rooms consist of three bedrooms and one bed sitting room. The first bedroom contains two full-size and one single bed which can sleep three persons, the second bedroom contains one full size and one single bed to sleep three persons, with a third bedroom containing two full size beds to sleep four persons. These rooms are for letting purposes and can sleep twelve, being generally full when the fleet is in. The bed sitting room is used by Mr Stokes and his wife with a full-sized bed.

It was suggested for closure as it was unnecessary, there being 19,843 people in town and 111 licences, or one to every 178 persons. In its defence it was stated that it was the only Devenish house on the street and very well conducted by Mr Stokes who had been there for 18 months and was a man of irreproachable character. £276 had just been spent on the house to meet the requirements of the justices. After some discussion the licence was renewed and the Stokes family continued until August 1919 when the Boot was one of several Devenish pubs to have their landlords returned to them after being away on active war service.

In 1923 attempts were made once more to close the pub, this time by local temperance groups fronted by a Mrs Hamlin. She more or less admitted that the Boot had been chosen at random as there were several others in the area that could have been considered. She also admitted that she had made no enquiries as to the occupants of the house and the effect that it would have on them. Horace Curtis the landlord had served with the Dorsets from 1914 to 1919 and was disabled with a gunshot wound to his wrist. The pub enabled him to support his wife and daughters, and closure would bring great hardship upon his family. It was agreed that the Boot be allowed to continue.

An amusing article from 1924 reads as follows,

'Sailors from the fleet like to sleep at the Boot Inn, Weymouth because the bedrooms have a list to port and they think they are on board ship.' This argument was successfully used on Wednesday at the licensing sessions when a renewal of the licence was applied for.

The Boot continues today as a fine quiet traditional pub selling draught beer and cider.

THE BRIDGE INN/OLD BRIDGE INN
Bridge Buildings, St Thomas Street, Melcombe Regis

THE BRIDGE INN stood right on the corner of the town bridge of 1827 on the Melcombe Regis side at the end of St Thomas Street. The drawing shows a fine square Georgian building and marks it as part of the portfolio of Eldridge Pope & Co the brewers. Its origins are unclear, and it was possibly constructed at the same time as the bridge. The census of 1851 shows it in the occupation of Henry Hayman beer house keeper aged 29 and his wife

The Bridge Inn from an old print

Mary. Being the only way to cross from Melcombe Regis to Weymouth and keep dry it generated a great deal of traffic and therefore more than its fair share of trouble. In 1853 John Edmonds, described simply as 'the keeper of a brothel', had a fight with Thomas Talbot a chimney sweep, after which Talbot's head required surgical attendance. According to the arresting officer the affair could have ended in manslaughter had he not been there. They were fined 8/- each with one week to pay. In 1862 the owners, now Eldridge Mason & Co., advertised the pub for rent and it was taken by James Strickland aged 50, a former collector of bridge tolls, whose office had been on the other side of the road. He applied for a spirits licence on the grounds that traffic had markedly increased since tolls had been abolished and he had been there for five years without incident; his application was refused. In 1865 Strickland was described as a beer retailer and dealer in glass, china and earthenware.

By 1870 the landlord was William Rashleigh, who applied for a licence to extend his hours on the grounds that it had been a beer house for many years and he had been there for three, during which time it had been well conducted and served his majesty's vessels. This obliged him to get up early and he did not mind staying up late. He also applied for a licence to sell spirits. The premises were described as having seven rooms, three bedrooms upstairs, a bedroom and drawing room, a smoking room, with a bar and kitchen downstairs, and both applications were granted.

There was a most unfortunate incident connected to the pub in July 1881 when a young woman who went under various names, including Fanny Sprucer, was found murdered in Woolwich. Fanny was 28 years old and had been brought up by her uncle James Strickland, who had run the pub and the toll house during the mid 1860s, as above. The story goes that she was expecting to inherit some property but it was all tied up in Chancery and she moved to London, where she took up with 36-year-old George Durling with whom she lived. Both were heavy drinkers and as a result had frequent drunken quarrels. On 20 July they had a fight in the street, during which Durling threw bricks at her and threatened to kill her before the night was through. They made up and walked home together, but on reaching the garden adjacent to their lodgings, the quarrel started up again. This time he picked up an iron carpet beater, swung it around and smashed it into her head with such force that it penetrated her skull to a depth of four inches. She died at once, and realising what he had done, Durling fell to his knees and began kissing her and begging her forgiveness. He was arrested and immediately confessed; he was hanged by William Marwood in Maidstone on the 23 August 1881.

Despite its prominent position little else seems to have disturbed the calm of this pub apart from an incident in 1899 when John Wootton a labourer was fined 2/6 for calling landlord William Hill a '...... gypsy'. In 1901 The Bridge closed down when the licence was transferred to Cook's Restaurant. The buildings were pulled down in 1928, as was the old bridge. At the time of writing the site is occupied by Prezzo restaurant with some new flats above.

THE BRIG INN
High Street/Trinity Road, Weymouth

According to the census returns this pub lay three doors to the right of the King's Arms, then known as 30 Trinity Road, and is probably the double fronted house at 19 shown below. The first mention comes from October 1870 when PC Bartlett saw two men go into the house at 3:30 on a Sunday afternoon. The landlord Joseph Hounsell, a bricklayer, and his wife Emma denied that they were there but after a diligent search the constable found them squashed together and hiding in a cupboard, Hounsell was heard to say to one of his guests, 'Did you leave anyone outside?' meaning a lookout to which he confessed that he hadn't. The case was disposed of on payment of a £1 fine and costs.

In 1874 Cecilia Rawson was charged with stealing 7/6d from an able seaman who had been drinking with her for three or four hours. When he went to the Brig she put her hand into his pocket and took his money, but he was convinced that an artillery man with whom they had been drinking had taken it, resulting in a fight in which he was thrown twice to the floor. Eventually Rawson was arrested and denied having any money on her. But when searched a two shilling piece was found, to which she retorted, 'I am not guilty, it was my own money, could I not have money without having stolen it ?' She was committed for trial at the sessions.

In July of 1880 the Brig was being run by Luke McCabe and his wife Eliza. They had been married for about 15 years and had four children, Luke was a pensioner having left the army as a sergeant with a good character. One afternoon he was attempting to evict a drunken woman and her baby, but the violent manner in which he did it was objected to by Eliza and they began to fight. He was drunk at the time and struck her in the face causing her nose to bleed, before catching her by the throat and attempting to strangle her. She ran from the house and did not return. She summoned the police saying that this conduct had been going on for some time but that he was becoming

The Brig 2025

more violent. McCabe denied that any assault had taken place, but said that his had been a military career and he was used to order and discipline; but his wife encouraged such disreputable characters at his house as went against his conscience, and she 'flew at him like a cat', breaking a cup over his head. Despite a witness saying that it was just a 'family affair' the magistrates found the case proven and fined him 10/-.

However, Mrs McCabe was not quite the victim she made herself out to be. In May of 1881 she was traced to Southampton, arrested and charged with keeping a disorderly and immoral house. The Brig had developed such an unsavoury reputation as a brothel that their landlord, brewers Reynold & Heathorne, had them evicted and the licence transferred to Stephen Fuszard, a cellarman, until a permanent replacement could be found. The couple went to Portland and continued their trade with some of the young girls from the Brig going with them, but the police managed to evict them from there and they went their separate ways. Two of the young ladies in question, Jane Keats and Maria Stone, gave evidence at the police court to say that they had been in highly respectable service in the town but were induced to go to the Brig in order to attend some dancing classes. This apparently caused them to become common prostitutes and for the use of the pub they paid Mrs McCabe 2/- per night. They moved on following Mrs McCabe to Portland and afterwards to 6 Myrtle Terrace, where the trade continued. They associated with soldiers, sailors and civilians, paying 2/- if 'with company' and 1/-if alone; the house contained a total of 16 rooms. The neighbours reported hearing cries of murder and much noise coming from the house, which was a complete nuisance to the neighbourhood.

Eliza McCabe was eventually arrested and sobbed continually throughout the hearing. She was most distressed to hear that she was going to be remanded to a higher court, exclaiming 'Oh! Oh! My poor mother! 'She was given bail to await her trial. Meanwhile the two girls were sentenced to two months hard labour each, with the magistrates hoping that they could be sent to a home where they might be taught a different life. To no one's surprise Eliza now aged 36 failed to answer to her bail in October and when caught and put on trial the evidence against her was described as 'unfit to publish'. But possibly an even bigger surprise was that counsel for the prosecution stated that since her committal the prisoner had been living very carefully and trying to make amends. The court took this into consideration and passed a much lighter sentence than they would otherwise have done; six months imprisonment with hard labour. Of Mr Luke McCabe nothing more was heard. Landlords Reynold and Heathtorne installed James Burgess, a 65-year-old ex prison warder, and despite its reputation the Brig continued, although by 1883 the police were less happy with the official choice of landlord, James Woodland, than they had been with Mr Burgess. The magistrates asked him to mind the way he kept his house in future but by the census of 1891 it had closed down completely.

THE BROWNLOW TAVERN
Ranelagh Road, Melcombe Regis

IN JULY OF 1880 it was announced that John Groves the brewer was to commence work on the construction of a new public house to be known as the Brownlow Tavern on part of the Park Estate owned by the Conservative Land Association. The story of this area is gone into in further detail in the Waterloo Stores entry. A patch of land had been allotted for a pub when the estate was being laid out. For one reason or another work did not begin until 1882, when a licence was applied for by Arthur Tom Meade, a brewers clerk, on behalf of the brewery. He did not know whether he would keep the house himself, he said, and building work had not yet been commenced. Mr Groves had purchased the site in the belief that he would have a licence granted to him, but at the hearing it was pointed out that no newspaper notices had been produced as required by law and therefore the application must fail. The applicant offered to hand over the required notices there and then but apparently the case could not be reopened. The applicants stated that they were prepared to give up the licence on the Welcome Home if the application was granted, which altered the magistrates attitude considerably, as they saw the advantage of replacing an old house in a bad area with a good one in a respectable area, which would meet the requirements of visitors to the town. The arrangements for stabling also formed an important ingredient in their consideration. The magistrates went against their natural instincts to refuse

Brownlow Tavern. The End. September 2010

all applications for new licences and made an exception, and by March 1883, newly built and fully licensed, the house was advertised to let by the Hope Brewery.

All the magistrates could wish for must have come true as there were no reported problems or incidents at this quiet pub throughout its long history – apart, that is from a serious controversy in 1938 when the then landlord Cyril Horace Frampton, licensed victualler, transport manager and mechanic, introduced racing tortoises. This took place on a billiard table with tracks laid out and toy jockeys fixed to the creature's backs. This outraged the local Methodist minister who objected to pubs being turned into 'funfairs', with the comment that 'if people who support this sport were made to crawl across billiards tables on their hands and knees themselves they would not think it all that funny.'

A customer reporting on the 'Pubs Galore' website just before its closure and conversion into flats in 2010 describes its last days,

> A detached corner pub in yellow and green, looking slightly tired currently, with a rear patio. The interior is a single open plan room with two areas, as there is a seating area and a pool table and dartboard in the other part. The decor is white and there is a brick fireplace, along with some wood beams. Interest is supplied by the few mirrors, some books, model greyhounds, brass ephemera, old photos of Weymouth and the fishing nets on the ceiling. The

TV wasn't on and the music was general and at an OK level. The service was really friendly and clearly this is a dog friendly place. A few locals were playing pool.

The Prince Regent 2025

THE BURDON HOTEL / PRINCE REGENT
Victoria Terrace, Melcombe Regis

James Yearsley announced that his new hotel, with 'spacious and convenient premises' was to open on 10 August 1858. He was a Dorchester man and former proprietor of the ancient Antelope Hotel in that town, from which he had run a successful carriage business. The Burdon had been under construction from early in 1855 under the informal name of the 'Railway Hotel', and in May of that year there were arguments with the builder Philip Dodson about its size, which appeared to some to be much larger than had been approved. Nevertheless, a fine building was produced to the design of architect Pierse Arthur. It was named after William Wharton Burdon who owned the gasworks in the town as well as coal mines in Newcastle, various other properties and probably the land upon which it was built. When its completion was announced the new assembly room was said to have an internal measurement of 88' x 35' and 25' in height with a ceiling of flowered glass.

The local press was enthusiastic from the beginning, stating that 'in addition to the old respectable hotels, the Victoria and the Royal, the erection of the Burdon with its extensive and beautiful apartments is quite justified and, with the splendid residences each side, fills a gap and completes a graceful sweep of buildings around the Esplanade'.

James does not appear on the 1861 census and was presumably away for the night. His wife Elizabeth, hotel keeper, aged 53, is shown as being in charge, along with a large complement of maids and guests of various descriptions. In the same year he announced that he had now purchased the hotel outright and was building up what must have been a very successful omnibus business attending the arrivals of every boat from the Channel Islands and every train. The following year saw a performance by the Female Christy Minstrels in full Indian costume, fresh from London to give their 'unrivalled Ethiopian Entertainment', front seats 2/6, second seats 1/-. He seems to have maintained a connection with the Antelope in Dorchester for a while and advertised good accommodation for gentlemen wishing to follow the hounds at either establishment for £2/2/- per week. During 1866 after he had left the Antelope he was in court summoned by Henry Barnes an architect who had a claim of £30/3/11d for dilapidations and injury to a brewhouse and other buildings at the rear of that hotel. Presumably Yearsley had left things in a bit of a mess but the judge wanted nothing to do with it and suggested that an amicable settlement might be reached if they were to engage a good surveyor.

The whole Weymouth enterprise seems to been a great success, but in a bizarre case during the summer of 1868 Yearsley, who was described as 'late of the Burdon Hotel', was fined 20/- for keeping pigs which, it was claimed, were a nuisance. When confronted by Superintendent Lidbury he denied that the pigs were offensive and said that they were there to be valued and that they were kept clean. He did not object to the fine.

By 1871 the Burdon passed to Mrs Jane Scudamore a widow of 40, who was described as no stranger to the hotel business, and the establishment continued its previous success. It had become a focal point for balls, exhibitions and events, including a magnificent 'panorama' of the late Franco-Prussian campaign by Poole and Young which drew in huge crowds.

The Burnaby Legitimacy Case provided some entertainment to the reading public. Margaret Burnaby left her husband on 20 December 1884 and did not return. Mr Burnaby obtained a divorce on 3 November 1886; the co-respondent was a Mr Willoughby and the two later married. Before the divorce Mrs Burnaby had three children, over the first there was no dispute as she was obviously legitimate. The following two were born in April 1885 and June 1886. In July 1884 Mrs Burnaby moved into the Burdon Hotel, where she was joined by Mr Willoughby who had booked adjoining rooms with a shared sitting room; evidence from others at the hotel claimed that they were obviously 'together'. Mrs Burnaby was attempting to claim settlement for the two later children from her husband who wished to have them declared illegitimate, with much supporting evidence from people who knew the individuals involved. Somehow the case managed to drag on for days with the pretty inevitable conclusion that the two later children were fathered by Willoughby and that there was no claim on Mr Burnaby.

Jane Scudamore continued to run things until 1896 when the reins were taken up by Frederick Sefton Smith, 39, a former counsellor from Lowestoft who took charge of what was now the Imperial Burdon Hotel and organised a concert to raise money for the Transvaal War Fund. In March 1917 the hotel was taken over as a military hospital and was not released until June 1920, when the huge task of redecorating over 100 rooms was accomplished in about eight weeks by 35 workmen. The hotel remained with the Smith family until 1929, and in 1954 there were proposals to turn this excellent visitor facility into council offices. Fortunately this idea came to nothing and it continued to serve its original purpose. In 1971 it became the Hotel Prince Regent which still operates today.

THE HOTEL BURDON TAP
Victoria Street, Melcombe Regis

SITUATED BEHIND THE Hotel Burdon in what was Victoria Street, the Hotel Tap was a small back street extension to the main hotel, where the working man could call in for a pint without contact with the well-to-do guests in the main building. It would have opened at the same time and under the same ownership but unfortunately, without the same licence, a fact seemingly lost on 26 year old John Collins the landlord. In September 1859 he was summoned by the excise authorities for selling beer and spirits without a licence, the maximum penalty for the first was £20 and £50 for the second. There was sympathy all round and at the police court, and both prosecution and defence urged the bench to treat the case as leniently as they could. Collins lived on the premises with his wife Maria with a large sign outside which said 'BURDON HOTEL TAP' indicating that there was no attempt to defraud the excise on his part. Any fault lay with James Yearsley the owner who had assumed that the Tap was covered by the hotel licence as were other hotels in town with the same set up. Collins was in Yearsley's employ and a licence had now been applied for but nonetheless expenses had been incurred and the law broken. Collins was fined the lowest amount possible £12/10/- for selling spirits and £5 for the beer – by way of a caution to others.

At the end of 1868 tragedy overtook the family which by now consisted of four children. Collins was driving back from Portland in his brougham when he had a fit, fell from the cab and was run over by the wheel, dying of his injuries later in the day and leaving his widow Maria as landlady in the employ of Jane Scudamore, now the owner of the main hotel.

The house seems to have been peaceful enough until 1883 when Henry Carter, a resident for the previous seven or so years, decided to blow himself up. He had been

Burdon Hotel Tap Victoria Street 1976 (Weymouth Museum)

a 'boatman' whose business had failed and a heavy drinker. The house was awakened at 2.00am by an explosion which blew off the door to his room and shattered the windows. Traces of chloride and nitrate of potash were found in the room. Why he chose this bizarre form of exit will never be known but it didn't work and he had to take the more traditional route of cutting his throat, with considerable success. Maria was still there in 1891 aged 59 and described as a 'hotel assistant'. This little house survived well into the 20th century and was described by one visitor,

> One of the smallest pubs I'd ever seen – the Burdon Tap. I could never believe that such a tiny premises could actually be a bar and I could scarcely wait until I was old enough to step through the door and see what it looked like inside. Only went in once though – once was enough: facing the bar was a single bench attached to the wall; no table. The sullen barmaid didn't get up from her stool to serve you, and on the counter was a glass case containing one sandwich and one meat pie, which I wasn't tempted to order. That's gone and not much missed.

The site is now part of the hotel car park.

The Butchers Arms (Weymouth Museum)

THE BUTCHER'S ARMS
West Street, Melcombe Regis

THE FIRST MENTION of the Butchers comes in the census of 1861 when the landlord was Henry Granville a widower aged 50. It was built on the site of a number of slaughterhouses, which probably accounts for its name. In August he had his application for a spirits licence refused despite his plea that there was a skittle alley attached to the premises and that access could be gained to the tramway, by the side of which it was 'not improbable that buildings would spring up'. He alluded to travellers and excursionists requiring more accommodation and was asked if it was customary for travellers to rush off to such places as soon as they got to Weymouth. Travelling, he claimed in response, was dry work and that a spirits licence would greatly enhance everything if the proposed theatre were to be built. 'As to the theatre, replied the opposition, it will be much the best course to wait and see if it really opened, and when that occurred the applicant could come again. At present it was not very probable that a large number would be drawn to the house to see the spot where a theatre was likely to be built'. Another application in 1865 was met with the observation that although the house was situated in a low neighbourhood it was nevertheless conducted very well, as the police agreed. Granville made one further point, 'we are happily very healthy at the present time, but if the cholera should visit the neighbourhood it will be important that people should be able to have a place where they might get a glass of brandy'. He added that a considerable amount of money had just been spent on refurbishment but despite his interesting argument the application was again refused.

In 1863 he managed to obtain a massive fossil from some labourers working on the railway lines at the Backwater. The monster weighed about 2cwt and measured 2'6" x 2' and about 17" in depth. He had bought it for a few shillings, although the corporation disputed his right to do so. Henry invited inspection by geologists and others despite an opinion that it was just a portion of a petrified tree.

In 1870 under the proprietorship of a Mr Meech, another attempt was made to gain a spirits licence which was denied on the grounds that his house was very near the poorhouse in the most impoverished part of the town and that having spirits would provide an inducement to make poor people poorer still. In 1888 new landlord Henry Croom was accused along with several others of receiving seven bags of wool from the wreck of the *Lanoma* on its way from Tasmania to London 'well knowing them to have been stolen' and taken from Chesil Beach. Croom was remanded on bail but I have not been able to find any report of his trial. Perhaps significantly he and his wife Eleanor were still running the pub in 1901, and so perhaps the case collapsed.

A notice placed by architects Crickmay & Son on behalf of the owner John Groves in the *Southern Times* during March 1895 invited tenders from builders to rebuild the pub, which presumably resulted in the rather drab red brick building shown above. This little local continued until very recent times in 1964 offering bed and breakfast at 5gns per week with sprung mattresses. The pub was closed by 1991 and the building demolished in 2003 to be replaced by a block of flats opposite what are now the Royal Mail offices.

THE CAMBRIDGE ARMS
St Mary Street, Melcombe Regis

THE FIRST INDICATION of a pub at 31 St Mary Street comes from the census of 1851. The house is not named but Charles Buckland aged 40, brewer and ale house keeper, is in occupation with his wife Eliza also aged 40. In 1858 a spirits licence was applied for on behalf of widow Elizabeth Hemingway, giving rise to strong objections from Joseph Farwell of the White Horse Inn next door but one, who said that another licensed house was not needed. He was overruled by the magistrates who said that a licence was promised to her late husband and granted the application. This was a good move as she ran the pub successfully until retiring in 1882, when the brewery put the pub up for rent. During that year a private soldier spent the night walking the streets before smashing three panes of glass at the pub. For some unknown reason he was convinced that his girlfriend was in the police station and so he broke the windows in order to get arrested and see her. History does not tell us whether he found her but he was fined 10/- plus the costs of the windows.

The Cambridge Arms site 2024

In 1907 the Cambridge, was run by landlord Alfred Wells for brewers Eldridge Pope & Co. and was to be closed by order of the magistrates. The White Horse was only one door off, and a within a radius of 50 yards there were 16 other licensed houses. The rent of the Cambridge was £21 and its rateable value £44 while that of the White Horse was £10 with a rateable value of £11; the Cambridge had no jug and bottle department and no stabling.

Wells said that a good many naval men stayed at his house and he had seven bedrooms furnished with double and single beds which could accommodate 17 men chiefly petty officers and seamen; 16 had slept there on the previous night. There was a great demand for beds and in the summer months one saw sailors lying about on the Esplanade as they have not been able to get beds. He did a good steady trade and had been at the house for only a short time, but during the past six months he had taken £13/9/- in December, £18/12/- in January £20/11/- in February £34.13/- in March £28/8 in April and £28 in May. Charles Morris Inspector of Police said that he had known the house for 26 years and that it was always thought of as a naval house, well conducted but unnecessary, particularly as the Sailors' Home had been built nearby and had 70 beds available. The brewery stated that during the past three years their takings had averaged over £389 per year and that they took the overflow from the Sailors' Home. It was asked if it was wise policy to shut up all small houses providing accommodation and drive the public into the glaring gin palaces? It was to no avail. The chairman of the bench stated that, 'We decided by a majority 8-3 to refuse the renewal of this licence and to refer it for compensation,' and the Cambridge was no more. In later years it became Bartlett the butchers and then the Oxfam charity shop.

THE CASTLE INN / GARDENERS ARMS
Horsford Street, Weymouth

IN THE CENSUS of 1841 a small but unnamed pub is listed at the bottom of Hill Lane near Hope Quay. Its occupants were Ann Warry, named as a publican aged 75, and Thomas Matthews a 45-year-old gardener and his wife Sarah. Nothing more is known until the following census when the Matthews are still there and the pub has a name, the Gardener's Arms. Three years later Matthews is at the Weymouth County Court having been summoned by the Earl of Craven and the other trustees of the Johnstone Estate, ostensibly over

The assumed site of theCastle Inn Horsford Street

the recovery of £8/16/3d for six months' rent, dilapidations and property tax. He was given notice to quit on 1 April 1854 because, claimed a witness, 'First of all he kept the premises dirty, and another thing, very often when I went to the house, I thought I saw light characters about the premises. Then I was told that he had expressed a wish to give up the house. Another reason was, I didn't think he made the most of the premises, he allowed the garden to remain full of weeds'. Questioning by counsel for the defence then took a strange turn.

> 'How did he vote in the last Municipal Election ?'
> 'I wonder if this has anything to do with the question,' asked those acting for the owners, 'you must not take up my time in this useless manner.'
> 'Did you not give my unfortunate client notice to quit because he voted for Mr Butt ? (George Butt was the successful Conservative candidate in the 1852 election).
> 'Certainly not, although parties have attempted to fasten it on me by handbills'.

The bench found for the plaintiff and Matthews was given one week to pay and presumably left shortly after.

The extensive gardens from the O/S map of 1864. The Castle is in the far left corner.

By 1860 the Gardener's had become the Castle Inn and in March 1861 a drunken John Winsor turned up at the house, challenged landlord Simon Wareham to a fight, swore at least 100 oaths, sang part of two songs, attempted a dance and broke a jug on the table in a demand for more beer. That little session cost him 6d for the jug 5/- for drunkenness and 4/- in court fees.

During an application for a spirits licence in 1870 the landlord John Tooth, a former horse soldier with decorations from the Crimea and other places, described the premises as having ten rooms and frequented by a large number of excursionists. His application caused great merriment, when asked to estimate the size of his bar parlour he said he could not, as although he had been in the army he was a horse soldier and it was not so easy to judge distances on horseback; however, he would estimate the parlour as more than two horses long – about 2 ½ horses depending, of course on, the size of the horse – his application was granted.

In 1875 the house was put up for auction and described as a 'substantial brick building of comparatively recent erection', in the occupation of Mrs Harriet Read as subtenant to Mr John Groves who holds the lease for the remainder of a term of 21 years from 25 March 1860 at a yearly rate of £35. The premises were held on a main lease dated 30 June 1817 for a term of 1,000 years.

The days of the Castle were numbered when in 1901 an application was made for the removal of the licence held by George Pearse to a parcel of land in Newbury Gardens bounded in the south by the road leading from Hope Square to Rodwell Avenue and the road opposite Dorset Place and Newberry Terrace to be called the Railway Dock Hotel. Plans had been submitted to the justices and agreed, the new house was built and the Castle became part of the Groves brewery site today converted into housing.

THE CHAPELHAY TAVERN
Franchise Street, Weymouth

THIS PLEASANT LITTLE pub is the result of two small cottages being knocked together probably in the late 1830s or 40s, and first noticed in the census of 1851 when it was occupied by Robert Grey, beer retailer 35 and his wife Virtue. They had gone by 1855 and after a couple of short-lived occupants, Frederick Caines took the licence in 1877 with his wife Frances Elizabeth. He died in 1888 at the age of 38 and Elizabeth carried on briefly before meeting and marrying William James Bagg in April 1890, who of

The Chapelhay Tavern 2017

course assumed control. In 1896 there was the inevitable case of selling beer on a Sunday, with four men caught sitting in the bar with beer in front of them. Landlord Bagg pleaded with the constable to 'look it over this time' but when that appeal failed he replied, 'It's a fair cop, let me down as lightly as you can. The men had come with mackerel to sell and had then stayed for some beer.' Bagg had been at the pub for seven years since he married Elizabeth, who had been there for 20 years with nothing against the house during that period. The magistrates imposed a fine of £5 with costs but did not endorse the licence.

William Bagg died in 1907 leaving Elizabeth to continue as a lone widow once more, she had now been there for 31 years and was known to be a very respectable lady; there had been no complaints against the house for a great many years. The owners were Eldridge Pope, who had at least 23 houses in the town at that time. The tavern was described as detached with three entrances and three rooms to let with a rent to the brewery of £21 pa.; included was a jug and bottle and two bars, with accommodation consisting of four bedrooms. The following year in their mission to close as many public houses as possible the police argued that the Chapelhay was unnecessary because there were far superior houses in the district, with the Albion (Eldridge Pope) 61 paces away, the Cornopean 84 paces and the Tivoli beer house 85 paces. Nevertheless, it survived with Elizabeth as the licensee until 1917, when it was taken over by her son Herbert Bagg who was there until 1923.

The Tavern is a flourishing local to this day and a report from CAMRA in recent times states that it was one of five Dorset pubs to be taken over by Admiral Taverns in November 2019 when the chain purchased 137 sites across England from pub group Marstons. It was described as a 'friendly locals pub, clean and well kept but unfortunately the skittle alley is now home to a pool table. (the skittle alley seems to have been reinstated recently). Walls are covered in naval and military memorabilia and the sloping bar counter on the front right could date from the inter-war period. The fireplace dates from 1973. Those who frequented the Chapelhay in the days of the Channel Islands boats may remember that it was the best place in town to purchase 'discounted tobacco and spirits'.

CHELMSFORD HOUSE
on the corner of Hardwick Street & Chelmsford Street

THE PUB THAT never was – but an interesting story nonetheless. In August of 1881 William Bennett who had been butler to a Major Sykes for 12 years applied for a full licence to sell spirits, wines, beer, porter, cider, perry, sweets and liqueurs from a house which he owned and occupied, on ground known as The Park Estate, an area whose history is explained in more detail in the Waterloo Stores entry. The house stood on the corner of Hardwick Street and Chelmsford Street in an area of development which had been laid out to include five new public houses. Bennett is shown on the 1881 census as aged 34, a butler in domestic service from St Neots in

Chelmsford House in 2023

Huntingdonshire, and living in the house with his wife Elizabeth and two daughters, . In August he applied for a full beer and spirits licence as he wished to open the house as an inn, ale and victualling house. His property had nine lofty rooms, two of them 20' x 15' front and back sitting rooms, a good kitchen 13' x 8' a scullery 8' square with an 18' frontage, three of the rooms are in the loft but flat ceilinged; he had no stable or coach house but might take the plot next door and build. The property was worth £30 a year and was structurally adapted for the sale of beer off the premises. The only other houses nearby were the Stag (200 yards) and the Ranelagh Hotel.

During his application it was claimed that Mr Bennett was a man of excellent character, but in cross-examination he was asked if he had offered a bribe of £30 or £40 to Superintendent Vickery if he would support his case. This he denied, along with claims that if he did get a licence he could sell it to Groves the brewer for £200 more than he would otherwise get. Whether there was any truth in this we will never know, but by August of 1882 Butler had moved out to Derby Street and a fresh application was made by Thomas Palmer, a tailor now residing in the house and paying £20 pa., on the grounds that since the previous application 20 new houses had been erected and the neighbourhood was growing daily. But despite the request having changed to a licence for a simple beer and cider house it was denied, as it was again in September. In evidence Palmer stated that he had six bedrooms available, he also had five children and the application was once more rejected, as there were 'no additional circumstances to warrant granting a licence'. There is no record of Chelmsford House ever operating as a pub and by the census of 1891 the property was occupied by Edward Lane, a brewer's clerk, and Bennett was living nearby at Southwick House in Ranelagh Road, and still working as a butler. On 25 November 1903 Chelmsford House was put up for auction as a leasehold residence.

THE CLIFTON HOTEL / RAILWAY TAVERN
Queen Street, Melcombe Regis

IN AUGUST OF 1869 William Williams reported two young women, 'whose dress and general appearance contrasted with the description given of them by the police as common girls of the town'. They were charged with loitering in the street, looking into his windows and behaving indecently. He had asked them to move on but they replied that they had as much right to be there as he had before moving off the pavement onto the road exclaiming to him, 'Now!

The Clifton Hotel 2023

you ---- ---- now can you move us?' Williams went briefly into the Somerset next door before returning to meet a train and found the girls back in front of his house, upon which he summoned a constable. When the case came to court the defendants said that Williams had called them, ---- ---- beasts. The superintendent told the bench that the Clifton used to be a bad house but Williams had to put a stop to it, causing the defendants and their class to take every opportunity to annoy him. Sergeant Harvey deposed as to the disgraceful way in which the defendants earned their living but the bench dismissed the case upon the defendants agreeing not to loiter in front of the house, and on their paying the costs of the summons to which terms they readily agreed.

Many landlords had second occupations or little earners on the side, and in 1874 William Lovelace was advertising space to rent for the erection of stalls at the Weymouth and County Races in September as the renter of stalls – details on application. In common with just about every publican in town Lovelace was arrested for selling beer after hours but because of the evidence given of his previous character – he had spent 3½ years in the police force, and had raised the character of the house in the five years that he had been there – and it being his first offence, they took a lenient view and fined him 5/-.

At the end of 1882 the owners were the local brewers Reynolds & Heathorn of 41 St Thomas Street. They had eight other tied houses in the town and were eventually absorbed by Groves and Sons in 1886 but on this occasion they were advertising for a new tenant, who turned out to be John Wills and his wife Jane. They didn't stay very long and the following year the licence was transferred to Albert Middleton, 29, a former a cab driver who had plied his trade around the railway station, often getting involved in heated exchanges with the other drivers. In 1882 he was prosecuted for keeping two carriages without a licence and had a number of previous convictions for the same thing. In court those acting for him claimed that it was rather a sad case because the man had an execution on his house and stables and had filed a petition for liquidation, having had to sell his livery business. The poor man did not have one halfpenny in his possession it was claimed. Middleton was fined £5 with a month to pay or 28 days in prison.

During 1883 Middleton, along with Thomas Le Warne of the Prince Albert, became the victims of fraud when a man named Charles Lambourne went about the country representing himself as a printer and publisher based in Plymouth who was soliciting payments for advertisements and entries in a series of local trade directories that he was producing, for Dorset on this occasion. Having been shown various prospectuses and mock-ups of the proposed directory Middleton gave him 5/-, upon which Lambourne left without paying his hotel bill of 14/-. During his trial it emerged that he had received well over £100, but because he had no previous convictions he was given a light sentence of six months hard labour. Despite his previous sob story Middleton seems to have become a very energetic landlord, organising many events, balls and dinners at the house and carried on as licensee until 1902, when he moved to the prestigious Gloucester Hotel. His place was taken by Captain and Mrs Harry Shrivell from the Channel Islands Hotel in Guernsey.

Bristolian William Robert Pruden became landlord in about 1907 and was summoned to appear before the magistrates, along with the licensees of the Victoria Hotel, the Sun, the Sailors Return and the Fountain, in November of 1920 for overcharging on spirits and passing off cheap whisky as Black and White. Also caught in the trap was barmaid Ada White. In his defence he claimed that he did not have cheap whisky in the house, only proprietary brands which on this occasion was Black and White. He was asked to produce his invoice books but as he failed to do so he was fined £5 plus costs. Pruden left shortly afterwards to take on the Golden Lion and was replaced by Frederick Woodward and his wife Rose Mabel.

The incomers situation was far from happy. Woodward was a former schoolmaster and serious gambler with a bad temper, and during their married life his wife Rose had had to find over £2,000 to pay his debts. He had frequently assaulted and burned all her clothes, driving her, at one point, to seek the protection of the police. She took on the Clifton in 1919 when he was demobilised to help him into a business but his behaviour became so bad, reaching the point of him carrying a razor in his pocket, threatening to kill her and commit suicide. She was granted a divorce and the pub licence was put in her name. Shortly after in 1923 she married a Mr Strange and they ran the pub together until 1931. Lieut. Commander Fred Mann soon took over and was by all accounts an interesting character and a genial host. He was also a collector of oddities, including a piffle snonker, all of which he donated to the Ex-Naval Association when he left in 1939.

Despite its unassuming exterior in 1968 the Clifton was described as having two bars, 24 bedrooms and an enormous ballroom overlooking the railway station with very old-fashioned tiled ladies and gents toilets operated by the old brass 'penny' locks. When the dining room was being reorganised, it was discovered that one room had once been the stables, and lots of items for silver service such as soup tureens and huge platters, as well as maids' uniforms with mop caps, were discovered. In 1971 the Clifton's name was changed rather unimaginatively to The Railway and it continues to this day.

THE COAL HOLE INN
South Parade on the Quay, Melcombe Regis

THIS SHORT LIVED beer house first appears on the census of 1851 situated on the corner of South Parade and Custom House Quay, a tiny street facing the water and occupied by Thomas Carter aged 41, his wife Sarah 28 and their daughter also Sarah eight years of age. His occupation is given as a coal merchant's clerk and the address as the Coal Hole beerhouse. He applied for a spirits licence in 1853 'endeavouring to make it appear that there was no public house near the Quay where ship owners, masters or brokers could resort for the indulgence in a glass of grog', but the reality was that 'if they looked out of any of the windows of the building in which they were sitting the eye would not fail to fall upon either the side, front or back of some respectable inn closely adjacent to the Quay and that three steps and a jump would bring

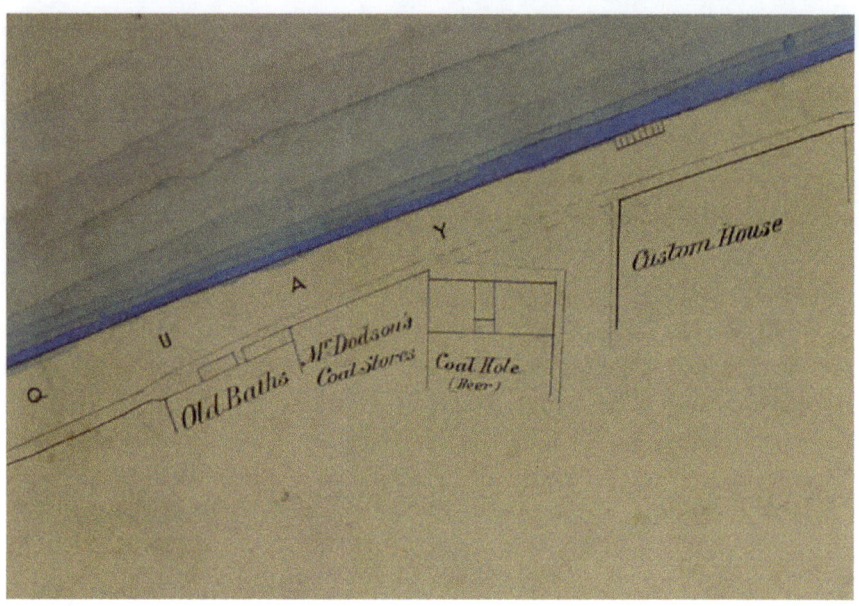

Site of the Coal Hole 1857 (Pierce Arthur)

to anchor any denizen of the salt water at the Quay disposed to indulge in spirituous liquors'. The licensed Globe was only '16 yards distant' and the George very close. The application was refused as it was again the following year.

Thomas Carter of the Coal Hole Inn was in the local obituary column during 1856, having died on 12 June 'after a lingering illness, late master mariner and an old inhabitant of this town'. His wife Sarah and daughter were still in South Parade during the 1861 census but the beer house business seems to be long gone. Today it can be seen that the building itself has been demolished and South Parade given a much wider entrance.

THE COOPERS' ARMS
Maiden Street, Melcombe Regis

THE COOPERS ARMS was first mentioned by name in an appeal by Thomas Bowyer Bower published in the *Sherbourne Mercury* of November 1790 for volunteers to join a mercenary army to fight in Spain, 'young fellows of spirit and high metal' which had to be '5'5" without shoes and 16 to 30 years of age'. The Coopers Arms was one of the assembly places of the appeal which covered the county. In 1813 the landlord and yearly tenant was George Milledge 35 and his wife Grace 31, he was noted for his splendid dinners and entertainments. The freehold was advertised for sale in 1833 but Milledge continued as landlord until his death in 1842, the only hint of trouble was in 1840 when he was fined £12/10/- for selling spirits without a licence.

In 1844 the old established and well accustomed inn was advertised for rent by the Wyke Brewery of Gillingham to include a coach house and stabling for 20 horses occupied by Levi Honeyborne. It was advertised again in 1847 this time described as 'old established but newly built' which would be the building that we see today. In the census of 1851 the landlord was 46-year-old Edward Cox with his wife Grace, who must have been the widow of George

The Coopers' Arms 2024

Milledge as stepsons George and John had that surname. They leave in 1854 after a sale of their furniture and effects as they are leaving the business. This was followed two years later by similar sale of the property of Edward Smetham also leaving the pub and could hardly have had time to move his furniture in. The Cooper's was looking for a new tenant again in 1875 and described as having an open bar, bar parlour, market room, large club room, sitting room, nine bedrooms, kitchen, cellar, and offices. There were two Forester's Courts, with Sheppard's and Oddfellow's lodges containing together between 300 and 400 members with regular meetings being held at the house.

Events took a serious turn in 1861 when a young man named Skinner whose father was a surgeon in Bath and who had been staying at the pub was discovered covered with blood in his room. As a servant entered he remarked 'Your nose, sir, has been bleeding!' No it hasn't' replied Skinner and the servant responded with, 'why sir, you have cut your throat!' A doctor dressed the wound and discovered that the young man had stopped slightly below the ear just missing the jugular vein. Suicide was of course a crime at this time and had to be investigated. His defence was that he had a headache and made the incision to relieve the pain which he claimed was 'quite in accordance with the rules of practice'. 'This maybe so for your part,' replied the magistrate, 'but if we had a headache we should decidedly objected to being sliced underneath the ear to effect a cure'. The young man escaped punishment. The pub is also home to a branch of the Loyal Order of Ancient Shepherds, a friendly society founded in 1826 with many of its meetings and celebrations being held there. The society's aim was to help the sick, bury the dead, and assist each other in times of distress. Members would pay a contribution, and the society would use the money to support sick members and their families, and to pay for funerals. An advertisement of 1874 seeking a new tenant claims that the pub was host to two Oddfellows Lodges and two Foresters Courts as well as the Shepherds. The pub was being let because of the ill-health of landlord Thomas Sherry who had been there for six years. The premises were described on this occasion as 'an open bar, bar parlour, market room, large clubroom, sitting room, nine bedrooms, kitchen, cellar and offices.'

There was an intriguing advertisement in one of the local papers during June 1882 when Henry Riggs placed a notice in the local paper regarding his wife of five years. Unfortunately, nothing further has been discovered about this intriguing story. But it seems that this pub was perhaps not the best place for marital harmony. In November 1925 Hilda Elizabeth White wife of landlord Wadham D White applied for a separation order on the grounds of his cruelty towards her claiming that he had been drunk continually for three months and

> **ROBBERY BY A WIFE.**
>
> LUCY RIGGS, the wife of Mr. HENRY RIGGS, was managing the Coopers' Arms, in Maiden-street, Weymouth, the property of Mr. Devenish, when she started on the 9th day of June, taking a large sum of money with her, while her husband was at work. I, the undersigned, Hereby Give Notice, —That I will not be answerable for Any Debt or Debts contracted by my Wife, LUCY RIGGS, from this date.
>
> (Signed) HENRY WILLIAM RIGGS.
>
> Dated this day, 9th of June, 1882, Coopers' Arms, Weymouth.
>
> Any Person who can give such information as will enable me to find the said LUCY RIGGS will be Rewarded.

Poole Telegram 23 June 1882

knocked her down twice in one morning. A doctor's professional opinion upon seeing him in this state was that 'he was going off his head'. He had threatened to kill her if she left him and she was now a nervous wreck. The bench granted her request and ordered the defendant to pay 30/- per week towards the maintenance of the wife and their five-year-old son.

THE CORNOPEAN INN
Concord Place, St Leonards Road, Weymouth

FIRST FOUND IN the 1841 census this beer house was run by 27-year-old Mary Winsford in Concord Place, Franchise Street but nothing has been discovered about its early years or how it came to be named after a large valved horn or trumpet, similar to the orchestral cornet and invented in the 1820s. *Robson's Directory* of 1839 has a Mary Winsford, beer retailer of Union Place but nothing else has been discovered about her. By the next census of 1851 the house was in the hands of the Tomkins family, William aged 33 and his wife Elizabeth 34. Their application for a spirits licence was refused as most were on the grounds that the Boot was only a short distance away and two others were within easy reach. The family were still there in 1861 now with four children.

This quiet little local was severely shaken in 1869 when one of its lodgers, a journeyman shoemaker, Robert Pouney was discovered in his room with his throat cut. A very intemperate man, he had not been sober for the last fortnight and when found it was apparent that he had been dead for some time, he was 35 years of age. At the inquest held in the pub some of the jurors complained that the coffin was too small and that the corpse had to be crammed into it. The coroner explained that the coffins were supplied by contract ready-made but the jury thought that the maker should be compelled to measure the corpse or at least send a coffin of the proper size.

The pub was, in the words of landlord William Sleep, 'rendered useless by enemy action' during the war and rebuilt at the corner of Granville Road at 16 Newstead Road only to be damaged again by further bombing. Applications

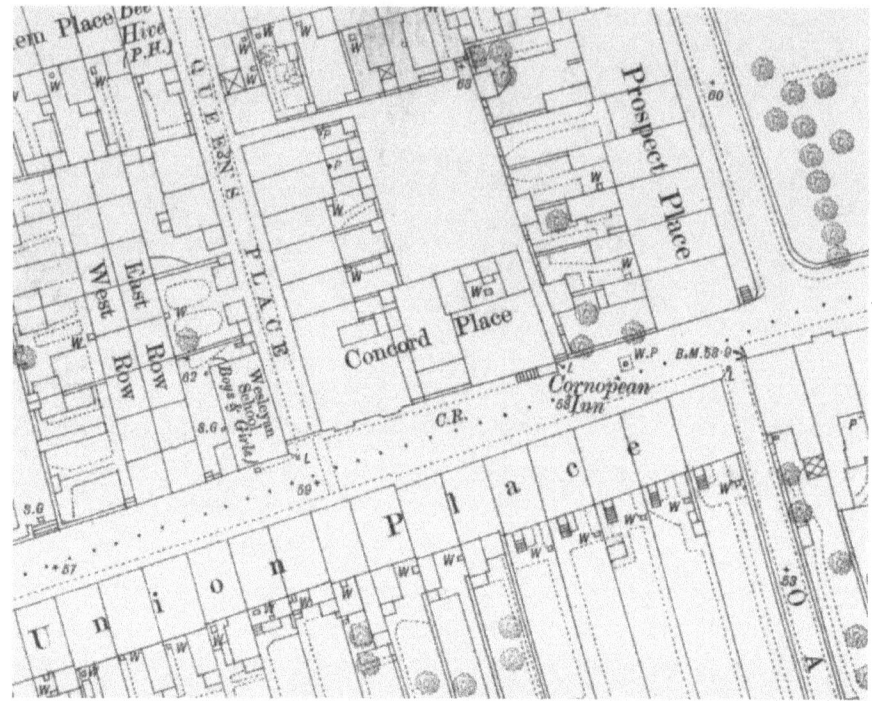
The Cornopean Inn 1864 O/S Map

to move the licence were refused as the neighbourhood was already well served. He and the Devenish brewery were referred to the Licensing Compensation Authority but the refusal meant that no compensation could be obtained.

THE COVE INN/ COVE HOUSE
Cove Row, Weymouth

This quayside beer house seems to have begun in the mid 1830s following the Beerhouse Act of 1830 which enabled anyone to brew and sell beer on payment of a licence costing two guineas, the aim being to increase competition between brewers, in the hope that people would drink beer rather than gin. The act resulted in the opening of hundreds of new beerhouses, public houses and breweries throughout the country, Elizabeth Bray is shown as a beer retailer at Cove House in directories of 1840 and was still there for the census of 1851 a widow aged 70. She died in 1854 leaving her estate and possessions to family members with the names Coleman and Newman who continued as licensees until around 1865.

Permission to sell spirits was strictly controlled by local magistrates and in 1855 there was an application for a spirits licence on behalf of the then landlord William Coleman who argued that the house was situated near the shipping on the Quay and in the event of steamers being re-established to the Channel Islands, passengers could land at the staging opposite the house. The application stated that 'This house has existed upwards of 20 years and during that period not a single complaint or irregularity had been made against it although there were nearly 4,000 inhabitants in Weymouth there were only four licensed public houses within those limits' the application was refused and it was not until the following year that his licence was granted.

The Cove Inn 1970s (Weymouth Museum)

There has been very little reported about this house. In June 1867 a drunken soldier stole 3/- from the till and made off but landlord John Otter Hawkin's 10-year-old son was able to give such a good description to the police that the thief was arrested and received six months hard labour. In 1870 the owner and master of a small schooner called the *Admiral Napier* were charged with scuttling her. Although worth only about £300 it was insured for £1,000. The owner, Hector Gillies had asked several people to help with his plan eventually engaging John Fitzgerald and the vessel was sunk by boring a hole in it from the captain's cabin. John Hawkins landlord, and a master mariner was called to give evidence. Gillies had lodged with him and he was asked to survey the vessel which he considered would be sound after a few repairs. The pair were arrested and the case went all the way to the Old Bailey where Gillies, as the owner and instigator, received five years penal servitude with Fitzgerald getting 18 months after a guilty plea.

In 1880 a letter to the local paper suggested that the entire road should be demolished to make the Nothe more accessible and it seems that the old Cove Inn, which was tucked away down Cove Passage, was demolished in around 1889 to be rebuilt in its present position, as the fine red brick building illustrated above. In 1923 the licence was taken by Bill and Lill Reynolds. Bill died in 1956 and the licence was taken by their son Roy who had been landlord at the High West Street Tavern until 1969 when he moved to the Mason's Arms at Upway. The Cove Inn had been in the same family for 46 years and closed in 1987 and is now a private house.

THE CROWN HOTEL
St Thomas Street, Melcombe Regis

THE CROWN IS one of the town's oldest named inns, the landlords in 1758 were John Staneway and his wife Edith. Staneway is named in the Dorset Militia List as an innkeeper and although the pub is not named, when he died in 1763 his widow issued a statement to the press saying that she was going to continue running the Crown Inn at Weymouth and that she had 'annexed the Three Crowns Inn where there are good stalls for 50 horses'. All that has been discovered about the latter is that it was run by a John Morris and his wife Mary, he died in 1753 and his goods were auctioned off, its location is unknown but presumably close to the Crown. Despite the loss of her husband Edith Staneway seems to have been more than equal to the task of running the establishment, not only did she, 'annexe' the Three Crowns but in 1773 she announced that 'she has enlarged her house with additional lodging rooms and commodious parlours, good grass and stalls for 60 horses.' Although it is quite possible that she had been running the place from the start as many landlords continued in their previous occupations while their wives run the pubs. One profitable side-line was holding auctions and in 1776 a schooner named the *Young Boston* of 45 tons was up for sale, another was transportation and beginning on 9 August 1779 a coach service was established between the

The Crown Hotel in 2022

pub and the Christopher Inn in Bath leaving there at 7 am arriving at the Crown on the same evening. For those with any illness or disability the 'Saxon Doctor and Oculist' Goergslenner was at the hotel every Tuesday and able to cure most complaints including a blind man who can now see, a bad harelip, and a girl who was deaf in both ears for many years but is now cured. There were probably others that have not come down to us.

By 1780 the inn was being run by John Loats, a former butler to John Williams Onslow Esq who laid in an assortment of the best wines and lost his dog, a one-eyed brown spaniel for the return of which he offered a 1gn reward or, 'the person in whose custody it is found after this notice will be prosecuted with the upmost severity of the law.' Auctions continued with 320 tons of French Bay Salt for sale along with the galliot the *Jonge Anne* at 180 tons taken by the *Friendship* privateer of Weymouth. In 1782 the pub itself is put up for auction together with coach house, stable and garden held on a lease for three good lives of which 13 years were unexpired. Loats remained as tenant paying an incredible £881 per annum, around £125,600 in 2024. In 1798 he moved to the Three Kings Inn, Wells, Somerset while the Crown continued to flourish with regular high-profile auctions and bankruptcy hearings continuing to bolster its status in the town. His place was taken by James and Elizabeth

Sketch of the Hotel in 1790 by Samuel Grimm

Cass and the 1813 Land Tax Returns show William Bower as the proprietor with James Cass as the occupier. December of 1815 saw the town visited by her Royal Highness Princess Charlotte of Wales and landlady Elizabeth Cass, now a widow, hosted her second dinner of the 'long established Gentleman's Beef Steak Club' at the inn which was been founded by Thomas Buxton sometime a local MP. This was followed later in the week by him giving a dinner to the gentleman of the Crown Club at his marine villa at Belfield.

In 1829 the Crown formed the last lot in a sale of the houses and pubs auctioned as part of the Fordington Brewery which is examined in more detail in the Bear entry. The property was held on three lives aged 10, 40 and 55 years and divided into several suites of rooms comprising 25 beds and still in the occupation of Mrs Cass at an annual rent of 100 guineas. It failed to reach its reserve but was sold after the sale to a Thomas Bennett of Weymouth for £1,404. Elizabeth Cass died on 9 July 1831 after a 'severely protracted illness' having held the hotel with her husband James for a remarkable 43 years and alone since being widowed in 1813 – about 18 years. Upon her death daughter her Charlotte Wilkinson takes over briefly having been involved with the business for many years.

By May of 1834 coaches were being run from the new more grandly named 'Crown Hotel and Guernsey and Jersey Tavern' to Bristol and Bath and in October of 1838 Nathaniel Roman took over saying that the premises have undergone a thorough repair with new lockup coach houses and a 'distinct room for the accommodation of commercial gentlemen' with coaches running through Dorchester to London. In July of 1842 Brother Roman hosted a dinner for the Provincial Grand Lodge of Ancient Free and Accepted Masons for the Province of Dorset at the Crown and in November 1845 Nathaniel and Eliza hosted their fifth anniversary dinner to celebrate the birthday of the Prince of Wales but within the year Eliza had died after a long illness at the age of 38 and the Crown was offered for rent within a few weeks, presumably Nathaniel feeling unable to carry on without her.

Thomas Bennet the owner, put the lease up for sale in May of 1847 containing '21 bedrooms, seven private sitting rooms, good commercial room, bar, larder, a large dining hall or ballroom, kitchen, scullery, cellars and other conveniences' which was taken up by 32-year-old Dominic Stone and his wife Fanny and in 1854 it was auctioned once more, 'The premises extend from Thomas Street to St Nicholas Street with another portion of the premises included a spirit shop all held for the remainder of the term and 99 years determinable on the lives of two persons aged 67 and 35.' By now it was trading by the name of the Crown Family and Commercial Hotel under George Frost who didn't stay long but was apparently the sole agent for 'Stogumber Medicinal Pale Ale' before moving to the Star and Garter in Andover leaving Walter W Commins as the new landlord. He was also an auctioneer and announced his arrival with an opening dinner on Wednesday 25 November 1863 at 6.00 sharp – tickets 10/6d including wine and the band of the 5th Dorset who will play during the meal. Apparently only 15 people turned up but 'a pleasant evening was spent'. Commins was another landlord to suffer the death of his wife who died in September of 1866 and he left soon after.

The opportunity was taken to rebuild the hotel 'in accordance with the spirit and requirements of the present day at a cost of several thousand pounds and elegantly furnished by an eminent city firm'. Opening day was 14 May 1868 by proprietor Edwin Dunn also of the Victoria and Great Western Hotel'.

At the end of 1887 the Crown was once again sold at auction, held on a lease for the residue of 99 years from 25 March 1866 and subject to an annual rental of £30. The sale this time included the contents of seven sitting rooms and 25 bedrooms, a bathroom two bars, kitchen, domestic and offices etc. Mr GP Symes secured the lot on behalf of Mr J Rowe of the Royal Hotel for what was considered to be a very low bid of £3,000. Elizabeth Stanbury was a single woman of 36 who ran the hotel seemingly single-handedly for around three

The Crown Hotel of 1868

years leaving to marry Quartermaster RH Luckham of the Broadway Flour Mills in 1893. There was much amusement in court when local businessman Thomas Hole appeared before the bench dressed only in a sheet and a rug with his face and hands blackened and being accused of being drunk and disorderly having been picked up naked on the ground outside the Crown. He put forward the perfectly reasonable explanation that it was Christmas and he had simply blacked himself up as a mummer. It is a great shame that no further questions were asked as to any friends he might have had with him or where the celebration took place – although they were doubtless many questions when he eventually arrived home. Fined 10/-

1900 saw a new century, a new landlord in the shape of Mr Nelson Bowes and a newly refurbished hotel including a doubling of the size of the smoking room to 24' x 15' a new entrance hall and bar and comfortable lounges in buffalo hide leather, the walls were decorated with lincrusta and anaglypta papers with a deep gold frieze. 'Electric light and bells have been renewed throughout'.

The late 1920s saw the rebuilding of the town bridge which opened on 4 July 1930 and yet another refurbishment and enlargement of the old hotel creating the one that we see today. This time expanded to include '40 bedrooms (h & c water in all rooms) lounges, smoke room, billiard room, restaurant, garage and every modern comfort'. The owners Devenish closed the hotel in 1974 but it was purchased by hotelier Leslie King and reopened two years later.

THE CUTTER INN
East Street & St Alban's Street, Melcombe Regis

THE CUTTER IS another of the town's pubs that go back a long way, the name being mentioned in 1790 as run by a William Payne. In January 1803 a Dutch brig named the *De Vrow Jacoba* then lying in Weymouth harbour was advertised for auction at the inn. Mary Mouat victualler of the Cutter was summoned to a bankruptcy hearing to take place at Luce's Hotel, Weymouth during March of 1827 and she is shown in *Pigot's Directory* of 1823 as having been landlady at the Cutter, East Street but nothing more has been discovered about her. Taking her place was Richard Clark who was landlord for 12 years before leaving to take over the Crown Inn, Sturminster Newton in April 1839. Immediately following was William Fowler who stated in his initial address that the house had received 'considerable attention and undergone a thorough repair for their accommodation'. Fowler was a former coachman on the *Magnet* taking people and goods from Weymouth to Basingstoke for 17 years, he died in March 1841 at the age of 50. In the same year Benjamin Young in prison for debt escaped from Ilchester jail by means of a rope ladder thrown over the wall by a friend, he managed to get to the Cutter and from there hoped to get across to the Channel Islands but by a stroke of ill luck he was recognised by a constable as he was sitting by the fire calmly writing a letter and was immediately returned to custody. 1845 saw a keen sportsman at the inn Edward Martin, an enthusiastic cricketer organised a grand pigeon match at Weymouth racecourse with a first prize of £7 for those who could shoot the most, shot was to be limited to 1½ oz. A report in the *Dorset County Chronicle* during March 1847 contained the following report:-

Monster Egg Club

We have seen an egg, which is now in the possession of Mr Stote of the Cutter Inn (who will be happy to show it to any person) measuring full 6 ½ inches in circumference and 7 3/4 inches in the oval, Weight within a trifle of a quarter of a pound, colour light brown. What renders this egg still more remarkable is it being the produce of a late last years pullet and the ninth egg laid. The hen is only of the common size and of the brown speckled colour. It has been shown to a number of persons several who have been regular dealers in eggs for the last 30 years and who have declared it to be one of the largest eggs that they ever saw as its size is little less than that of a turkey egg'.

In 1848 William Stote offered the pub to let with immediate possession claiming that a good trade had been carried on for the past 20 years. Stote was ambitious and declared himself to be moving on to a larger inn taking over the Bear with his wife Harriet which they ran successfully for many years leaving the Cutter in the care of James Sly 36 and his wife Harriet 30. The pub organised a trip to London to visit the Great Exhibition at Crystal Palace including transport, board and lodgings which proved very popular but there does not seem to be a report of how well it went. There was also a trip to Bindon Abbey near Lulworth Cove and possibly many others showing that the pub had been taking interest in exploring the wider world. Other Sly innovations included dealing in cigars and organising a Christmas raffle for

The Cutter Hotel 2016

which 500 tickets were sold with prizes to the value of £50 including ducks, turkeys and of course, cigars. During the summer months he organised horse racing events.

Sly took a man to court for creating a disturbance and refusing to leave the pub for which he was fined 5/- or six hours in the public stocks an entertaining but declining form of punishment, which alternative he chose is not recorded. He and his wife were presented with a silver claret jug and goblets to match in Feb 1861 as a mark of respect and esteem; all indications are that this was a very popular and well run local pub. An advertisement of 1862 shows the pub rebranded as *J. Sly's Cutter Hotel* but within a few years by now around 60 years of age he had moved on to the Antelope Hotel in Poole, a sad loss to the town. The *Southern Times* gave the Cutter an enthusiastic review during July of 1864 describing it as 'the best of all snuggeries' during Sly's occupation.

Although it is very common for landlords to continue with a previous profession while pulling pints the case of Mr Charles John Dring, his wife Annie and their seven children must have been quite unusual as he was also a member of the Royal College of Veterinary Surgeons who continued to offer his services while occupying the Cutter, he moved to take over the Victoria Hotel on the Esplanade which he held for many years.

Dring's tenure was followed briefly in 1879 by the occupation of Jeremiah Chapman who didn't stay long as he was arrested for being in possession of 12lb of tobacco and several boxes of cigars all smuggled from one of the ships in the harbour, his exit was followed by a period of some confusion. It appears that when Dring left the licence had been split, half of the property licensed and the other half not. The unlicensed half was occupied by a John Case and his wife Fanny who attempted to start the Cutter Temperance Hotel, and had spent about £500 in furnishing the place. The ancient walls must have blushed with shame. He made a rule that people must have a dinner at his house before he would send out for beer or spirits which he obtained from the licensed part of the house. In August 1882 Case applied for a beer and wine licence, 'he at first attempted to conduct the hotel on temperate principles but found that his customers were constantly asking for wine and spirits'. The magistrates considered this arrangement to be quite sufficient and declined to issue a new licence. During 1884 the licensee was a William Palmer from Hoxton in London who ran the pub until 30 Oct 1887 when he was killed on the yacht *Laureate* in Weymouth harbour during a severe storm, nine others lost their lives with him.

In 1890 owners, Devenish & Co advertised the property for rent and things continued under the direction of Frederick Glanville before he moved to the Black Dog in 1907. The house seems to have carried on without complaint until 1939 when Police Sergeant Stickey heard voices coming from the pub at 11:20 pm and suspecting that a crime was being committed he knocked on the door which was opened by landlord Frank Roe. Drinking at the bar, by now in darkness, were five RAF men. Roe trotted out the usual defence that they were guests having been invited to stay for the night as their car had broken down. The sergeant gave evidence to say that he had heard the words, 'One for the road' quite distinctly which Roe claimed came from the radio (!). Amazingly they got away with it, had they not been in uniform and during peacetime the verdict might have been quite different.

A post on the Pubs Galore site during 2012 gives the flavour of the place at that time

> The Cutter Hotel is a small boozer located down a small side street off the main Esplanade. There are two small rooms and the right hand side is a seating area that houses a dartboard. There were a few women throwing some arrows on my recent midweek evening visit. The bar is located to the left. There is a plasma screen that was showing muted Olympic coverage whilst the jukebox was playing. Children are permitted but a sign on the wall states 'unattended children will be given a free puppy, a litre of Pepsi Max and their bus fare to Portland.

THE DOLPHIN INN
Park Street, Melcombe Regis

SINCE 1834 WORKS had been carried out to infill an expanse of river known as the Backwater which included an area known as the Park District so named because the original intention was to create an extensive park for the enjoyment of the people in the town and its visitors. This never materialised as there was too much money to be made by having the land developed commercially causing much scandal and controversy, further information can be seen under the Waterloo Stores entry. The name Park Street is one of the few remainders of that period and the street itself was probably constructed during the 1840s. The census for 1851 shows George Smith, bricklayer, and his wife Hannah living there, no pub is mentioned but two years later he applied for a spirits licence for the Dolphin Inn which was refused on the grounds that he had been caught for Sunday trading within the last 12 months and that his house was too small to accommodate a sufficient number to justify the licence

The Dolphin 2024

and despite Smith offering to 'make it larger' his request was refused. There was a strange case in March of 1853 when one Sunday morning Sarah Spranklin went to the pub on three occasions looking for her husband, there were three men in there drinking who assured her that he had not been seen whereas in fact they were covering for him having slipped out the back just before one of her visits. Suspecting a conspiracy and wanting revenge she took landlord Smith to court for serving outside of legal hours which resulted in him being fined 40/-. But that wasn't the end of the matter, Smith summoned her in return saying that she had turned up drunk looking for her husband and was very abusive and would not leave, scratching his face as he tried to turn her out, hammering away at the door and breaking a window. She was fined 6/- and given a week to pay.

Thomas Bennett the landlord during 1866 was caught selling beer after hours when the police discovered several men and women drinking together after 11.00pm. He explained helpfully that they were friends up from London and that no beer was drawn and that it was a private party. He was then asked if all of the five or six railway porters present were from

London? Fined 10/-including costs. In November of 1880 the Manchester Unity of Oddfellows organised the funeral of former landlord and carpenter, Brother Emmanuel Ricketts who died at the age of 38 after a long and painful illness. The licence passed to his widow Hester who was there until 1885 when Devenish advertised the premises to let and the Dolphin passed from carpenter to stonemason in the shape of Simon John Rabjohns Lock 37 and his wife Ann who run the pub with little incident until 1912 when the Kirkaldie family took charge. Landlord William was called away on military service while wife Alice run the pub having his licence restored upon his return in August 1919 and they were still there at the outbreak of the Second World War in 1939. The Dolphin was one of several Devenish pubs that had their landlords returned to them after being away on active service.

A contributor to the Pubs Galore site describes the situation in November 2016

> 'A basic drinkers' pub on the end of a Georgian terrace, currently operated by Hopback. There are two bars downstairs, and rooms to let upstairs. A former skittle alley is now used as a function room. Recent refurbishment as removed unnecessary clutter, and the front bar is now a wood-floored drinking area, while the families' room at the back is more of a saloon. The bar had four pumps on it, but there were only two ales on draught, plus a selection of bottles. An old customer remarks further that, 'The back bar of the Dolphin was an addition that was put in in the mid 1950s. We know this because there's a photo that was taken by Weymouth photographer Graham Herbert from the old Christ Church tower. You can see that the back area of the pub wasn't there before 1955.'

The Dolphin still operates today as a friendly local.

THE DUKE OF ALBANY/ NEW ARRIVAL
Park Street, Melcombe Regis

FIRST MENTIONED IN August of 1870 when William Oliver applied for a spirits licence for the 'New Arrival' beer house in Park Street. In his application he stated that he had just purchased these premises but had kept two licensed houses before and as a measure of his respectability he added that he was a fish agent for the London and South Western Railway Company which seemed to work as his application was granted. In 1882 he moved on to the much more central and prestigious White Hart in Lower Bond Street.

Next up was Ambrose Charles Orchard who got off to a rather rocky start when he was summoned for 'allowing his premises to be open for habitual resort of prostitutes, and also for keeping it open beyond the hours allowed by law'. Orchard did not appear in person due to illness but sent his wife instead who appeared in floods of tears saying that it was her that sold the beer and that she did not know the girls were prostitutes. She had shut up for the night when two ship's captains arrived looking for beds, they had some girls with them but because she had just taken over the pub and not had one before she did not know that they were such characters. Mr Orchard, it emerged, had been a prison warden and had not run a pub before. The owners, Messrs' Newman of Sydling said that they would be removed from the house and on that basis Orchard was fined £1 including costs. But the matter did not end there here. When the owners tried to have Orchard's licence revoked the magistrate took the view that he was of good character and had just arrived. 'It was the innocent person who gets caught', he stated, 'while the knowing thief stays clear', if the publican and had been an old licensed victualler then what had happened would be fully considered by the bench but in this case

The Duke of Albany 2024

if Orchard were to be kept on the matter would not weigh against him and his licence was renewed'. Despite such wisdom and understanding from the bench, within a few weeks Newman and Sons had advertised the now renamed Duke of Albany to be let. The challenge was taken up by George W Burch formerly of the Clifton Hotel and the licence was transferred in November. Orchard moved to the Steam Packet Inn in January 1883. Burch and his wife Ann served out their time until 1897 when he retired at the age of 68. In 1912 the Albany was taken over by Henry Coleman.

In February of 1923 in a move reminiscent of 20 years before an attempt was made to close down six public houses, the Bird in Hand, Duke of Cornwall, Turks Head, the Boot Inn, the Phoenix and the Duke of Albany. The move was made by local temperance organisations fronted by a Mrs Hamlin the wife of a Baptist minister on the grounds that these premises were 'surplus to requirements' and based on an Act of Parliament which allowed magistrates to close pubs that they considered unnecessary. The proceedings were adjourned until March when it emerged that landlord Henry Coleman was now in his early 70s and in very poor health with heart problems . Apparently he had not been told of the attempts to close his pub and out of sympathy for him this case was withdrawn and he died very shortly after but the Duke remained in the same family until at least 1939.

THE DUKE OF CORNWALL/ DUKE OF CUMBERLAND
St Edmund Street, Melcombe Regis

IT WAS THE Duke of Cumberland who put down the Jacobite rebellion at Culloden in 1746. He died in 1765 and perhaps it is not too big a stretch of the imagination to think that the pub was named in his honour shortly after his death. That was certainly the name of the inn until comparatively recent times. Records going back to 1790 show Rob Ford as landlord from 1790-93 and from at least 1813 until 1827 the land tax returns show the Cumberland to be owned by William Bower who had a number of pubs in the town with his tenant being John Robbins or Robens. In 1829 it was one of the houses auctioned as part of Fordington Brewery. (see the Bear entry for more details.) On 25 October 1831, it being St Crispin's Day, the Weymouth Benefit Society of Cordwainers held their third anniversary at 'Mr Read's the Duke of Cumberland Inn' and the following year the Mechanics Benefit Society held their first meeting there, all good for business.

From 1836 until 1853 the house was run by a William Chalker and when he retired John and Elizabeth Phillips took over; John died within the year and the licence passed to his widow. On 4 January 1857 she married local photographic artist Theodore Brunell originally from Corsica – this did not begin well let alone end well. On the morning after the marriage he became violent towards her when she refused to pay his debts throwing cups and saucers at her, striking her violently and threatening her with a carving knife. They lived together for only three weeks before he left her for 'a female of bad character' and the following May Elizabeth took him to court, requesting a divorce on the grounds of cruelty and adultery which was undefended and granted. While they were separated Brunell was apprehended on a warrant for failing to attend court to answer a charge of creating a disturbance and abusing Mrs Seaman wife of the landlord at the Baltic Inn. Brunell had once

The Duke of Cornwall 2024

made an income of several hundred pounds a year and if he had been able to remain sober might have lived in comfort. As it was he was an incorrigible drunkard constantly before the magistrates for brawling. On this occasion he was ordered to enter into his own recognisances of £50, to find two sureties of £25 each and to keep the peace for 12 months but as he was unable to find two people with sufficient confidence in him he was 'locked up'. In the census of 1861 the occupants of the police station, which was right next door to the Cumberland, record only one prisoner on the night, Theodore Brunell, photographer aged 39.

Elizabeth left the pub shortly after her divorce in favour of James White Board, his wife Eliza and their family. Board was one of those landlords that not only run their pubs well but took an active part in the local community. He took over in 1859 at the age of 29 and was still there when he reached 60. Among his early achievements were to expand the local rifle corps band into a band for the whole town and host dinners for the local police force and the local football team. By 1877 he had been appointed the local rate collector and took this role so seriously that he made alterations to the pub replacing the east window with a doorway in order to give a separate entrance and office for those coming to pay what they owed. His alteration can still be seen today with the door on the left-hand side replacing the window and spoiling the symmetry of the frontage.

In May of 1893 the licence passed to Charles Hughes a worthy successor to James Board a keen sportsmen from Kew whose achievements included winning cups for rugby, being recognised as one of the finest fast bowlers of his day as well as being secretary of the Weymouth Football Club. In a rather unusual departure from the usual activities of a public house an advertisement in November 1895 offered 'Thorough instruction in all modern Ballroom dances, Syrian, Barn Dances etc lessons private or class apply to Mr C Hughes Duke of Cumberland.' Hughes was a leading Freemason and tireless political worker for the Conservative Party. There was an interesting civil case in August of a 1906 when a Mr G Chandler and family of Barnes Common, London stayed off and on during the summer months. Their total bill came to £7/7/8d which Hughes agreed to make £7 even money and was paid most of it by cheque -which Chandler cancelled when he returned home resulting in a court case to retrieve the outstanding sum. The charges had been 30/-per week for the rooms and 4/6 and 2/6 for meals each day, no complaints had been made about the rooms or the food. The problem was that nothing had been agreed beforehand and Chandler found the bill excessive. The judge found in Hughes favour and the case had enabled him to tell the story of Emperor Charles V and the innkeeper who charged him a florin each for eggs, 'Eggs must be very scarce here' said the Emperor 'No your Majesty' replied the innkeeper 'but Emperors are'.

Hughes died of influenza and gastritis in January 1915 and it was during the following year that the name of the inn was changed to the Duke of Cornwall. No explanation for this has been discovered but it was during the

*The Duke of Cornwall in the 1920s beside the Guildhall
(Weymouth Museum)*

tenure of Charles's widow Agnes before she married Albert Frost who became the licensee in 1919. In 1923 valiant attempts by the temperance movement to close the pub along with five others were abandoned when the applications for the previous five had failed. Reginald Bugler became landlord in around 1935 and like many licensees he had been involved in the carriage trade and was apparently the town's first motor car taxi driver. Continuing the sporting theme of previous landlords he was a founder member of the Weymouth Swimming Club and one of the originators of the Christmas Day swim when in 1948 he made a wager with his successor at the Duke, Mr RS Laker against each others ability to swim across Weymouth harbour on Christmas Day, both made the other side successfully thus starting the tradition. In 1944 Arthur Richard Hunt was fined £10 for selling rum which was 13.5% added water after the landlady admitted that she poured spirits left over in customers glasses back into the bottle. The pub continues to be run very successfully to this day.

THE DUKE OF EDINBURGH / BRIDPORT ARMS
St Thomas Street, Melcombe Regis

VERY LITTLE HAS been discovered about the early days of this house first known as the Bridport Arms. The 1841 census names a Christopher Goodwin innholder and former cabinet maker aged 42 and his wife Sarah but no pub name is given. Sarah was in charge ten years later as a beer shop keeper aged 49 and now a widow following her husband's death in 1846. A Ruben Hillier took over in 1852. Walter Alfred Fitch applied for a spirits licence after spending much money refurbishing the place in the hope of impressing the magistrates. A memorial or petition had been signed by a county magistrate and numerous others, and there was no disputing his respectability but he did not put forward any reasoned argument for granting another licence in the area. A similar application in the following year received some sympathy from the bench but as the landlord had changed once again they felt unable to grant it. The nearest licensed houses were the Gloucester Hotel and the Cross Keys opposite the Masonic Hall and it was said that one more would be a serious nuisance in that respectable neighbourhood. Net and twine maker Mathew Dix Roberts also applied unsuccessfully for a licence before moving on to the Portland Railway Hotel in 1867. A licence was finally granted in September 1869 and the following February Alfred Neale of the 'Bridport Arms' was able to advertise his 'Wine and Spirit Vaults with foreign and British spirits of a very superior quality and first-class wines at the lowest possible price'.

1870 was the turn of 42-year-old George Woodridge, a pensioner from the convict service, who applied for the name of the Bridport Arms to be changed to the Edinburgh Hotel which was granted. His reasons for doing this are not known, he was from Hampshire himself. Another slight adjustment to the name perhaps made more sense in April when his widow Emily gave up the licence to Henry Dibben, changing the name from the Edinburgh to

The Edinburgh in 2025

the Duke of Edinburgh. In all probability this was to celebrate the Duke's marriage to Her Imperial Highness Grand Duchess Marie Alexandrovna of Russia in a much-publicised event in January of that year. In an advertisement Dibben offered 'good accommodation to the offices and servants of the Yeomanry Cavalry'.

In an indication that standards are not quite as high as they once were, a man named Ford dropped in for a glass of beer which was served by Dibben's niece as the landlord was drunk which resulted in a brief altercation and appearance before the petty sessions with each accusing the other of provoking the fight. Dibben admitted giving Ford half a sovereign to keep the matter out of court but to no avail. Sensibly the court dismissed the case on condition that each pay 1/- for the cost of the summons – although Ford thought that he was entitled to another half sovereign for his days work...

In 1888 landlord Charles Acock left a soldier alone in the bar for a few moments and upon returning found that nearly all the silver had gone from the till as had a bunch of fine cigars. When apprehended later private Tiff said 'If have done wrong . . . I must put up with the consequences' before going on to say that he had bought the cigars in a nearby shop – there wasn't one, and that he had the £1/10/10d in silver on him when he left the barracks. Unbelievably, he was given the benefit of the doubt although it was agreed that his case was a very weak one.

For such an old and prominently sited establishment there is a remarkably small amount of information available about its later years, presumably the sign of a well run pub which continues today as a free house specialising in live music.

THE EAGLE TAVERN / GOLDEN EAGLE
Lower Bond Street, Melcombe Regis

THE EAGLE TAVERN in Lower Bond Street, formerly Conygar Lane, was one of the new beer houses which grew up to take advantage of the 1857 railway station, so new in fact that it was still being built at the end of 1858 a situation which did not deter prospective landlord Mr Hurdle from applying for a spirits licence anticipating that the building would be 'finished in a fortnight'. He was advised to try again the following year. In June of 1869 the town was visited by Jenkins and Morgan two 'smashers' a term for those who live by making and passing fake money. Having tried to pass varying amounts without much success at several pubs they handed a dud shilling to Mrs Forsey the landlady who tested it with her teeth after which they were arrested and received 12 months hard labour each. The owners of the house, brewers John Groves and Co put the Eagle up for rent in September 1873 along with the Red Lion at Portland and the Kings Arms at Portisham. February 1884 was the time of the great Publicans Measures Raid during which at least ten licensed premises were searched for having incorrect measures but on this occasion all cases were dismissed with warnings. To avoid repetition a more complete account can be found under the Royal Oak entry.

The Golden Eagle 1998 (Weymouth Museum)

Not all husband and wife partnerships were suited to the pub trade, Edward and Mabel Collins were a case in point. A Mrs Spranklin went to look for her husband at the Eagle to find him drunk and asked him to come home, he refused and ordered another quart of beer for himself and his mate which Mrs Collins poured in defiance of his wife's wishes. The magistrate said it was a most disgraceful thing to sell beer to a man who was already drunk and that Spranklin should go to prison without the option of a fine but realising that he only took home £1 per week and that the burden would fall upon his wife, he was fined 10/- for riotous behaviour and although the fault lay with Mrs Collins for serving a drunken man her husband was responsible as licensee and was fined 30/- with his licence endorsed. By the summer of 1884 things deteriorated badly behind the bar when Collins appeared in court with a black eye charged with assaulting and beating his wife. She said that she was afraid to live with him and wanted a separation, they had been married for 13 years and had seven children. She claimed that she did not know how her husband's face became bruised, possibly when she was defending herself. All parties agreed that a separation was the best course and that Collins should make some agreement with his wife and if he didn't the court would.

Alfred Legg and his family rented a room in a house adjoining the Eagle and a late one evening he was observed to climb out of the top floor window of the pub, clamber along the roof and climb back into his own window. The neighbours summoned the police who found him in bed pretending to be asleep. When questioned he claimed firstly that he had climbed onto the roof to have a smoke, and secondly that he had climbed out to ask the price of some fish that some men were selling in the street below. Despite these preposterous stories nothing seemed to be missing from the pub and so he was discharged with a caution.

In 1893 the Eagle was pleased to host meetings of the Amalgamated Society of Carpenters and Joiners who were much distressed to learn that the contract to build the new Westham Church had been given to a firm from Exeter despite the bulk of the money having been raised by local subscription and the building trade being somewhat depressed in the town at the time and there being little difference in the two quotes.

The landlords in 1905 were Mr and Mrs William Andrews who temporarily took in 12-year-old girl Nellie Sergeant whose parents had died recently Mr Williams had been a close friend of her fathers. A little later the girl was passed onto Robert Jolliffe a railway guard who had promised to look after her as a companion for his wife Alice who had lost her right arm, but the reality was very different and the poor girl was treated as a servant being frequently beaten and starved, Mrs Jolliffe was described as an 'exceedingly irritable and bad tempered woman'. The couple were arrested and Charles was charged with causing unnecessary suffering and injury to her health on diverse dates in the previous six months. The court was given detailed accounts of beatings and ill treatment despite a promise to the Andrews that they would settle £100 on her and keep her at school until she was 14. Nellie was examined at the Eagle by the police doctor who found extensive bruising all over her body which must have caused great pain and suffering. The magistrates found the case of unjustifiable cruelty proven and the pair were fined a total of £9/19/1d. Remarkably, the Jolliffes were back in court a few months later charged with assaulting another girl of 20 who they employed as a companion and to undertake general housework despite hearing much evidence as to the way the girl was treated, the magistrates concluded that she was 'difficult' and this time Alice Jolliffe was fined only 5/- plus costs.

Trouble of a different sort came back to haunt the house in 1910 when Thomas Gibbs landlord from 1888 -1901 contested the will of his wife Mary Ann who had left money and property to her daughter, which he said, was his, although in his wife's name he claimed that the property had been bought with his money. He lost with costs awarded against him. 1918 saw John Bush prosecuted under the Beer Prices (Description) Order of that year. Bush had been charging 5d per pint for beer that was below the limit for that strength and should have been 4d as the specific gravity was 1026.6 degrees rather than 1030 degrees. Bush was awarded a rather hefty fine of £5.

Sometime later the pub became known as the Golden Eagle and scene of legendary performances by showman 'Jumpin' Jimmy Thunder' before being demolished in 1998 to make way for the Debenhams development.

THE EAGLE TAVERN
High Street, Weymouth

THERE WERE TWO pubs named the Eagle Tavern, one each side of the river and the earliest known mention of the one in Weymouth High Street comes from August 1859 when Andrew Lane was granted a spirits licence. During the same year a John Lane advertised his new gas fitting service for which orders could be taken at his house in Town Lane or at the Eagle Tavern in High Street.

In 1861 local worthy and sometime counsellor Jeremiah Hibbs proposed that the Tavern be purchased and demolished to facilitate the widening of the street which will be of great public benefit and a great improvement on the approach to the bridge. The matter had arisen about two years ago and the present owner was a John Tizard himself a member of the town council who was quite prepared to sell at the right price despite the jokes that he become

High Street, Weymouth

a public benefactor and hand it over gratis. A small committee was formed to negotiate and decide whether this should be done by subscription or paid for via a loan from the local board extended over 20 to 30 years and as the road was so narrow at that point payment at public expense was certainly justified. Two surveyors were appointed to value the premises one said £350 and another £375, neither would give way and so a Mr Barnes of Dorchester was called in who came up with a very unhelpful £550, the press were rather disgruntled after being excluded from council discussions on the negotiations.

Early in the following year Mr Tizard agreed to take £400 but was hoping for a favour in return. Removing the pub meant that there was one less licence in the area and he hoped that the Council would look favourably upon a licence being granted in lieu, either for his Rodwell Tavern or a house he was preparing on the Quay. It was agreed that this recommendation would be put forward and despite the usual opposition the Rodwell Tavern obtained its licence in August of 1862, a tender of £21 was accepted from a Mr Chalker for the demolition contract and the Eagle was no more.

THE FISHERMAN'S ARMS
High Street, Weymouth

IN THE CENSUS of 1851 the licensee of the Fisherman's Arms was Samuel Scott a local man and his wife Ann at 44 High Street, Weymouth. By the following year the licence had past to John Cooper 'lodging house keeper' who was fined 5/6 for having bought a pair of boots from two private soldiers

The Fisherman's Arms shortly before demolition

who had intended to desert. Trouble was never far from this unfortunate beer house. In the summer of 1856 George Hodger, 'a desperate looking fellow, an itinerant who had lost an eye and appeared not to have had his hair combed for a twelvemonth' entered the pub and become abusive. Cooper tried to evict him but fared worse in the fight, finding himself flat on the floor with Hodger's arm tightly clamped around his throat, Hodger's free hand was also clasping the hair of two women who had come to Cooper's defence. When arrested he fought with the police despite which the bench was less than sympathetic implying that Cooper and brought the situation upon himself by continually allowing such a bad class of person in his house. In 1860 Cooper himself appeared before the Bench charged with 'permitting persons of a notoriously bad character to assemble and meet together at his house'. He claims that he had kept the pub for six years without a complaint being made against him and promised that it will not happen again and that he had turned every one of the disreputable women out. The magistrates wished him to make the same promise about another pub, the British Queen kept by his mother and sister to which he agreed. Cooper had gone by the following year but its reputation didn't improve under the occupancy of the Talbot family with various court appearances concerning drunkenness and minor theft.

On 5 May 1875 landlord Charles and his wife Marianne were arrested and charged with 'feloniously receiving from Sarah Frickus one towel, one knife and fork, two cups and saucers, the property of Richard Rolls well knowing the same to have been feloniously stolen'. Frickus was a 50-year-old laundress who was charged with stealing various items from her employer over a period of time and selling them. Seven people were charged with receiving stolen property including Benjamin Ireland landlord of the Portland Arms and his wife Jane. Marianne was accused of exchanging various items from Frickus for beer. The matter came to trial but in the end, it could not be proven that the recipients knew that the items were stolen and the jury acquitted them but with grave reservations from the judge. Frickus received 12 months hard labour followed by a two-year supervision order.

In 1877 Arthur Lloyd a musician and actor asked for accommodation for himself and a private in the Royal Marines. They were shown to a room but Lloyd run back down stairs after a short time claiming that the marine had taken indecent liberties with him, he also seemed to have fled with his bed mate's money. 28 days hard labour. At the annual licensing meeting during August 1883 the Fisherman's was mentioned as one of those houses most complained about and their licence was suspended. Talbot had occupied the house for 23 years and he now applied for a licence to keep a common lodging house which was granted and regularised what was already going on as well as placing it under the supervision of the police who had the power to go into a lodging house at any time and make enquiries which was not the case for a public house. There was a strange little incident in 1884 when Thomas Vallance who owned the yard next door to the pub summoned Talbot for using threatening language. Vallance was apparently happily working away when Talbot came out and told him that he didn't know how to saw. He went in when it rained but popped out once it had stopped for a bit more sawing only to be accosted again by Talbot claiming that he and his father were thieves. Costs were ordered against Talbot as it was known that Vallance was an old townsman and an upright citizen in every respect.

Smashing pub windows was a pretty regular occurrence but in June 1889 Felix Summers managed to get 13 panes in one frantic spell smashing them with a stick as fast as he could according to one witness. He said that he had a grudge against the landlord but Charles Talbot claimed never heard of him but nonetheless his exertions earned him a month's hard labour. 'That Fisherman's Arms! exclaimed one magistrate 'The sooner we get rid of that the better!' And so it went on, a catalogue of petty crime, drunkenness, violence and poverty with the pub described as a 'lodging house for tramps'.

On the night of the census 1891 the house contained 13 members of the Talbot family and an incredible 31 lodgers including labourers, hawkers and musicians. At the licensing hearing of March 1903, the Fisherman's was one of several considered for closure but surprisingly, was allowed to continue on condition that it passed an inspection by the Medical Officer of Health, presumably its large intake of undesirables was seen as a public benefit – they had to go somewhere. Charles died in around 1905 and the house passed to son Herbert. At the annual renewal of licenses session in 1907 the authorities wanted insurances that certain sanitary alterations had been carried out and that notice had been served to bring the premises up to the correct legal standards. In August of 1919 the Fisherman's Arms was one of several Devenish pubs who had their landlords reinstated after being away on wartime service. The pub was rendered uninhabitable during the bombing raids of the Second World War and finally demolished during 1958 and the site is now part of a carpark.

THE FORESTERS ARMS / BRITISH QUEEN
Great George Street, Melcombe Regis

T HE EARLY DAYS of this house are rather sketchy. It seems to have started life as the British Queen and in 1854 landlord James Coombs had a rather strange side-line in that he also sold pickaxe handles, and in September a railway worker, Robert Miller, was seen to take one from the workshop. His house was searched after reports from witnesses and the handle was found underneath the floor of his privy, valued at 4d – he was committed for trial but the result does not seem to have been recorded. 42 builders engaged in constructing the new church at Preston were treated to a dinner at the British Queen provided by the Revd. Baker. The Queen was mentioned briefly in January 1860 when John Cooper, licensee of the Fisherman's Arms was taken to task over the disorderly state of his pub and the women that frequented it, 'do you not have another house of the same character in Weymouth? Cooper replied that he had 'but no girls were allowed there. It was kept by his mother and sister.' He was then made to promise that his undertaking to clean up the Fisherman's Arms would also apply to the British Queen. He would not have had time to make good his promise as he had left the Fisherman's by 1861 and is mentioned in an attack on one of his female servants by a jealous wife who had discovered that she was seeing her husband.

By the census of April 1861 Cooper had gone and the Queen

The Great British Pint

had been changed to the Forester's Arms run by 70-year-old widower Jeremiah Dean. As usual several applications were made and refused for a spirits licence until 1870 when Edwin Taylor England was at last successful. As well as the pub he was employed as foreman for William Reynolds a successful local builder, a responsible situation which spoke greatly in favour of his respectability and within the last few years a considerable sum of money had been laid out on the premises both by the himself and the freeholder. It now contained a large number of rooms perfectly adapted for accommodation and the area was increasing in size with many new houses being built. A branch of the Ancient Order of Foresters held regular meetings there. In his application the property was described as clean and commodious with a club room that could accommodate 60 people with a dining and a smoking room that could hold 20. As the house was situated at the back of the terrace, gentleman's servants often came for spirits and on this occasion the application was granted.

Little more was heard of the place until the census of 1871 when Edwin England aged 42 had become a builder in his own right employing four bricklayers, two masons, two plasterers, five labourers and two boys as well as being inn keeper of the pub. It seems that he had massively overstretched himself as he was out by 1877 and bankrupt the following year. George Seward was there in 1878 and summoned by his neighbours as his newly installed skittle alley said to be the cause of noise, drunkenness and bad language, he replied that he was considering installing some rubber pads.

In 1896 Eli Roberts of the Waverley Arms at Westham applied to remove the licence from the Forester's to his house under an act of 1872. Objectors said that was no need for a full licence there as the Rock Hotel was only 405 yards away. The bench reserved its decision and the case dragged on but presumably it was eventually agreed despite the objections as there is no mention of the Forester's after 1897.

THE FORESTER'S RETREAT
St Thomas Street, Melcombe Regis

THE FINE RED brick building described as, 'muscular Venetian Gothic' that is now 61 St Thomas Street seems far too grand to have been home to a short lived beer house which existed on the site the 1860s although it is correct for the period. The Retreat is first mentioned in 1865 when a stolen mantle was offered for sale at the house. It was run by Edward and Louisa

Site of the Forester's Retreat in 2025

White and in its brief existence saw the usual round of petty theft, drunks and reprobates. In June of 1867 Edward was summoned for allowing persons of a notorious character to assemble at his house contrary to his licence, fined 40/- and cautioned. There is no mention after 1868.

THE FOUNTAIN HOTEL
King Street, Melcombe Regis

DESIGNED BY THE architect George Crickmay and financed by brewers JA Devenish & Co. the Fountain was built by Reynolds & Son to be completed and fitted out by1860. The hotel became home to Solomon Sly, wife Elizabeth and an impressive brood of five children, four servants and staff, it's a wonder that they had room for guests. Sly had moved across the road from the Half Moon Hotel where he was described as a beer house keeper and this change must have been a big step up. The local paper announced the birth of a daughter at the Fountain in early August but the official opening was not celebrated until 10 January and then in great style with guests including the local military, businessmen and the architect himself, George Crickmay. During his time Sly hosted many dinners and celebrations and in April 1864 he was involved, probably unwittingly, in a strange hoax. The great Italian leader and revolutionary Giuseppe Garibaldi was on a visit to London and some wag had started a rumour that he was about to visit Weymouth which caused huge crowds at the station and a notice was affixed to the front of the pub say that he would be arriving at 7:30. Business was undoubtedly increased during that evening... Despite what must have seemed like the foundation for an extremely lucrative business – a brand new purpose-built hotel just yards from the railway station, Sly moved to the King's Head in East Street in July of 1866 and what is known of his life is recorded in that entry. When he left the Fountain was advertised to be let with immediate possession 'having a corner situation in Richmond Terrace opposite the railway station comprising a bar, parlour, three sitting and eight bedrooms, with convenient cellarage and outbuildings'.

His replacement was William James Rogers, late chief steward of the Peninsula and Oriental Steam Navigation Company's Service. He died of a heart attack two years later at the age of 33 and the licence was taken over briefly by his wife Elizabeth with the news that a 'first class American Bowling Saloon now adjoined the hotel'. She continued until 1874 when owners Devenish & Co advertised the pub for rent 'having a splendid open bar, bar parlour, coffee room, large smoking room, two drawing rooms, ten bedrooms, kitchen, yard, and offices. On the market in consequence of the death of the late proprietor'. The hotel passed to Richard Hardy formerly of the Star Inn who ran a livery business alongside the pub. He hadn't been there long before he was summoned for 'causing a horse to be worked while in an unfit state' it having been ridden from Weymouth to Dorchester by an employee in a very emaciated condition. Hardy managed to get away with it but his driver was fined £3 or one-months hard labour.

March 1874 saw a most unpleasant incident, a fight in the Victoria had resulted in somebody being severely slashed in the face with a glass thrown by a local businessman named Hibbs. The victim was staying at the Fountain and was assisted back there after the attack. After a long trial taking up two full pages of the local paper Hibbs got away with a £5 fine. The matter is considered in more detail in the Victoria entry.

The Fountain Hotel 2017

In June of 1876 Richard Hardy along with wife Jane and brother Walter were summoned for assaulting a police officer. They had been granted an extension during Yeomanry Week but when the constable arrived at about 1.30 am he found the place packed with revellers and demanded that the pub be closed upon which he was assaulted by the three defendants in a violent attack which continued out into the street. The Hardys accused PC Cooper of being drunk and abusive when he arrived. Much conflicting evidence was taken but, in the end, the two men were fined 10/- each with costs. Hardy spent much of his time building up his livery business offering dog carts, pony phaetons and picnic breaks from the hotel.

In June of 1878 two men on the way to work saw a woman in the sluice near Greenhill Gardens, they managed to pull her out and it was realised that she was Mrs Elizabeth Rogers former landlady of the Fountain who had been running a lodging house in Brunswick Buildings. She was charged with attempting suicide with the magistrates concluding that, 'There is a man at the bottom of it, she has been in trouble and had her goods sold away from her'. In the end she was bound over in the sum of £20 and to keep the peace for three months on condition that her relatives look after her which was agreed.

The tenure of the Hardy family seems never to have been without incident. They employed a vocalist named Fred Card who in turn employed two sisters named Hitt aged 10 and 16 to sing and dance at the Fountain for 12 nights at £5 between them. After the first night Card told them not to come again as Mr Hardy was not satisfied with their performance. When they approached Hardy he denied all responsibility, offered them 8/6-and referred them back to Card. Meanwhile two other girls had been engaged at a cheaper rate. When they asked how they were to get home they were advised to contact their parents for the money. Hardy and Card continued to blame each other for the state of affairs but the documents were in Card's name and with the magistrates expressing their disgust at this, 'most disreputable and unmanly treatment of two defenceless girls,' Card was ordered to pay the £5 owing plus the costs of the case.

Soon after, Hardy was summoned for keeping his house open after hours, several people had been found in the bar and Hardy was asked to close up. Returning sometime later the constable found that the landlord had indeed closed up – but with the customers inside. He gave evidence to say that he had great difficulty getting other public houses to close when they pointed out that, 'the Fountain was still open.' The situation led to an interesting legal argument. The defence case was that the Fountain had been built especially for the accommodation of travellers upon their arrival in Weymouth Railway Station with the platform, only 150 yards from the pub and very often the last train arrived at 11.00 and if the house was shut up and arrivals left to wander the streets the intention of the act of parliament would not be carried out. In this case there was no evidence to show that the sale of beer or spirits had taken place outside of permitted hours. Surprisingly the magistrates agreed and the charge was dismissed.

Small victories aside Hardy's time at the Fountain ended in failure. In June 1879, described as a, 'livery stable keeper etc' his business was put into liquidation. He immediately advertised in the press as continuing his livery business and giving riding lessons from premises in King Street. In October this rather unpleasant man took out an advertisement apologising and expressing sorrow and regret for an unprovoked assault upon a Mr Curtis promising not to repeat such conduct. Yet another case arose when one of Hardy's drivers was accused of maltreating a horse this case was even more serious than the previous one and the man was sentenced to 14 days hard labour without the option of a fine.

In November 1881 there was an auction of what must have been the entire contents of the pub from horse carriages to salt sellers and in 1883 Edwin Dunn took control after many years at the Victoria. He died in May of 1896 described as a fish and a game dealer who had been laid up with severe jaundice, he was 65 years of age and had for several years been a member of the Weymouth Town Council. From a tenancy agreement drawn up in the late 1880s we learn that the hotel contained gas chandeliers, a 22ft circular bar counter, an eight motion beer engine with china handles, a Brussels carpet in the coffee room and an oak hat stand in the entrance hall.

At the close of the 19th century and into the 20th things seem very quiet at the Fountain with nothing reported in the press apart from the occasional drunk and several changes of landlord all of little note until November of 1902 when James Petty a travelling brewery salesman was found dead in one of the rooms having taken poison with an unused five chamber revolver beside him. Brothers Edward and Percy Hardy were summoned to appear before the magistrates along with the licensees of the Victoria Hotel, The Sun, The Sailors' Return and The Clifton in November of 1920 for overcharging on spirits and passing off cheap whiskey as Black and White a proprietary brand which commanded a price of 1/1d. Upon conviction the brothers were fined £10 each plus costs. The matter is considered in greater detail in the Victoria Hotel entry. In 1946 interest was reawakened when the hotel was taken over by Billy Kingdon the retiring manager of Yeovil Football Club and former Villa half back.

THE FOX INN
St Nicholas Street, Melcombe Regis

THIS OLD INN lay on the east side of St Nicholas Street opposite what was once John Street but now the bowling alley car park. Its history can be traced back to at least 1813 when land tax returns show that it was owned by William Bower and occupied by John Caddy who by 1827 had been replaced by Mary Haylor. She remained until her death in 1831 at the age of 53 after a lingering illness. There was a strange court case in 1852 when landlady Sarah Spencer brought charges of being drunk and disorderly against Catherine Bradshaw who was fined 10/- nothing unusual in that but she told the police that her husband George, was concerned with a notorious gang of burglars who were now in Dorchester jail awaiting trial. When questioned further she reminded silent and the pair were ordered to leave the town immediately.

The Fox passed to Harry and Mary Hayman in the same year. Harry was a very keen sportsman and soon organised a monthly auction of horses and stock at the inn as well as regular pigeon shoots for which he supplied the birds. In July of 1864 he became involved in a rather complicated civil suit when he was taken to court by gentleman's outfitter Newington of Bond Street over an unpaid bill of £3/13/11d. Harry did not dispute the debt but claimed that he was owed £4/2/- board and lodging for a dog that he had been asked

The Fox Inn 2nd April 1942

to look after as he did for many local sportsmen and his invoice should be set off against the amount owing. It seems that the dog did not live up to its owners expectations and when presented with a bill he denied that it was his. Several witnesses were called for and against but in the end His Honour found for the plaintiff and the set off was not allowed. In 1878 Harry found himself out of pocket again this time by £36 when an acquaintance or business partner in London, was made bankrupt in the sum of over £4,000 a huge amount in those days but there are no further details.

In 1866 a Mr Scattergood brought a thoroughbred horse which came with a serious warning. 'It was a kicker,' he was told, 'never use the horse without a breeching strap and kicking harness'. A couple of days later Scattergood made his way to the Fox and agreed to borrow Henry Hayman's dog cart to go for a ride. He also borrowed Henry's ten year-old son Charles. Scattergood stopped at the Ferry Bridge Inn and met local baker Hann leaving young Charles in charge of the horse and after a few drinks they agreed to ride on to Portland together. Once they reached the Chesil Beach Road Scattergood turned round to Hann and shouted 'Come on I'll show you the way to gallop.' and whipped his horse which took off down the road at a furious rate, Scattergood tried desperately to slow down pulling on the reins but to no avail. A terrified Charles was hanging on to the cart's sides for grim death. Galloping unchecked into Victoria Square horse, cart and passengers teetered to one side and the already panicked horse reared in fright throwing the couple out. Thoroughly battered and bruised Charles survived to tell the tale but Scattergood was killed outright. At the inquest Hann insisted that no wager had been made over their beer at the pub and that they honestly hadn't been pitting horse against horse in their race to Portland.

Hayman rented out rooms and one of them was to Hugh Merriman, his wife and daughter. He returned one night to find that his wife had made him a pie for his dinner at which point he knocked her onto the floor, possibly he didn't like pies. They had been there for some weeks paying 8d per night for one bed and the use of the kitchen. The following day there was another almighty row during which the police were called and tried to evict Merriman but his abused wife grabbed hold of his neck in such a way that he could not be arrested and when it came to court he was fined just £1 for causing a disturbance.

As part of his interest in sport Hayman had a collection of guns and somewhere safe to keep them which meant that he was sometimes asked to look after them for other people. On this occasion he had an old shotgun that he was looking after for a Mr Legg who sold it to Alfred Hines of the George. Hines fourteen-year-old boy took it from him to put away but it went off and killed his little brother. Initially charged with manslaughter young William was let off with a caution. Further details are included in the entry on the George.

During March 1881 the circus was in town and Henry became the proud keeper of an elephant along with 50 horses and had to take the owner to court in order to get is invoices paid. ('I assume the elephant had packed his trunk', commented the witty the old judge) in fact the elephant did more than that having become restive causing a certain amount of damage and to make matters worse the elephant was not a fan of rail transport and had to travel by road. The number of small amounts of money for expenses added up to an amount that the circus master thought excessive and would not pay but in the end judgement was in Henry's favour.

Hardy died in February 1900 at the age of 78 and after almost 50 years at the pub. There were a succession of publicans after him but none could replace him. The Hewlett family took go over in 1915 with Thomas Hewlett 33, being granted exemption from home service until the end of November due to domestic and other circumstances. In August of 1919 the Fox was one of several Devenish pubs who had their landlords returned to them after being away on active war service. They remained until 2 April 1942 when a German bomb demolished the building. Landlord Thomas was injured and survived but his son William was killed.

THE FREEMASON'S ARMS
High Street, Weymouth

THE FIRST NAMES to be associated with the beer house that was to become the Freemason's Arms were Thomas Bonella and his wife Maria in the 1841 census when they were living in East Street, Bridport, he was a mariner aged 46 from Scotland and she was born, 'within the county' aged 42. The pair next appear in the census of 1851 having moved to Weymouth, Maria is listed as 'general shop keeper' at High Street, Weymouth, no pub is named but it can be assumed that one was in operation as in the local paper for February 1852 they were running an unnamed beer house, presumably the Freemason's Arms. The Bonellas are inexorably linked to their rivals across the street, the Prankards who ran the Weymouth Arms. Both houses appear to have opened at around the same time and a serious and violent dispute arose between them during the early part of 1852. Samuel Prankard, listed as a baker, accused Mrs Bonella of having sent the police to his house as a result of which he threatened her resulting in an appearance at the police court. They asked if she ran a beer house to which she replied, 'no but my son does, I am a servant for him.' Prosecution alleged that the dispute had arisen because Prankard had taken away some of her custom and that she did not sell as much beer as she had 'two or three years ago'. The bench decided that they were as bad as each other and dismissed the case.

High Street Weymouth

On Good Friday 9 April two neighbours were accused of attacking Maria Bonella over drawing water from a pump, and there were more than a few hints that she was rather fond of a drop of gin and when it came to court she perhaps misunderstood the point of a question in cross examination, when asked, 'Did you strike any of them? she replied, 'I don't know, I tried my best I suppose'. The case was again dismissed but she was ordered to pay costs.

This end of the High Street was already resembling a battleground but later in the month things became much worse and involved John Prankard, master carpenter of 53 High Street the 56-year-old father of Samuel and his younger son James. Sargeant Wooton entered Prankard's beer house towards closing time and was subject to much abuse from Samuel who amongst other things suggested that he go and 'turn the whores out of Bonella's'. Insults flew in all directions and pretty soon there were three constables and a crowd of about 30 or 40 onlookers. Samuel was taken into custody despite a rescue attempt. Constable Mitchell was attacked receiving extensive injuries to his head and was taken to the Bonella house to be patched up. At the police court they were all convicted and fined a remarkably lenient 10/- each plus costs. In August an Italian hawker, was fined £5 for attacking Maria and the following July (1854) she was taken to court after a fight with a prostitute who she had attempted to evict for 'manifesting great curiosity respecting the kilt of one of the Highlanders in the bar', case dismissed.

The first mention of the Freemason's Arms by name comes in May of 1856 when they are summoned for serving out of hours. Two men were caught in the house with one of them drinking at 12.30 in breach of the licensing laws. Bonella 'came to his own rescue with undiminished vigour employing the 'lodger' plea with ingenuity and success'. He claimed that the man had lived with him for the last nine months and was in the habit of assisting him on Sundays by looking after the horse etc in order that he might go to a place of worship in return for which the lodger received his breakfast which on this occasion had included a pint of beer. The mayor told the ingenious Thomas that he had saved himself again and had managed his court cases extremely well but warned that the police would have him yet. Bonella politely wished the magistrates 'good morning' and retired.

It was in the general election of 1857 that the family made the headlines. Petitions were put in after the event alleging bribery, treating and intimidation. Bonella was alleged to have been bribed to vote a certain way by his stepson Thomas Newman and the affair was examined by a House of Commons appointed election committee. Two Whigs, Freestun and Campbell were elected with the Conservative George Butt who had lost his seat trailing far behind. The committee discovered that Bonella owed money for beer supplied by Henry Devenish the brewer and ultimate owner of the beerhouse, – possibly as much as £40. Bonella had the right to vote but it was Newman who called the shots, eventually things were settled and £6/10/- was paid off the debt, Bonella went to vote for the candidates preferred by Devenish and 36 gallons of beer and 18 gallons of ale arrived the next day. At its conclusion on 30 July the committee decided that there was evidence to prove corruption but nothing to say 'that these acts were practised with the knowledge or consent of the sitting members or their agents', and the election result was allowed to stand, which makes one wonder why they bothered to investigate in the first place.

This house never appears to have been a particularly happy place with fights, arguments and summonses for serving after hours, thefts and other minor matters occurring at frequent intervals. Maria died in 1861 and that same year Thomas Bonella, master mariner, was admitted to Wyke Road workhouse as a pauper and widower aged 71. He died in 1865.

The next family to try and make a go of the place was Job Short, 43 and his wife Charlotte, who appear on the 1861 census as beer house keepers at 82 High Street. Short applied for a spirits licence as his house served a great many commercial travellers of a 'certain class' and that a 'glass of spirits was as necessary for the poor man as the rich especially the poor traveller.'

Refused. Despite the new landlord the catalogue of petty theft violence and disorderly conduct continued but no accusations appear to have been launched against Short and the small matter of keeping a horse in his kitchen was to be overlooked. He gave up the tenancy in 1874 in favour of William Stanley and appeared in the census of 1881 as a milkman. At the annual licensing meeting of September 1885, the superintendent of police described the house as being 'in such a dilapidated condition that it was not fit for the accommodation of the public.' Very shortly after brewers Devenish agreed that the pub should be closed within three months with no reflection at all upon the character of the landlord who had 38 years good character and who they wished well.

THE FRIENDSHIP INN / THE JOLLY SAILOR
Park Street, Melcombe Regis

THE JOLLY SAILOR was one of the Park Street pubs which grew up along the street when it was built in the 1830s and stood opposite the Duke of Albany on the corner of Clifton Place. Kelly's Directory has a James Staines beer retailer in 1840 but no pub is named and the census of the following year has Staines aged 24, a painter with his wife Eliza and their young daughter also Eliza. By the next census of 1851 he had become a coach painter employing one man and one boy but by 1861 Eliza was a coach painter's widow at 30 Park Street but still the beer house remains unnamed and does so until a report in the local paper of March 1870 when James Fulljames, 'landlord of the Jolly Sailor' in Park Street took a seaman to court for assaulting him and his wife in the pub. Fulljames was summoned for an assault on nearby shopkeeper, Mary Pollard who he threatened with violence and accused of encouraging policemen to watch his house saying that he was going to burn her shop down, it seems that Mr Fulljames was rather fond of a drink which in this case cost him a 10/- fine. The Jolly Sailor is mentioned by name again in the census of 1871when Fulljames 45, is described as a mariner out of employ originally from Greenhithe in Kent.

In August of 1873 the owners, Reynolds Brothers brewers, put the house up to let and the next landlord was William White, and it is almost certain that this is when the name was changed, the maybe not so jolly sailor having left. 30 Park Street is next reported as the Friendship Inn when White is caught serving after hours at 11.40. Mrs White's explanation that she had been trying to clear people out of the house but her husband was too drunk to assist was possibly not the best defence that they had heard but as he had conducted the house for the past two years very well he was fined only 17/- including costs.

The Friendship Inn 2023

The last landlord to serve at this rarely mentioned pub was 55 year old army pensioner Frank Summerfield who had been a licence holder for almost 20 years and had run the Friendship for seven of those. He applied for a spirits licence saying that he did a very good steady trade and was the only house belonging to Messrs' Groves in Park Street. He provided food when required and described the Bridge Inn and the Clifton as several hundred yards distant. There were only two beds for the public and turnover was about £450 per year. His application was refused and in 1907 the Friendship was referred to the Compensation Committee for closure, then described as a tied house with a bar, smoking room, passage, kitchen yard, outside urinal and WC. On the first floor was a sitting room, two bedrooms a WC for public use with one large bedroom on the second floor. There was no stabling and only two rooms for the use of the public. It closed in September and the following month the building was advertised for sale as 'Freehold Business Premises until lately known as the Friendship Inn otherwise 30 Park Street'. It was later renumbered as 60 Park Street and is now a private house.

THE GENERAL GORDON
Franchise Street, Chapelhay, Weymouth

MAJOR-GENERAL CHARLES GORDON was a British army officer who was killed in 1885 while organising the evacuation of over 2,500 soldiers and civilians from Khartoum in the Sudan which was threatened by the Muslim army of Muhammad Ahmad. Gordon stayed to defend the city despite the wishes of the government who were far too late in sending a relief force which arrived two days after he was killed. He became a national hero and many pubs and societies were named in his memory.

Awaiting the hammer 1956

The pub was open by 1890 as an inquest was recorded there on the body of an 11 month old boy who had to been scalded to death. The landlord from the beginning was Edward Sly, 28 from Hampton in Middlesex and his wife Fanny who died in 1905.

In 1900 a strange notice appeared in the local paper asking for signatories for a petition protesting against a sentence passed on a William Lumley which many considered excessive. Briefly, Lumley and his wife ran a bakers in Mary Street with their son, also William, who liked a pub and a drink which caused him to abuse his wife so badly that she left him and he wanted revenge on her and her family who had given her refuge. Lumley bought a gun and fired at his brother-in-law who he blamed for all his misfortunes. He was arrested and received five years for the serious assault which had led to the petition but why so many respectable people should take an interest in such a violent alcoholic whose family lived in terror of him is not known. His sentence doesn't sound too bad if all the accounts of his violent behaviour are true. It is believed that he moved to Canada and joined the armed forces at the outbreak of war. There was what sounds like a very harsh punishment in 1905 when Nellie Wallbridge picked up half a crown outside the pub having seen somebody drop it. She denied having had it but at the police station it 'dropped from her mouth' and she was sentenced to an incredible one months hard labour. Other than the occasional drunk the hotel passed its time pretty uneventfully remaining in the same family for most of its life. In 1956 it was bought by the local council as part of the redevelopment scheme following the bombing the Second World War and demolished.

THE GEORGE INN
Custom House Quay, Melcombe Regis

A PLAQUE ON the wall of the present building states that the original George Taverne was bequeathed to the town of Weymouth and Melcombe Regis in 1666 by Sir Samuel Mico a merchant trader based in London who did much of his extensive shipping business in Weymouth. Upon his death he left the George to a charity in his name which still continues today. The inn was established before the first King George came to the throne and probably takes its name from St George the patron saint of England. It would be reasonable to expect that many of the town's earliest pubs were right on the Quay to cater for the fisherman and dock workers of the time, but records from the early days are very sparse. There was a John Hardy from 1710-18 and Joseph Langrish was paying £15 in rent during 1775 when regular auctions of ships and goods were held there. One story is that the pub was once owned by a Jack Randbury a former smuggler who once hid up the chimney when the revenue men were chasing him.

A remarkable discovery was made hidden in the stone walls of the old building when it was being demolished during the 1880s. The landlord in 1776 was a Matthew Voss who, it seems, had a great interest in smuggled goods and even kept a set of accounts recording the large amount of brandy that he received at that time. The casks usually contained four gallons and he paid from 17/- to 18/6d per cask to a Peter Le Cocq who seems to have been his main supplier and it looks like business was brisk. Voss died in 1784 at the age of 38.

James Talbot was landlord from 1837-1845 and the following year the 'old established free public house' then occupied by Harry Hayman was offered at auction to be let by the trustees of the Mico Charities who by 1850 were able to announce that they had sufficient funds to apprentice a number of poor boys paying 30/- for their clothing and £1 each per annum during their apprenticeship, all to be run from the George Inn and premises on the Quay.

In May of 1853 the long-anticipated invasion by the French finally took place. Nine crewmembers of a French fishing smack became extremely drunk, started a fight with the locals and tried to break into the George upon which Thomas Gardener, the landlord summoned the police. The French had armed themselves with bludgeons and a long boat hook which they used as a battering ram on the door of the pub. In the general melee PS Wotton had his collarbone dislocated and others were seriously knocked about. The captain, 'a herculean fellow' was arrested with ten others after a great struggle and the assistance of the Yeomanry Cavalry, and taken into custody. In court the following day they were fined from between from £1 and 5/- causing the captain Jean Mathion to declare, 'Je n'ai point d'argent, de tout, de tout! (I have no money nothing nothing!) upon which they were ordered to the cells. No sooner had the policemen begun to remove them than the 'obese captain' produced a leather purse full of gold and silver exclaiming, 'mais je paierai, Monsieur, je paierai (I will pay Sir! I will pay!) and as soon as he did so the prisoners were released. Gardener did not last much longer, being summoned for 'entertaining company on a Sunday' he pleaded ignorance of the law, proof as the chairman observed, that he had not read his licence despite his wife having been cautioned several times before for the same thing. He was fined £2 and his licence taken away.

An emergency council meeting was called in May of 1873 to discuss the deteriorating state of the Quay in front of the George which the town surveyor reported was in danger of collapse and it was agreed that oak piles should be

The George Inn c.1884

inserted to shore it up to a depth of about 18 feet where solid clay could be found at a cost of about £130.

Tragedy struck on 20 September 1879. Landlord William Hines had bought an old shotgun from Harry Hayman of the Fox Inn which was delivered to the pub while he was out. His 14-year-old son Willie took it upstairs where he was playing with his brother nine year old Alfred and sister Florence aged eight. Not suspecting that it was loaded he pointed it at his younger brother saying 'Bertie I will shoot you', which he did. The shot went straight through his neck killing him instantly. The inquest was held at the Guildhall, where it emerged that Willie had put a cap on the gun which prepared it to fire and that he had served three customers in the bar before taking the gun upstairs and firing it. Florence gave evidence to say that the gun had hit the floor and gone off accidentally but a forensic expert said that this could not have been the case and she had probably been coached by her father. There was much confusion over when and by whom the gun had been loaded which remained unresolved. The jury brought in a verdict 'that the deceased met his death by the explosion of a gun through proper precautions not having been taken'. The coroner explained that this was a verdict of manslaughter by the person handling the gun and young William was released on £50 bail. At the police court it was accepted that the death was an accident and Willie was released with a caution.

In February of 1882 the George was raided in a search for contraband tobacco which was soon discovered, the affair is considered in the Globe entry.

That same year it was proposed that the Council come to an arrangement with the Mico Trust to demolish and rebuild the George setting it further back from the shore in line with the fish market to allow more space for the growing passage of traffic on the Quay. This prompted an editorial in the *Southern Times* who were outraged at the cost, £700 to be paid for a strip of land 60' x 12'to be paid for by the Corporation and set by the Mico Charity. After much negotiation this was agreed resulting in the handsome building that we see today. In February 1884 the George was subject to a raid by an inspector looking for illegal weights and measures during which many unstamped cups were taken away and Hines appeared in court along with nine others. In the end they were all dismissed with a caution and more complete account is included in the Royal Oak entry. In September 1885 Devenish & Co advertised the fully licensed public house to let and George Davis took control but in 1895 his son William was arrested for setting fire to a nearby yard with an oily rag and some matches, it seems that the lad was not quite *compos mentis* and his father could do nothing with him and the case was adjourned for medical reports. During the early part of the 20th century the inn was taken by John Baugh from Cambridgeshire and his wife Louisa who had moved from the White Hart in Lower Bond Street, the family continued there until around 1915. The George continues today popular with locals and tourists the year round.

THE GLOBE INN
East Street, Melcombe Regis

THERE IS MENTION of a Samuel Martin of the Globe ale house being granted a licence for beer and brandy in 1730 situated at Governors Lane/ Maiden Street and possibly still going in the 1760s but by the 1790s we are on firmer ground with a John Mansell holding a licence on The Globe, East Street and by the 1813 land tax return the pub is owned by William Bower and occupied by Benjamin Kerridge. In November 1829 it was one of nine public houses auctioned as part of the late William Bower's Dorchester Fordington Brewery estate. (see the Bear entry for more details.) and at the first census taken in 1841 the occupier is Hannah Kerridge aged 70. Benjamin died in 1832 at the age of 60 and Hannah in 1845 at the age of 74 having passed the inn on to her son James 27 a sailmaker in 1841 and described as a licensed victualler. James continued until his death in 1870 when his sister Hannah took over until 1871 the pub having been in the family for about 70 years.

But to retrace our steps. In 1844 the Conservative Convivial Association held a meeting at the Globe to raise a petition protesting against the anti-Corn-Law League interfering in elections, and in 1854 while doing over £600 worth of restoration work a cannonball thought to have been fired during the Civil War was discovered imbedded in a wall but there is no record of what happened to it. Sometimes the most trivial offence can bring forth some fine descriptive writing. 'John Knaresborough, a staid personage of unshaven aspect, attired in an antique swallowtail coat, with the lappets cut about three inches below the armpits, thereby developing a waistcoat of ancient pattern decorated with brass buttons.' His crime was to obtain 7/6 worth of board and lodging and to decamp without paying, the police caught up with him at the Old Rooms where he was trying the same trick. A tramp named John Adams was suspected of stealing three sixpences from the till at the Globe and Kerridge summoned a constable. Back at the station Adams was searched but nothing was found, he wasn't saying much and was asked to open his mouth which he refused. 'The constable forced it open and after some difficulty found two sixpences which the prisoner was endeavouring to swallow but which were

The Globe Inn 2017

successfully retrieved. Adams was sentenced to one months imprisonment with hard labour.

It was not at all uncommon for landlords to have a trade or second activity outside of the pub and sailmaker Kerridge also owned a ketch named the *Express* which sank when carrying Portland stone to Greenhithe. The crew were saved but boat and cargo were lost. In 1869 the Globe played its part in the rescue of two Dutch sailors whose schooner capsized with the loss of four of their fellows. The two survivors had lashed themselves to the mast and remained there for many hours until rescued by the customs boat which got them to the Globe and fortified them with whiskey. They had another visitor in 1873 when a Mr Luce of Jersey started looking for his father who had left the island by steamboat and could not be found. He turned up at the Globe not speaking a word of English but when taken to the police station he produced papers written in French claiming that he was a prophet sent by the Almighty to tell the Queen that there was going to be war and that he had to light walls of fire around London for her protection. He was looked after and returned to his son, he was apparently a highly respectable and wealthy farmer.

James Kerridge died in 1870 and his role was taken over briefly by his sister 67-year-old Hannah Strachen until in 1876 owners Devenish advertised the house to let and there followed at least ten different names one after the other in the licensing sessions record until in 1882 when the house was settled on George William Parkman who had no sooner taken the job than he was raided by the Inland Revenue and caught with 25 ounces of sweetened Cavendish tobacco on the premises. There had been 19 seizures in five days around the town and apparently, this type of additive to normal tobacco was prohibited being described as 'mixed with some kind of saccharine matter contrary to the Manufactured Tobacco Act of 1863 which stated that,

> If any tobacco called Cavendish and Negrohead whether of foreign or British manufacture, containing or being mixed with any material or ingredient prohibited by any act in force.... not being enclosed in a wrapper securely fastened by a label... (which) has been cut, torn, obliterated or cancelled or bears any other mark or appearance of having been opened or tampered with, shall be sold exposed for sale or be found in the possession of any importer or manufacturer or dealer he shall forfeit either treble the value thereof or a penalty of £20 and all such tobacco shall be forfeited.

It seems that the adulteration had taken place at the customs warehouse and then enclosed in a false wrapper showing that duty had been paid. The magistrates claimed that an extensive system of fraud had been going on as they found original packages at the warehouse imported from America. Parkman pleaded guilty. When the George was raided landlord Hines had denied that he had any in the house but a diligent search revealed a surprising 17lb of Cavendish for which duty had not been paid still in its original packaging. Hines said that he was neither the smuggler nor the buyer despite such a large amount being found on his premises and was liable to a fine of £18/14/- but was treated leniently with a penalty of £5.

Ellen Keeley landlady of the Sun Inn was similarly summoned for possessing three ounces of the same. Her son Thomas who now ran the pub attended court and pleaded guilty saying that it was given to him and was for his own use adding that the officer had turned the house upside down but found nothing more. The magistrates said that he had no right to have it on him in the first place and added that in his position he could not be ignorant of the law. Charles Masters of the Market House Tavern was caught with nine ounces and again a guilty plea was entered but he said that he thought that it was only four or five ounces which he had bought at a rate of 4/- per pound. They were treated with great leniency, Parkman, because he led the officers directly to the tobacco which they may not have found otherwise, was fined £1 and Tom Keeley even more so being fined just 1/- including costs and Masters was also fined £1. Hines suffered most because he denied having any on the premises. It was a first offence for all of them.

The pub was again advertised to let in 1886 and by 1891 was in the hands of 66-year-old Moses Moore formerly the captain of a Jersey cutter and landlord of the Castle Inn, Portland. He died at the pub of pneumonia the following year and his wife Annie took charge for a brief period until Richard Theophilus Williams took up the reins and announced his retirement with an unusual advertisement in the local paper in June of 1894,

> LANDLORD LEAVING – should like a Village or Roadside Public House with the garden attached. Seven years and four months under brewer. Pensioner. Apply Globe Inn, Weymouth.

Whether his dream was realised is not recorded. John Wilkins was landlord in 1900 when his 27-year-old son Sidney got a young lady in the family way. It emerged that she sometimes assisted at the inn and it was there that she 'got into trouble'. Foolishly he let the matter go to court and was ordered to pay 3/- per week until the child reached the age of 14. The Wilkins family had run the pub from the late 1890s until January 1904 when Mary Wilkins dropped dead of a heart-attack at the age of 64. The Globe continues today as a quiet family run local.

THE GLOUCESTER HOTEL
Gloucester Row, Melcombe Regis

THE ORIGINAL PART of this prestigious building was constructed in around 1780 for the Prince William Henry, Duke of Gloucester, younger brother of George III who used it himself between 1789 and 1805 as he thought that bathing and sea air was good for his health. George purchased the property from his brother in 1801 and in 1804 a contemporary newspaper reports that, 'His Majesty gave orders for immediate and considerable additions to be made to Gloucester Lodge as it was found to be incapable of accommodating different branches of the royal family independently of their attendants who were 'boarded out' in different parts of the town last summer to their great

The Gloucester Hotel in 2014. The original lodge is on the right

inconvenience. To this end the King has purchased four adjoining houses. The Lodge is to undergo complete renovation with respect to its hangings and furniture and is to be fitted up for the sole residence of the Queen, the Princess and attendants. The principal house, which is contiguous to the Lodge the King appropriates to himself and his attendants the next is for the accommodation of the Royal Dukes and two others are intended for the equerries and servants. His Majesty has desired that the architecture of the whole pile of building may be exactly uniform, both in height and in exterior ornaments'. King George spent his last summer at Weymouth in the following year and upon his death in 1820 the property was auctioned along with the four adjoining houses on Friday 14 July 'containing upwards of 100 beds and the sleeping rooms contain 70 wardrobes besides chests of drawers and other chamber requisites in the same proportion'. Also included was a mass of furniture and effects. The successful bidder was William Young Esq. who paid £4,000 for the lodge. The individual houses went for £600 each.

The property was used for many years as a private residence before being 'fitted out at great expense and put in complete repair with new grates and other features', by new owner J Henning who in 1854 applied to open the building as a hotel, his application was at first refused but the decision was reversed the following year and after the renovations were complete it was back on the market in May of 1857 with a reserve price set at £4,600. It was purchased by Thomas Dorney Luce who also owned the Royal Hotel next door and advertised its availability in 1859 as a private hotel and boarding house. The census of 1861 records Mary Groves a single woman of 28 as hotel manager describing her relationship to the head, presumably Luce, as 'servant'. A large and attractive red brick extension was added in what had been the gardens at the southern end in the 1860s to accommodate the Weymouth and Country Club dwarfing the original. The newly set up hotel played host to the Duke of Cambridge during 1866 and in that same year John Bevar was summoned for 'bathing without drawers', he did not attend court.

The census of 1881 shows that Luce, hotel proprietor aged 69 and unmarried had moved into the Gloucester where he died in 1886. Probate was valued at £30,885 and he left the Gloucester to Catherine Sampson a single woman of 66 who had been his manageress there for a good number of years and had worked for him at the Royal Hotel before that. Described as a genial hostess and kind hearted lady treating her employees with great consideration and generosity she died of bronchitis at the age of 75 having been confined to her room for several years. The freeholds of the Gloucester and the Country Club which had been run separately were put up for auction in London selling together for £10,300 in August 1900 to Albert Middleton of the Clifton Hotel. Weeks later the entire contents were put up for auction in separate lots.

Gloucester Lodge before the Country Club addition

The Gloucester Hotel before the fire of 1927

It seems that Mr Middleton was as much a businessman as a hotelier as by the following April he was offering to sell the entire premises to the Council for £16,000 to provide a site for the proposed new pavilion at an estimated building cost of another £10,000. They were sorely tempted and much discussion ensued but in the end the scheme was thankfully rejected and Middleton reopened his new purchase with its 70 rooms artistically refurbished by the London firm of Oetzmann. How Middleton was able to afford such a large and expensive residence is something of a mystery, a former cab driver whose business had had to be sold and who was threatened with prison for being unable to pay his cab licenses somehow acquired one of the most prestigious hotels in the town, not only that but he was elected onto the town council by a substantial majority in 1906. He was still at hotel until 1911 when the business was taken over by his daughter Lillian May. In 1914 the licence was transferred to Arthur Clayton secretary of the Gloucester Hotel Company and by 1924 it has become part of the Honywood Hotel group of which Lady Honywood was the managing director.

In March 1927 disaster struck when a massive fire broke out in the linen room in the old part of the hotel which was completely gutted with much of the very old furniture destroyed with damage amounting to many thousands of pounds. Residents had to be rescued by ladders as their escape was cut off and the hero of the hour was the hotel boots William Dicker who climbed up a drain pipe and along a ledge to rescue a lady and her nurse amidst loud cheering from the crowds. It was back in business by 1929 with two extra storeys and bought by Devenish Brewers in 1966 but various ideas failed and in 1984 it was rented out to DHSS tenants before in 1988 it was converted into flats and offices with a pub and restaurant below.

The Gloucester Tap: Like most of the large hotels the Gloucester had a 'tap' or pub tacked onto the back of it for the hotel staff and the public in general. This one was extensively rebuilt in the 1860s.

The Gloucester Tap

THE GOLDEN LION INN / HOTEL
St Edmund Street / St Mary Street

ORIGINALLY KNOWN AS The Feathers and run by Gregory Babbidge in the 18th century its fine Georgian front masks what architectural historian Eric Ricketts describes as an 'old coaching inn that has internal dimensions, lower storey heights and an internal structure which suggest a date as early as the first quarter of the 17th century'. Until research reveals more the first mention we have is a possible entry in the court records from 1720. In 1730 a Robert Saxon had a 'brandy and beer house' on the site, then, in 1749 the Golden Lion was sold as part of the estate of Mr Richard Jordan deceased, and included stables, a brewhouse, other outbuildings and a garden. Part of the property was freehold and the other part offered for the remainder of a term of 999 years. Philip Adams moved down from Ilford Bridges, Somerset in

February 1753 and in July of 1764 he put a notice in the local paper claiming that, 'Some ill disposed persons have given a report that the smallpox is now in Weymouth, this is to certify that it is not neither has it been in town for this 11 months. Any gentleman or ladies may be provided with good lodgings, a plentiful supply of good fish and an excellent bathing machine'.

Stephen Spicer was the owner from c.1772 until his death in 1793 during which period the inn continued to run coaches to the Saracen's Head in Bath and conduct auctions of ships, property etc and in 1784 he auctioned the right to the tolls at the local turnpike at Weymouth Gate 'the receipts of which in the previous year came to £422/17/4d above the expenses of collecting them, bidding to start at that sum'. Things did not always run smoothly, William Iveney 'late of the Golden Lion Weymouth' went bankrupt to the tune of £2,000 not necessarily all to do with the pub but he ended up in the Fleet Prison, London unable to meet his debts.

William Bailey was proprietor by 1816 and running the coach business. In October at 1818 his coachman took some Methodist ministers from the town to Tolpuddle to attend the opening of a new chapel in the village which provoked a serious anti-Methodist riot. As they were leaving about 100 people were found assembled near the chaise and behaved in a 'most turbulent manner'. For more than two miles on a very bad road to Piddletown drivers, horses and carriages were pelted by the mob with stones, mud, dung and exposed to the most brutal insults. 'The carriage windows were broken, one side of the chaise was pierced by a stone and the lady beside the driver received a severe blow to her head. The driver was confined having received a blow to his neck which, were it not for a large neck-cloth, would probably have proved fatal.' Bailey offered a reward of five guineas to anyone offering information about the perpetrators which would lead to a conviction.

In 1823 Joshua Hide moved from the Antelope and set about a complete refit of the inn with well aired beds and a good larder while maintaining the coaching business. George Pearce Scott took over in 1828 also moving from an Antelope but this time the one in Dorchester. In 1832 a sumptuous dinner was organised to celebrate the passing of the 1832 Reform Bill at which TF Buxton future MP for Weymouth was present. Scott was still there in the 1841 census aged 60 with his wife Mary. By the census of 1851 the inn was owned by John Pothecary aged 32 and his wife Mary. He was also an auctioneer and seems to have run both enterprises extremely well until he retired as inn keeper in August 1864 after almost 20 years. He offered the free house for rent and describes it as having, '17 bedrooms three of which are double, eight servants' bedrooms, a commodious coffee room, three sitting rooms, commercial and

The Golden Lion 2024

smoking rooms, excellent spirit bar, doing a good business over the counter, two parlours, two kitchens, spacious cellarage, at houses, and extensive commercial showroom, stabling for ten horses, and a coach house with convenient lofts'. In October he put himself forward for election to the local council, 'having had the honour of representing you in the council chamber and in the offices of auditor and assessor'. Presumably he was still the freeholder and continued to hold auctions there until at least 1868.

Robert Felton, 'late of the great Western Railway' took over the licence in 1876 and fell prey to the 'Gillingham Cheat'. A man impersonating a very wealthy and respected farmer and cattle feeder named Charles Benjafield of Gillingham who had obtained board and lodging from Charles Jones of the London Hotel spinning a yarn about having a horse named Gertrude which he was to enter in the Weymouth races ordering straw and stabling for the non-existent animal and borrowing money from Jones. He was exposed when no horse of that name appeared on the race card. He moved onto the Golden Lion, again using the Benjafield name and borrowing money because he had 'left his cheque-book behind'. He pulled off various other scams around the town including obtaining a large ham on the strength that he was doing a large cheese deal worth £220 -a sample of which could be seen at the railway station, there was nothing there of course. It emerged that he had carried out similar frauds all over the West Country and that his real name was Charles Hiscocks and when eventually arrested he pleaded guilty to all charges and was remanded to the assize court for sentence. Felton left the pub the following year due to ill health and was followed by William Charles Davis and his wife Harriet in January of 1878. Formerly at the Spread Eagle Hotel in Gloucester, Davis also took over the Voss lodging house and turned it into a new establishment which he named the Marine Hotel. However, things were not happy in the Davis household. Davis it would seem had a weakness for barmaids and was once taken to court for an assault at the Marine Hotel, not only that but he liked to knock his wife about frequently and threatened to kill her on a number of occasions. Harriet applied to the court for a divorce, William did not appear and she was granted a *decree nisi* in July 1880 and custody of their child with costs awarded against him. In the census of 1881 he is shown as living at the Marine Hotel and the Golden Lion passes briefly to James Symes whose main achievement was to introduce a billiard saloon and organise professional matches.

Ernest Clapp was the proprietor from 1883 until he moved from the town in 1901 to be replaced by Mrs Mary Dunn and while she was there the hotel was almost destroyed by a massive storm in August of 1903 which flooded the ground floor with water three feet deep. In May of 1920 the freehold was put up for auction as a fully licensed premises comprising, entrance hall, cosy lounge, bar, commercial room, 27' x 17', office, private sitting room, housekeeper's room, pantry, storeroom, large kitchen and offices. On the first and second floors there was a coffee room 25' x 14' a large bay window, reading room and 28 bedrooms. The property was on a lease for 21 years expiring at Midsummer 1922 at a rent of £120.

In August of 1927 in a daring move a local constable climbed a ladder at 3.00 am and peered through the pub window discovering, presumably to his horror, the landlord and four commercial travellers playing pontoon! 'One said Twist and another said Stick,' the officer reported gravely to the court. The licensee, William Robert Pruden was fined 50/- for gaming and his guests were dismissed on payment of costs saying that they thought they were playing in a private room, one reporting that the officer scooped up the money and the cards and tried to stuff the lot into his coat pocket.

October of 1944 there was trouble of a different sort when some overexcited American soldiers broke the curly tail off the lion sculpture that sits above the main entrance and took it back to camp, it was speedily replaced by an axe handle until years later Devenish brewery restored the curl with a new tail. The Golden Lion continues to thrive to this day and is now owned by Greene King.

THE GREYHOUND
St Nicholas Street, Melcombe Regis

A RATHER LATE arrival to the town's drinking establishments. In August of 1866 the Greyhound was described as having been newly fitted out at a cost of between £1,500 and £2,000 and an application for a spirits licence was made by a Mr G Parker who, it was stated, had been a licensed victualler for 20 years, possibly the George Parker who had run the New Inn on North Quay previously. It seems that the building ran from St Nicholas Street to St Thomas Street and was linked to an establishment known as the Victor Emmanuel. It lay almost opposite the Fox but as there was some confusion over who was responsible for what, the licence was refused. Parker died in 1868 and this place was taken by George Cox Forse a cordwainer formerly of the Royal Engineer, Chapelhay. He hadn't particularly distinguished himself there as numerous complaints had been made about the way in which it was conducted. Surprisingly, Forse aged 41 and his wife Mary Ann were described as having nothing against them when they applied for the licence – but the application was still refused, as most were, to safeguard the trade of existing houses.

The following year accounts began to circulate that a private of the 13th Regiment stationed at Weymouth had tried to hang himself in the pub and was cut down just in time almost black in the face but when he was returned to barracks he tried it again by jumping off the bridge. Reports of his arrest and sentence where eagerly awaited until it was revealed that after a mammoth drinking session and spending all this money he had tried to suspend himself with a woman's waistband from a nail in the pub wall causing hilarity rather than sympathy from his comrades; he was confined to barracks for six days.

> Robert Richard Forse, of the Greyhound, was next objected to. Mr. Vickery had had a report day by day, for the last 28 days, of the number of prostitutes harbouring there.—Mr. Howard asked that the case might not be adjourned, but a licence granted to the present occupier, in order that the house might retain the licence, and the owner have an opportunity of changing the tenant, which he would do unless the house were properly conducted.—Mr. Groves promised that if there were any future complaints, he would change the tenant next quarter. - Adjourned.

A Disorderly House 1869

In April of 1868 Forse was summoned for two counts of selling spirits without a licence and fined the huge amount of £12/10/- in each case, he also lost his beer licence and his place seems to have been taken by his brother Robert possibly in name only as in August of 1869 Superintendent Vickery, who had ordered daily reports of the number of prostitutes harboured there objected to the pub continuing. Nonetheless, they allowed it to carry on so that the house might retain its licence giving the owners, Groves & Co a chance to change the tenant should things not improve, which they didn't as on licensing day in September 1871 Vickery described the house as 'a common brothel'. Some of the girls were brought to court and 'disgusting scenes' were described with women, soldiers and sailors brawling in the streets at all hours with half naked women frequenting the Greyhound late into the night. Forse was soon out and there followed a succession of landlords without any improvement, the final licensees being William and Jemima Randell and in 1877 the Greyhound was ordered to be closed giving rise to some quite amazing scenes. Following the closure order the property had been sold to a Mr Elliott who quite understandably wanted his property empty. Mrs Randell claimed that her husband was too sick to move and refused to go demanding that they be allowed to stay until their lease had expired. Negotiations having failed Mr Elliott took a rather 'robust' view of the situation and sent his men in. They ripped out the lower windows and gained access to the roof and by removing part of it then worked their way down through the house taking out more windows ripping up the floor and actually pulled down the staircase. The Randells were joined by a friend who came to help in the fight but it seems that the workmen accidentally spilled a bucket of water over him and he didn't stay long. The siege lasted for a week before the property was given up and the short but unfortunate life of the Greyhound was no more.

THE HALF MOON HOTEL
King Street, Melcombe Regis

THE FIRST DEFINITE mention of the Half Moon comes from 1837 when it was owned by a James Richardson Hendy followed by the census of 1841 when James Puckett takes control followed by Solomon Sly aged 30 and his wife Elizabeth who in 1853 declared that 'his house is now complete with every comfort to be desired in a small inn and from his long experience in the trade and he flatters himself that there is no one more up to the mark in the domestic matters that himself. Stabling for six horses'. On Whit-Monday

The Half Moon 2024

of that year he organised a marquee, Maypole and a band of music for the entertainment of visitors and guests. The Sly family had been in Weymouth since the 18th century and were seriously involved in the hospitality and business activities of the town. In 1860 Sly moved just across the road to the newly built Fountain Hotel, a bigger and far more prestigious establishment to be replaced by the Roberd family. Landlady Jane took a Mrs Knight to court for using threatening and abusive language calculated to provoke a breach of the peace. Knight came in looking for her husband, a not uncommon occurrence but on this occasion threatening to break her windows and 'put her house down', for allowing him to spend three days in there drinking. Mrs Roberd claimed to be 'very much frightened and cried a great deal as she had never been used to such language' which was rather unlikely given her profession, Knight was ordered to enter into a reconnaissance of £5 to keep the peace with 12/6 costs.

In 1876 Joseph Keeley landlord of the Sun Inn on the next corner was summoned by Thomas Kellaway of the Half Moon for threatening behaviour. Unfortunately, they were persuaded to settle their differences in private 'to the disappointment of an expectant audience who had assembled in the court' and so we shall never know what it was about. Each party to pay their own costs. That same year, Thomas Jollife, a 35-year-old pot man at the pub went for a 'bit of a lie down', he seemed in his normal good health and was soon fast asleep on a settle in the tap room snoring very loudly, attempts to raise him failed and by the time the doctor arrived he was dead from heart failure. In 1883 Keeley became one of the victims of Charles Lambourne a conman who went round various pubs and businesses claiming to be producing a directory of goods and services in the county and ended up 5/-poorer on the directory scam and stuck with a 14/-unpaid bill for accommodation. The full story is told in the Clifton entry.

In 1901 Henry William Banks a convict serving the last 18 months of a five-year sentence on the Isle of Portland made an ingenious bid for freedom. An intelligent and trusted prisoner he had more freedom than most and used it to gradually acquire a set of clothing from the officers quarters, a frockcoat, a black silk hat, a silk handkerchief and a pair of gloves – he had even managed to steal £14 in cash and having donned his new attire he used a ladder to get over the wall and made his way toward Weymouth. Banks 'borrowed' an old grey horse and two wheeled trap. By now of course all hell had broken loose at Portland and the hunt was on. Making his way towards the railway station he called in at the Half Moon where he was supplied with a brandy and lemon and appeared to be in a very agitated state. He paid the landlord, Fred Taylor, with a sovereign and left in such a hurry that he did not collect his change. Having been spotted coming out of the pub and going up Crescent Street he was pursued until eventually captured after a violent struggle. His comment to his captors was, 'If I'd had good nag instead of an old crock I would have got away!' Upon leaving the police station he was cheered by the crowd, he acknowledged the salutations and bestowed a gracious grin' and later in the year he received an extra four years-the price of his adventure. In 1904 the pub was allowed to carry out extensive alterations by the magistrates and in August of 1919 the Half Moon was one of several Devenish pubs who had their husbands return to them after being away on active service.

After a spell as a gift shop and chemists it is a gaming centre at the time of writing.

HIGH WEST STREET TAVERN
High West Street, corner of Love Lane Weymouth

IN THE CENSUS of 1851 the property on the corner of Love Lane and High West Street was occupied by William White Board a 30 year old cordwainer and his wife Ellen. There is no pub mentioned but they may have already started selling beer as by the next census his wife Ellen is described as a beer retailer. As with most publicans he fell foul of the beer act and was fined 5/- plus costs for serving a couple of pints of cider on a Sunday in 1864. In 1870 he placed an advert in the local paper thanking his customers for their attendance over the previous 16 years and said that he now has a spirits licence adding that he will continue to sell the beers of John Groves and Sons. In his application he states that he pays £15 rent but is rated at £20; the house has four rooms on the ground floor, a bar, parlour and five rooms upstairs, his wife and four children also were also living at the property. This enables us to date

High West Street Tavern on the corner of Love Lane

the opening of the house to about 1854 and in the following census of 1861 he is still working as a journeyman shoemaker and continued to run the pub until his death in 1892 at the age of 72. His son Joel a cabinet maker took over until 1901 and in 1903 architects Crickmay & Sons carried out some alterations to the front of the building.

Things did not run quite so smoothly when Henry Winzar took charge in 1905. He was summoned for having sold a half pint of beer to a boy ten years of age without sealing the bottle which should have been closed with sealing wax. The boy said that he often picked up beer for his mother in this way but that it was normally sealed properly. Winzar said he was distracted when some customers came in and the boy left. The police said that they were not entirely happy with the conduct of the house but Winzar was released upon payment of costs. Two years later Winzar was convicted of selling a large amount of whiskey to a tramping hawker who was already so drunk that he died in his sleep of alcohol poisoning that night. He was given a very heavy fine of £10 with £4/18/-in costs and despite putting in notice of appeal he was given notice to quit by the owners. The tavern passed the next few decades without incident finally closing its doors in 1981.

THE HOPE TAVERN
Hope Street, Weymouth

THIS BUILDING HAS been assumed to date from around 1800 but nothing has been discovered before the 1841 census when a Thomas Hunter aged 40 his wife Mary Ann and an impressive tally of nine children is listed as a publican in Hope Street this is certainly the Hope Tavern but the house is not named. By the 1851 census Robert Brinsley is named as a beer house keeper, aged 28 unmarried, and living with his mother Jane Brinsley who was herself a retired inn keeper the family having moved from the Portland Arms in Maiden Street. In 1857 an advertisement in the local paper states that Elizabeth, sister to Robert, had been subject to deafness since a child but had her hearing perfectly restored after a very short and painless treatment by a Mr Downing who specialised in treating ailments of the ear.

In August 1861 the Hope Tavern was raided by the police and the Collector of Customs who after a vigilant search found an impressive 37lb of foreign manufactured tobacco hidden behind some beer casks in the cellar. Brinsley pleaded guilty to possession of the contraband. He could have gone to prison but in mitigation it was stated that he had always conducted himself

The Hope Tavern Undergoing Restoration 2017

in a respectable manner running his house properly and supporting his aged mother. The bench with great leniency inflicted a fine of only £25 plus costs or six months imprisonment in default. In the census of that year the licensee is Robert's 75-year-old mother Jane with Robert shown merely as 'publican's son'. Two years later Robert was in court again but this time in the role of prosecutor when three soldiers were convicted of stealing a looking glass as well as a quantity of lard and bacon from the house to the value of 7/-. They each received six months imprisonment with hard labour.

Elizabeth died in 1866 at the age of 81 and the licence passed to her daughter also Elizabeth. By the census of 1871 Robert is recorded as 'Sergeant of the Mace' a ceremonial officer who carries the mace, a symbol of authority, during civic processions and meetings, he is responsible for ensuring that the Mayor is appropriately robed and other ceremonial civic functions. He is still living at the pub with his sister.

By 1881 the licence had passed John Perks a widower who was still there twenty years later aged 79 along with his 37-year-old daughter Frances now married as Mrs Carter. In November of 1901 she was summoned by the NSPCC for cruelly beating her five-year-old daughter Ethel May to 'correct her dirty habits' several neighbours were called as witnesses to prove cruelty and she received three months imprisonment.

Shortly after this the licence was transferred to James Burt a fisherman at a rental of £1/6/8d and a turnover of about £25 per month. The ground floor consisted of a bar and smoking room with a kitchen at the end. The bar was 16' x 9' x 7'6" high, there was no jug and bottle, customers being served in the passage. The first floor consisted of three bedrooms and one bed sitting room occupied by Mr and Mrs Burt and their little girl. In the attic there were two small rooms with full size beds in each, lodgers were not taken in. There are two entrances to the house one from the street into the bar and the other side entrance from the yard which was a nice size containing an old skittle alley and a sanitary convenience but no separate WC for the occupants of the house. There was also a four roomed cottage in the yard included with the property. By 1909 the Hope Tavern was owned by brewers Eldridge Pope & Co. but was refused a licence under the act of 1904 and closed for good eventually becoming a private house.

JERSEY HOTEL / CROSS KEYS
St Thomas Street, Melcombe Regis

THE CROSS KEYS was definitely established by 1840 when John Thomas beer seller was convicted of selling spirits without a licence and fined £12/10/-. 30-year-old Thomas was a baker by profession and was running the pub in the 1841 census with other members of his family, the Besants were also bakers and it was William Besant aged 29, baker and victualler who had taken over the show by 1851. During their tenure an 11 month old baby was discovered abandoned in the passage. Apparently, the mother, Amelia Edwards was unable to cope and had tried to leave it in the church but had been turned away leaving the little mite in the pub as a last resort. The child was taken to the workhouse the following day having first being refused entry because 'it was too late to be admitted'. She said she had left it in the pub for the father to keep it; she was sentenced to two months imprisonment with hard labour.

Landlord Thomas Hann applied for a spirits licence in 1858 and denied that he had been refused the year before, claiming that there had been no application, because he and been in prison for beating his wife. The bench thought this irrelevant and granted the licence. Hann aged 24 was another

The Jersey Tavern 1998

baker from Beaminster and had received three months with hard labour for the assault on his wife Sarah. She stayed with him and their two daughters until she could no longer take his constant violence and adultery and in 1868 she obtained a divorce and moved to London, Hann was out of the pub shortly after and continued as a baker. Successor Levi Bartlett was attacked by two sappers after they refused to pay and told him to go to 'a warm place' after which a fight broke out and Levi and his wife were knocked to the floor and had their windows broken for good measure. The pair were fined a total of 30/-between them. Owners Eldridge Mason and Co. put the pub up for rent, and in 1871 it was occupied by John Rodberd aged 48 and his wife Jane who sometime previously had run the Half Moon in King Street.

By the end of 1872 name had been changed from the Cross Keys to the Jersey Hotel and Francis Spring a former gamekeeper from Gloucester took charge in 1874 but was dead within six months and the pub advertised for rent again by the brewers but within a couple of years complaints were starting to be made about the way in which it was run. In December 1882 John and Margaret Ewings were arrested for being drunk and disorderly having just come from the Jersey where they 'abused the landlady dreadfully'. They were rowing in the street and with them was a pretty curly haired boy about three years old crying bitterly. They were perfectly fit but had gone around the streets begging using the child as a 'prop'. The magistrates wanted very much to take the child from them but after some discussion realised that there was nothing they could do and were reduced fining them 5/- each. After the death of Francis Spring in 1875 and his successor Frederick Knight in 1882, Charles Tompkins formally a sergeant in the medical corps became the third landlord to die on the premises in April of 1889.

In 1890 there were many complaints about the way in the pub was run and fears that it was becoming a very disorderly house with uproar and fights in the streets, so much so that there was talk of the house being closed completely. In hope of a new start the owners Eldridge Pope carried out some extensive rebuilding resulting in the property we see today.

From 1909 the landlord was Sidney Loveday and in August of 1918 at the age of 47 he was granted a temporary exemption from national service and continued on at the pub until the 1935 during which time he found one of his guests wandering about the hotel in his underpants with two bottles of whiskey under his jumper saying that that he was going to join the Royal Ulster Constabulary the following year, he was fined 15/- plus costs. An even more bizarre event occurred in 1921 when two privates of the Royal Enniskillen Fusiliers were seen to smash two plate glass windows of a nearby shop and then lie on the pavement pretending to be unconscious. Possibly some sort of performance art? Whatever their reasons, John Spring, landlord of the Lamb and Flag, and Sidney Loveday of the Jersey apprehended the pair who were sober, and commandeered a passing fish lorry which drove them to the police station. They were remanded to the quarter sessions and each received one calendar month with hard labour their bizarre behaviour unexplained

Loveday must have had some enemies because in 1933 a yacht that he owned, an auxiliary cutter named the *New Moss Rose* was set on fire and destroyed in Osborne Bay, Cowes the three man crew having to be rescued by a passenger steamer but there are no further details. Two years later the landlord is Martin Burnell an enthusiastic collector of matchbox tops whose time at the pub did not end well as in December off 1939 he was arrested along with two leading stokers and charged with stealing 25 gallons of petrol from a patrol vessel property of the Admiralty. It was a very sad case, Burnell had joined the army at 15, been wounded twice and was in receipt of a 25% disability pension, a man of unblemished character who had run the pub for five years. He was convicted and fined £20 losing his licence as well. He died in 1941 at the age of 40. In 1979 the name was changed to the Jersey Tavern presumably because they no longer took paying guests and by 2000 it had closed and become part of the Café Nero chain of coffee shops.

THE KING'S ARMS
Trinity Road, Weymouth

Thought to date from the 16th century but remodelled in the 18th and 19th centuries, little is known about the early years of this ancient inn now Georgian fronted with some Victorian alterations but retaining a much earlier interior. It would have been one of many small beer houses on the less fashionable side of the river serving sailors and working men with no flash coaches or important events to draw attention to itself. There is mention of a Nathaniel Lewis at the King's Arms Ale House, High Street, Weymouth from the record of those eligible to vote in 1760. He wrote his will in 1765 as an 'innholder' leaving everything to his wife Amy and died in 1768. The auction

The Kings Arms 2018

of a captured enemy ship, the *Rosario* with all its cargo was held in 1808 and a large property on the Esplanade was auctioned there during January of 1810. We are on firmer ground from 1813 when an Edward Mace is shown as occupying a property owned by Thomas Gear. No property or occupation is specified but in 1820 he is shown in the land tax records as occupying a public house now owned by Elizabeth Arbuthnot. The 1825 jury list has Mace as an innkeeper and leaseholder but the following year he has become the freeholder of a still unnamed inn on High Street, Weymouth. His last entry is on the

1837 list of those eligible to serve on a jury where he is described as a publican and freeholder in High Street he died in 1851.

By the census of 1841 James Bartlett 30 and his wife Mary have taken charge but the premises are put up for rent in 1846 and 'satisfactory reasons for leaving can be given' but these of course remain unknown to us. The house is up for sale again in August of 1850 this time as part of the extensive estates of Taver Penny of High West Street which also included the freeholds of the Black Dog and the Golden Lion. It was then in the occupancy of Joseph Yates and family which continued until 1891 shortly after which the licence was taken by William Rex and his wife Sarah. Rex was subject to a vicious and unprovoked attack in the pub after asking four Australian servicemen to moderate their language, as a local paper reports, 'A scene of the wildest confusion and excitement followed in which everything available was hurled at him and the destruction of a considerable amount of property resulted. Assistance of the military and civilian police was involved and while one of the four desperados escaped the three others were got to the police station and put securely under lock and key'.

It emerged that Mrs Rex, who had served them, reported their language to her husband who, 'had a word' which resulted in him being smacked in the face followed by a barrage of anything that came to hand one of the men jumped over the counter and smashed a whole shelf of mugs and glasses. Large panes of glass and windows were smashed before the civil police assisted by the military police arrived and made the arrests. Rex was so seriously injured that he required five stitches in his head, more in his neck and face and some to his finger. By now a large crowd had gathered and surveyed a scene of absolute devastation. At the police station three men claimed that they were so drunk that they could remember nothing – but all witnesses stated that they were perfectly sober. The three were charged and bailed to appear at the next Assizes but of course when the court assembled in October they had long gone back to their native country and all the judge could do was issue warrants for their arrest should they ever return. Mark and Mary Rex were still there in 1926 after which the pub is run by the Garnett family until at least the 1939 register.

THE KING'S HEAD INN
East Street & Market Street, Melcombe Regis

THE KING'S HEAD was built as a replacement for the ancient inn in Maiden Street of the same name which was demolished in 1866 to make way for road improvements and the new Wesleyan Chapel. Its first landlord was Solomon Sly son of William Sly who was briefly landlord of the original King's Head. There is so little information available about the lives of the landlords that it seems reasonable to record what we do know of the more interesting ones when information is available.

The King's Head Inn 2024

A fascinating character, Solomon Samuel Sly was born in 1815 and was 11 when his father died at the original King's Head in 1825. He was at first destined to become a musician, he performed well on the violin and possessed considerable musical talent but it was as a publican and host that his destiny lay. He began at the White Hart in St Nicholas Street in about 1836 the same year as he married his wife Betsy Ann Percy followed by the Royal Oak on the Quay, the Half Moon in King Street and the Fountain Tavern where he had also been its first licensee. Why he felt the urge to move so many times is not known. He was a short burly figure with a resounding voice and a dedicated

Conservative who made his presence known at every meeting and with a fast and ready wit he was a match for any heckler. After the death of his first wife he remarried Elizabeth Bowring in 1847.

One of his other business interests while at the King's Head was as custodian of the bathing machines on the beach which gave rise a very curious case of assault heard before the borough magistrates in September of 1869. The main question was whether Weymouth Sands was or was not public property. From contemporary reports, a Mr William Wynn, on a visit to Weymouth, summoned Solomon Sly, the custodian of the bathing-machines, for assaulting him. Mr Wynn was playing on the sands at trap and ball with his son. At this time the water was low and the machines which were not in use lay some 30 or 40 yards distant from where they were playing. Mr Sly came up to him in a very authoritative way, and told him to get off the sands. Mr Wynn demurred, saying that the sands were public property, whereupon Mr Sly, who was in a very excited mood, told Wynn that the sands were his, as he paid £40 a year for them. Mr Wynn refused to leave, upon which Sly thrust him aside in a violent manner, hit him, and kicked over the trap. Wynn had a small bat in his hand, with which he struck Sly, who put himself in a fighting attitude, offering to fight for £5. The assault on either side was not a violent one, and Mr Symonds, who appeared in support of the charge, admitted that if the case had been one of common assault only, his client would not have troubled the bench with it, but he came forward on public grounds, in order to ascertain whether the public had a right to the sands or not. If they had not the sooner it was known far and wide the better, so that persons might not be deprived of that which they visited Weymouth to enjoy.

Mr Howard, who appeared for defendant, said that of the thousands of persons who visited the town, this was the first case which had ever been brought against his client by one of them. The facts of the case, as he was instructed, were simply these—Mr Sly, perceiving Mr Wynn and his son playing trap and ball near the machines, asked them to desist, giving as a reason that only a day or two previously a lady, whilst in the act of crossing the sands, was severely struck by a ball in the face. On Mr Wynn refusing to leave, Mr Sly pushed him, using no more force than was necessary. He (Mr Howard) contended that Sly had a perfect right to the sands, because as one of the proprietors of the machines he paid the corporation £40 a year for the licence to run them from the sands to the sea. There was no doubt that the sands were open to the public, but it was at such times when they were not required for the purpose of bathing. The Mayor said the bench were of the opinion that an assault had been committed, and very much regretted it should have occurred.

They, however, thanked Mr Wynn for coming forward on behalf of the public, for he could assure him that he had as much right to the sands as any other person. The bench were aware that Mr Sly, or those whom he represented, paid a licence to the corporation, and they would give him every facility for using the sands for the purpose of bathing. Sly was fined 10/- and costs. In May of 1871 returning from a trip to London he complained of shortness of breath which had plagued him for some time despite every appearance of robust health. A doctor was called and he was given medication but died within the hour asthma being described as the cause of death. His obituary said that he had *about* 10 children and the licence passed to his widow Elizabeth who ran the establishment until 1905 and lived to be 95 dying in 1921. A brief entry in the theatrical paper The Era for June 1901 contained the following, 'WANTED, Good Comedians, Used to Sketches write Jack Sly King's Head Hotel'.

In the 1911 census 37-year-old army pensioner Frank Devin Roe took over but was called away for active service during the war and returned to his wife and eight-year-old son Leonard in 1920. Leonard had served briefly in the Royal Tank Corps but changed from a 'good tempered sporty lad' into a 'nerve ridden man' who disappeared without leave, with 'several matters concerning money and other valuables which would have to be investigated'. Roe was found in a gas filled London hotel room with his throat and wrists cut in February of 1935. The licence was taken over by their eldest son Frank Ernest Roe who was running the pub when the 1939 register was taken.

THE KING'S HEAD HOTEL
Corner of Maiden Street & Helen's Lane, Melcombe Regis

MEETINGS OF A charity called 'Clergy and Sons of the Clergy of the County of Dorset' were held at the King's Head regularly as advertised in the local paper for the 1756. The first name to be associated with this ancient coaching inn was Robert Knight who is on the list of those eligible to vote during the 1760s as living at the King's Head, Maiden Street. He appears again for the same period in, 'A List of all Persons now Dwelling within the Town of Melcombe Regis between the age of 18 and 50 years', Robert Knight innholder'.

This inn and the Bear were probably the largest and most important in the town with the King's Head holding regular auctions of ships and all things marine, including, in August 1773, six fine fresh turtles newly arrived at Bristol weighing from 20lb and selling from 1/4d to 2/- per pound. 1780 saw the

The King's Head Hotel 1860s

sale of 67 tons of French claret and 11 tons of French white wine, part of the cargo of the Dutch galliot or cargo boat *Jonge Ulbe* captured on her way from Bordeaux. In 1786 the lease was up for sale and purchased by Thomas Luce formally a waiter at the Crown Inn, Blandford, 'fitted it up in a genteel manor with stabling for 70 horses'. He is there until 1792 when he moves on to the White Lion Inn and coffee house in Bristol. In around 1798 the Wesleyan Methodists held their first local meetings at the old assembly and billiard room at the inn before moving to larger premises.

In April 1800 the hull of the schooner *Hercules* which lay full of water at the entrance to the harbour was up for auction and immediately after, the sale of the hull 'will be sold the materials of the said schooner consisting of masts, yards, sales, anchors cables standing and running rigging with various ship's stores saved from the wreck'. During 1804 the inn received a very distinguished guest in the shape of the Revd John Skinner vicar of Camerton in Somerset and one of the founders of British prehistoric archaeology. He was there to visit his brother on board the yacht *Royal Sovereign* and after visiting a play, 'I slept on a mattress on the floor of the King's Head Hotel'. 1809 was the 50th anniversary of the reign of King George and the 'All Souls Lodge of Freemasons' organised a march from the inn to the laying of the foundation stone of the King's Statue, 'dinner on the table at 3 o'clock'. In March of 1811 a dinner was held for the local hunt with the pub now referred to as The King's Head Navy Tavern. The Union Weymouth Coach began running to London on 22 July 1811 to which 'the strictest attention has been used in selecting sober and careful coachmen and guards and purchasing able and steady horses'. Serial 'pub hopper' Joshua Hide moved from the Antelope in June of 1820 promising that his public dinners on market days will be continued as usual with an Ordinary (a plain cheap meal) served every day, during 1823 he moved once more taking over the Golden Lion before he died in 1826.

There is an excellent watercolour of 1825 by John Upham which shows the inn adjacent to the original Guildhall building, the name W Sly can just be made out above the door. This was William Sly landlord until his death in July of that year at the age of 44 leaving his widow Frances. An auction was held the following March to dispose of the brewing utensils, casks, furniture etc property of Mrs S Sly who was to leave the premises on 20 March, there are no

John Upham 1825 the old Guildhall with the King's Head in the centre distance

further details. The following year the pub name seems to have been elongated to the, King's Head Navy Tavern and Guernsey and Jersey Hotel by a Richard Gaulton, he didn't stay long and was replaced by Thomas Willis, followed by John Soper and William Roll, until in 1839 William and Jane Dyer take over followed by their son also William. The inn became the unofficial headquarters of the local Conservative Association taking an active part in politics and after one enthusiastic report of a meeting during 1837 the writer ended with 'The Whig-Radicals held a meeting the same evening, but proved a complete failure.'

In July the inn was advertised, 'TO LET with immediate possession All That old established and well accustomed inn and market house called the King's Head situated in the marketplace where extensive business has been successfully carried on for the last century the tenant Jane Dyer is retiring from ill-health', She died in August 1843 aged 62 and son William took over.

William Dyer jnr and his wife Maria continued behind the bar with a slight hiccup in 1852 when William was caught on a return trip from Guernsey with his pockets bulging with 100 cigars and over half a pound of tobacco. He was fined a total of £2 with 4/6d costs. Upon which he declared that 'I think this is sickening; I should be more careful next time.' Which could be interpreted in a number of ways… By the census of 1861 William and Maria are still at the pub but William is described as a coal merchant perhaps leaving Maria to serve the customers which was quite common. In March of 1866 the Dyers put the entire contents of the pub up for auction so presumably it had closed shortly before and in the same month it was announced that the old inn was to be demolished seemingly on the grounds of road improvements making a thoroughfare from St Edmund Street to East Street on behalf of the Johnstone Estate although very little discussion seems to have taken place. In April the licence was transferred to a new building in East Street, keeping the name of the King's Head and a new Wesleyan chapel was proposed for the site of the old pub with the new road alongside. All being approved, the cornerstone of the magnificent new chapel was laid on 28 June 1866.

THE LAMB & FLAG
Lower Bond Street, formerly Coneygar Lane, Melcombe Regis

THE FIRST MENTION of the Lamb and Flag, then described as at 12 Coneygar Lane comes from 1851 when it was leased to Samuel Flood by the owners, local brewers Eldridge Pope. Flood was summoned for selling

The Lamb and Flag (Weymouth Museum)

beer during divine service on Sunday the following year but was let off with a warning despite this being the second time that he had been accused of the offence, but the matter didn't quite end there. Flood was taken to court by George Westcott a short while later as he had observed people buying beer outside of permitted hours and taking it across the road. He ordered some himself via somebody else and gradually build his case. In court there were various witnesses for and against, was it beer ? wasn't it beer ? was it paid for or not ? Eventually the true meaning of the case came to light. Westcott had a long-standing grudge against Flood and had set him up. Magistrates expressed surprise that he had fallen for it but nonetheless the crime had been committed and Flood was ordered to pay a mitigated penalty of £3 plus costs.

It wasn't long before he was in much more serious trouble being charged with selling spirits without a licence and fined £12/10/- he appealed to the higher court and brought a case of perjury against George Curling who claims to have bought a quarter pint of gin from Mrs Flood for which he paid £4/1/2d. This was on 4 September 1853 which just happened to be the date upon which the Floods buried their adopted child. After the service Mary Flood retired to bed and remained there for the whole day – the very time at which she was alleged to have been dispensing gin. A number of witnesses were called to prove that this was indeed the case and that Curling was lying. No motive was revealed but the jury found him guilty with a recommendation for mercy. The judge was having none of it and declared that perjury was one of the most serious offences to come before the courts and sentenced Curling to 12 months with hard labour.

Some people seemed to put much effort into their dislike of Mr Flood but his tenure continued until after the census of 1861 at which, still at the Lamb and Flag now aged 46, he gave his occupation as a sawyer and wife Mary Ann 42 as a dressmaker. It was quite common for licensees to have more than one occupation.

The next landlord was Joel Board a journeyman baker from Portland and his wife Grace. Joel died in 1867 at the age of 34 and the pub was taken over by Grace who was granted a spirits licence in 1870 with comments that the establishment was extremely well run and described as situated at the bottom of Conygar Lane near a large building lately converted into industrial dwellings for the working classes. The pub had eight rooms, was four storeys high and rated at £20 per year. Her husband had once been a cook on the Channel Islands boats and she was bringing up her four children alone. Grace was still there in 1895 having run the pub with far less drama than the Floods. In 1898 Eldridge Pope & Co submitted plans to expand the premises by incorporating two cottages in Harmony Court and spent £737 on the alterations. From around 1910 until 1926 the Lamb was run by John and Annie Spring until it passed to former master gunner at the Nothe Fort, Joseph Hannan who was still there for the census or register of 1939. The building was damaged by enemy action in 1941 and again in 1942. Its last tenants were Joe Meakin and his wife Nina who were there from 1956 to 1958 when the pub was finally closed and the licence transferred to the new Admiral Hardy pub on Chickerell Road, the Meakins went with it as the first landlords. The former Lamb was purchased by the Royal Sailors Rest in 1960 for £6,900 to be converted into a 15 cabin sailor's home which ran from 1961-1974 until being finally demolished in the 1990s to make way for Debenhams and the New Bond Street shopping development.

THE LONDON HOTEL
Upper Bond Street,/ New Street corner, Melcombe Regis

LOCAL ARCHITECTURAL HISTORIAN Eric Ricketts in his book *The Buildings of Old Weymouth* estimates the London to have been built or re-fronted in the 1840s which fits in well with the documentary record beginning with the census of 1851 when it is occupied by George Read and family, beer house keepers. Before long it was being run by Robert Baxter a farmer's son from Yorkshire who moved from The Fox, he was there until 1860 when he sold up having built his own 'Stores' in New Street just across the road from the London.

The pub is advertised for rent by owners Devenish & Co. in 1868 and is taken by Vincent Newman late of London town who advertises a 'thoroughly renovated hotel with a new refreshment bar added similar to the London luncheon bars', a large smoking room, coffee room, 13 bedrooms with good cellars and offices with five entrances. He is only there for a few months before the pub is advertised to let again and taken by FW Bunyer another one up from London this time from the Old Bell Hotel in Holborn. He didn't stay long either dropping dead from heart attack in May 1873 with the licence passing to his wife Sarah.

The London Hotel 2025

Charles Jones takes charge in 1876 giving the name a slight tweak and calling it 'London Hotel, Jones's Café Restaurant' eggs and bacon 1/6d tea or coffee 2d. During October there was a fire that could have been disastrous, clouds of smoke were seen to be pouring out from a first floor window above which the landlord's three children were sleeping. They were quickly rescued although almost suffocated by the smoke and the fire put out with buckets of water from obliging neighbours. They left the following year and were replaced by Henry Abbey with a letter from the Commissioner of Police stating that they had known Abbey for 16 years at Islington and knew him to be a very respectable man and the owner of a large property. He seemed to possess more staying power than the other Londoners and was there for about ten years. Scandal hit the pub in 1884 when 'boots' Charles Woodsford was convicted of an indecent assault on an 11-year-old girl, he offered her and her mother money to say nothing about the matter but it was reported nonetheless. Woodsford was a married man of 49 who has spent 21 years in the Royal Artillery with very good character. He was sentenced to 12 months imprisonment.

In 1889 George E C Collinson described as 'late of the Great Yarmouth Aquarium Orchestra' offered sitting rooms from 2/6d and double bedrooms with attendance for 4/-but he was gone within two years. It is interesting to note that with the increasing use of photography simple matters like references and previous experience when advertising for staff could be dispensed with as this advert from 1891 illustrates, 'Barmaid and Waitress wanted – send photo, age, and terms to, Proprietor, London Hotel Weymouth'.

Collinson was replaced by the double act of proprietors Walter Wright (late Comedy Theatre, London) and Captain WH Johnson. By 1899 the reign of the London theatricals was over but the London Hotel still attracted those from that city this time in the shape of 30-year-old John Thomas Baugh from Bermondsey, his wife Sarah and young family who were to play a large part in the public houses of the town. For a brief period in 1901 Weymouth had its own giant but things didn't end well. A Frenchman named Baptiste Hugo was 22 years of age and 7'6" tall weighing 401 lbs. He was on show for eight days in a tent on the beach and staying at the London. Everything went well until a little girl received a slight abrasion on her leg, opinions differed greatly on how this happened but one of the many rumours was that she was being a pain and the giant had kicked her and broken her leg, the mother reported the incident to the police. This was the version adopted by a gang of boys aged about 16 who attacked the tent cutting the ropes and throwing stones at Mr Hugo who retreated in a cab to the hotel followed by a noisy crowd some of whom returned to the beach and attacked the manager who was trying to re-erect the tent. Meanwhile a howling mob developed outside the London attempting to force their way in but were repelled by a study bunch of locals.

There was a tragedy in the Baugh family in January 1919 when one of his sons, a 17-year-old second class air mechanic was killed riding his bike across a railway line near Doncaster. The family continued to run the London until the 1930s without any further incident and after brief periods as wine bar at one time the 'Twenty Twelve Bar ' it closed permanently in 2001 and is undergoing renovation at the time of writing.

THE MARINE HOTEL
Bank Buildings, Esplanade, Melcombe Regis

THIS IMPOSING GEORGIAN building known as the Bank House was put up for auction while still in the process of construction following the bankruptcy of the owner John Puckett in 1802. Described as 'an excellent situation for a hotel' and with a 90-year lease the sale took place in November 1803 with the consent of mortgagee John Puckett. Opinions differ but it seems probable that it never was a bank but may have acquired the name from an adjoining building and was initially a private house said to have been occupied by the mother of local MP Thomas Fowell Buxton sometime after her husband died in 1793. She remarried Edmund Henning- a banker in 1806 although there is no evidence that they actually lived there together but it seems like the closest the building ever got to banking.

Although never strictly a public house it began life as the Marine Hotel and was occupied by JB Luce who moved to the Castle Inn, Kingston upon Thames in the early part of 1833 after which it became a boarding house run by Sarah Clark in the 1841census followed by George Voss and his wife Mary who ran it as Voss's Private Hotel until around the mid 70s when it was described as ' an eyesore, begrimed with dirt and dust'.

In 1878 William Charles Davis of the Golden Lion who had once kept the Spreadeagle in Gloucester and produced many glowing testimonials from his time there, rented the property from one of the owners, John Wimble general manager of the Weymouth and Channel Islands Steamer Company. Davis renamed it the Marine Hotel and furnished it in the 'most modern style'. Presumably it was Wimble & Co who had spent the large amount of money on the refurbishments as this report in the local paper indicates,

'The bar is very beautifully fitted up in the main hall there is a lift which reaches from the kitchen up to the second storey a coffee room, a ladies

The Marine Hotel 2023

waiting room, a space set aside for the use of Customs Inspectors as soon as passengers leave the boat. The staircase long admired for its beauty has been freshly decorated; there is a fine billiard table on the second floor. The sleeping accommodation is first class with light enameled suites and marble top dressing tables, all the beds are fitted with a patent spring mattress and every bedroom has a bath in which either a fresh or salt water dip maybe taken; pneumatic bells are fitted throughout the house and there are wonderful views over the new gardens'. All this was of course to catch, and hopefully keep, travelers from the steamers coming from the Channel Islands and France day and night and one of the terms in his lease was that every boat was to be met and prices charged were to be the same as those aboard ship.

That August began a battle of epic proportions to acquire a spirits licence. The process is very much like a trial with solicitors for and against. Those against were in the main paid for by the licensees of nearby houses fearing the competition which in this case was bound to be fierce. Those for Davis said that the excise authorities were delighted to have the use of the hall and those against found it extraordinary that customs examinations would be allowed in a public house. A bell was rung ten minutes before the arrival or departure of the boats and the 'boots' met the needs of every one. Davis had taken over the lodging house on 13 May and had since then provided 566 beds, he had also held the Golden Lion since 9 January for which he had a 14 year lease and was run by his brother while Davis himself lived at the Marine. As there was no logical real reason why Davis should not have a licence the opposition resorted to obscure points of law and the arrangement of the various rooms dragging the process out over two separate sessions. In the end he got his licence amid much applause in court which was quickly silenced. The building may have been splendid but the same cannot be said of its landlord. In March 1879 Mr and Mrs Davis were taken to court by Elizabeth Ware a 'smart but pert looking damsel' employed for a fortnight as a servant. One of a number of complaints against her employers was that Mr Davis had repeatedly tried to kiss her and she had to fight him off. Of course, she was not believed and the case was dismissed. The misadventures of William Davis are gone into in more detail in the Golden Lion entry.

It is said that the much-acclaimed Jersey actress and a socialite, Lille Langtry stayed there in about 1881 and commented in a letter, 'We got in at two and went to the Marine Hotel which turned out to be a pot house of the lowest description in which people shared beds between six and the proprietor was quite drunk and would not show us our rooms...'

Davis appears in the census of 1881 aged 37 but gave up the licence in 1883 to JW Blackman 'a gentleman of high position who had formed his own estate but was a stranger to these matters who had come down to find out exactly what would be required by the magistrates and as the answers to enquiries had not yet arrived he was granted a temporary transfer and called his new venture the Marine Channel Islands and Cherbourg Hotel. Concern was expressed regarding premises known as 'The Dives' at the back of the hotel. Letters had been received complaining about activities there which were said to involve instrumentalists and which were apparently 'causing dancing and subjecting residents to great annoyance'. To their credit the magistrates chose to ignore this particular complaint.

By 1890 the house was taken by two sisters Jane and Harriet Bowles from Sussex, who almost lost their investment in December 1893 when there was a terrible gale which ripped the slates and lead work from the roof scattering it far and wide. There are no details, but in 1894 there was County Court judgement against them in the sum of £38/16/9d and the pub was put up for rent by brewers Groves & Son to be taken by Ernest Clapp who had also run the Golden Lion since 1883. He renamed the pub the Royal Marine Family Hotel and there was another name change in about 1911 when it was strangely renamed, Hotel Edward by that then landlord Albert Whaley who moved to the Queen's Hotel shortly after.

The house had been requisitioned during the war and was returned to service in 1946 and after a period during the 1980s as the Hotel Dumont run by Philip Dumont it was closed and converted into flats.

THE MARKET HOUSE INN
St Edmund Street, Melcombe Regis

THIS SMALL BEER house was first recorded in 1844 when it was owned by John Hancock and the licence held by George Male, by the end of the decade it was being run by Ann Hine a 60-year-old widow. Daniel Dober a cooper and his family came next but had his application for a spirit licence deferred for one year because of complaints of noise and an 'unfavourable police report.' By 1861 Dober had moved to the Porters' Arms.

His place was taken by John Nicholls a former sapper in the Royal Engineers now retired with a pension. He had also been a steward on one of the Jersey steam packets and tried his luck at obtaining a spirits licence in 1866 on the reasonable grounds that as the nearby King's Head Inn had been removed there was one less licensed house in the area but he was unsuccessful and the inn had to wait until 1870 when Andrew Guy applied, describing his house as having seven large bedrooms three of them double bedded and it was pointed out that it was so close to the Guildhall that the court would take advantage of it being licensed. Granted.

Living next door to the pub a Mrs Rogers was surprised to find two men in her room having just climbed over the wall from the pub, presumably they didn't expect anybody to be in. She reported the matter to Martha Baggs the landlady who had been in charge with her husband William since 1874. Baggs was very abusive but eventually went to the police. The two men appeared in court claiming to be fisherman who had 'got lost' trying to find the way out which had caused them to climb over a six foot wall.

The police described the reputation of the house as a very low one and the men were fined a total of about £3 for damage to the wall and various articles. In fact, 1874 was quite an eventful year for the Market House. Henry Pitman a coal porter and Elizabeth Standon were arrested for assault and robbery on George Hollister a stoker from HMS *Achilles*. Standon had known Hollister for

The Market House Inn 2025

some years and they met at the Market House with some shipmates of his having just been paid and come ashore. After a while he left with Standon and Pitman and was found lying in the street a short time later having received a severe blow to the back of the head which rendered him unconscious with blood pouring from his head and mouth. He was taken to the hospital and it was thought that it would not survive. The pair were arrested and after a lengthy trial Standon was acquitted while Pitman was convicted and sentenced to seven years penal servitude. In February sailor Joseph Randall who had known William Baggs for some time persuaded him to part with £1/17/6d for an advance note which he had been given by his ship for half a month's wages as he needed to buy some clothes. Baggs reluctantly agreed only to discover that Randall had no intention of boarding his ship which had already been delayed from sailing three times due to his actions. He was convicted at trial and as he had been to prison seven times before he was sentenced to 12 months hard labour. In May Martha Baggs had a clothes brush stolen by prostitute Amelia Cornick who shortly after tried to exchange it for beer or 2d (its true value was about 1/6d) at the Portland Arms saying that she had found it in the road but she was convicted of theft and sentenced to one month's hard labour. During that same month William Baggs himself was in trouble for supplying intoxicating liquor, half a pint of rum and peppermint, to a drunken sailor who was afterwards found unconscious in the pub doorway. Baggs was told that he was liable for a £10 fine but was only fined £5 plus costs, and lucky to get away without his licence being endorsed.

The Baggs had moved on by 1878 and after a few short termers the Brake family ran the pub from 1901 until 1922 when it was taken over by Arthur

William Taylor a reasonably famous footballer for Dorset County, who went by the name of 'Ginger'. Disaster was averted in October of 1926 when the place was pretty much destroyed by fire and complete tragedy avoided only by the three children being awakened by Sam the family cat clawing at their bedclothes and scratching the daughter's face. The family were trapped because the staircase was on fire and the upstairs rooms a furnace. They were rescued in the time-honoured fashion by being thrown out of the window into the waiting arms of Police Sergeant Richardson. This probably accounts for the rather bland looking exterior when compared to the Georgian frontage of number 22 next door.

1938 saw the demolition of the old Market House building in St Mary Street and to mark the occasion Major Devenish commissioned a striking new sign for the pub painted by FG Biles of Bridport which depicted the old Market House building and replaced a plain sign which just had the name on it. The new one caused much comment and admiration but its present whereabouts is unknown. The original iron bracket for the sign exists to this day. Landlord Kenneth Owen Austin was quite surprised when arrested for keeping a common gaming house in 1959 claiming that he thought the machines were legal. He was advised to get a solicitor.

MARKET HOUSE TAVERN
Maiden Street, Melcombe Regis

WILLIAM LONG WAS the first known landlord, at the Market House Tavern when he applied for a spirits licence in August of 1864 he had only been in possession of the house for about three months but had been a rate payer for several years and formerly a steward of the Channel Islands steamers. His application was refused as the house was judged not have the accommodation or stabling and might be said to be nothing more than a 'front' having no back entrance. One year later William Jolliffe applied, reasoning that it was close to the Market House trading centre where much business was done, this time describing it as 'a very commodious establishment with six rooms upstairs and four on the ground floor'. Mr Jolliffe was a 'highly respectable man who had conducted the house most satisfactorily for the past five to six years. The place is very convenient for market people although it might be argued that there is the Bear Inn on the other side'. The request was again refused along with that of many others because the bench considered that with a population of 12,000 there were already 61 spirit licences one, for every 200 persons which was quite sufficient – and there were seven houses within a stone's throw of the place to which it was remarked that 'people would not leave their carts to go as far as that'. His application was finally granted in 1870.

John Palmer took the licence in 1874, he had once been a messenger in the House of Lords and the Metropolitan Police gave him a good character reference, upon moving to Weymouth he was an assistant warder in Portland Prison. In 1878 the house was extensively rebuilt by owners Eldridge Pope & Co. In 1882 landlord Charles Masters was caught with nine ounces of illegal Cavendish tobacco and summoned to court along with publicans from the Globe, George and the Star. The tobacco had been smuggled without the duty being paid on it and there is a more detailed report in the Globe entry. In 1880 landlord James McBean took up the offer of a hawker, Alfred Collins, to mend some chairs for him at 1/3d each but the work was so bad that he refused to pay upon which Collins removed his hat put his hand inside it and smashed the glass panels in the door. When convicted of wilful damage to the extent of £3/10/- he was unable to pay he was sentenced to one month's hard labour.

Market House Tavern 2016

Owners Eldridge Pope & Co offered the house for rent at the end of 1883 and despite quite a rapid change over of landlords the house seems to have been very quiet and well run. In 1919 there was a dispute between landlord Alfred Holloway and his brother William over a property in St Alban's Street, Alfred wanted it for his son who was intending to open a restaurant and the judge found in his favour.

In 1924 the licence was transferred from Alfred John Holloway to 30-year-old Charles Edwin Dunford late steward of the Weymouth Working Men's Club with an excellent war service record despite which he became bankrupt in August of 1925 with liabilities amounting to over £234. He blamed his predicament on a falloff in trade. He was paying £150 per month to Eldridge Pope and had spent about £200 on furniture but did not keep any books and had been forced to sell the furniture for £14. There were some complaints to the police about the conduct of his house but he did not see that as the cause of his problems. Examining what records there were the official receiver said that he should have made about £400 a year to which Dunford replied ,'Well sir, I don't know where it is, all I know is that I have not got it'. The conclusion was that he had frittered the money away in a business that he did not understand and in 1932 he was killed when a car in which he was a passenger overturned near Dorchester, he was 40 years of age and left a wife and two children. In December of 1962 Louisa Blanche Matthews made the local paper when she retired from the pub at the age of 88 after running it for 40 years before and after the death of her husband Dan in 1944. Known to all as 'Mother' she said' I'm not as fit as I used to be, only the other day I had to go to bed in the daytime!'

The pub continues today as a cosy local and friendly free house described in 2010 as, 'A 1930s looking corner pub, which is mainly in undressed brick, part white render and with some blue paint work. The interior is a U shape around the bar that is in front of you on entry. The decor is white and a toffee coloured wood panel, with stone flag floor a little tired, but not shabby. There are no real pictures or ephemera, leaving the place a little bare, but it has a dart board one end and a pool table at the other, with screens showing the footy. There was no music. The service was friendly and the clientele seemed a mixed bunch of locals and friendly enough'.

THE MASON'S ARMS INN
Petticoat Lane / St Alban's Row, Weymouth

VERY LITTLE HAS been discovered about this house even its precise location in Petticoat Lane/St Alban's Row is unknown. The census return for 1851 has John Richard Glasson aged 40 a married beer house keeper and stone mason from North Petherton in Somerset living there with his unmarried sister Elizabeth 22, and niece of one year plus two lodgers. In February 1852 Glasson appeared at the Weymouth Petty sessions accused of keeping a disorderly house. Sergeant Wotton entered the premises looking for a young man called Ford who was alleged to have beaten his mother. In two rooms below stairs he found him along with 18 to 20 prostitutes and nearly

Sarah Bilke, a servant at the "Mason's Arms," in Petticoat Lane, deposed that the prisoner was drinking at their house on the night in question. He was left alone in one of the rooms, where two shawls, belonging to the witness, were lying on a piece of furniture. The prisoner left the house soon after nine o'clock, and was intoxicated when he left. Soon after his departure the two shawls were missed. Those produced by the police-constable were the same.

P. C. Hounsell found the prisoner lying on the pavement near the King's Statue, in a state of beastly intoxication. On searching him at the station, the shawls produced, a piece of new flannel, and a quantity of onions and other articles were found upon him.

The prisoner, on being questioned by the Bench, said that he "was so beastly *intosticated*, that he did not know how he came by the shawls. The flannel and other articles he had bought." Committed for trial at the next sessions.

Inspector Morris stated that several navvies who appeared to be "chums" of the prisoner, had been attempting to bribe the prosecutrix with a sovereign not to appear against the prisoner that morning.

Beastly Intostication 1853

50 men some of whom were intoxicated. They dragged him out and police had the house cleared but he refused to go home with his father. The Glassons were accused of keeping a disorderly house and Mary Glasson, who appeared before the bench on behalf of her husband, denied this but the magistrates disagreed and fined her £5 plus costs to which she replied, 'Very well, I shall pay it. but we shall appeal to the Quarter Sessions. There are several persons of respectability who are willing to speak as to the good order of the house and they would have been here today had not business compelled them to go out of town'. There are strong indications that the pair sailed off to Australia onboard the *Meteor* in July of 1853. They do not appear to have had any children.

There is a report of the theft of two shawls in November of 1853 and a spot of dangerous driving in March of 1854 along with a fight outside in 1859 when three soldiers of the 42nd Highlanders came out of the Masons and attacked the police as one of them tried to arrest a prostitute in their company. PC Curtis was severely beaten about the head with sticks. One of the witnesses describe the attack is taking place near 'Grinter's beer house' who may have been the landlord at the time but no other evidence has come to light to confirm this. Other constables joined in, drawing a large crowd of spectators and eventually four men were convicted and fined the maximum of £5 each which they were not prepared to pay and so they were sent to Dorchester jail for a fortnights hard labour. It seems probable that the Mason's Arms closed down very shortly after.

THE MILITARY ARMS
Barrack Road, The Nothe, Weymouth

THE MILITARY ARMS was described as newly built in 1854 when landlord Dennis Luce applied for a spirits licence, he was a gentleman described as without a stain upon his character and in a much better situation and superior building than the nearby Canteen who applied at the same time. One big advantage, claimed Luce, was that being close to the barracks soldiers could be more subject to surveillance then in a more distant part of the town. Both had their applications refused but the pub soon became a popular destination for those fed up with being confined to the barrack canteen. Beer money was part and parcel of a soldiers pay, and so it was not surprising that drunkenness was a major problem. The licence was soon transferred to William Puckett a tailor by profession who wasted little time in serving beer outside of permitted hours and was fined 5 /- as it was his first offence. After Puckett came Thomas Sherry a man more than equal to the job of running a public house right next to the barracks. In October of 1862 he was attacked by six sailors who had ordered copious amounts of beer but refused to pay for it, smashing the jugs, throwing them at the landlord's head, jumping over the bar and giving him a 'tap' on the nose. The police arrived and joined in the melee eventually drawing a crowd of some 200 or so people including soldiers from the barracks. Somehow a full-scale riot was averted and the miscreants were transported to the police station ending up with fines of around 5/- apiece.

Violence soon broke out again, this time between Mary Sherry the landlady, and a female customer with Thomas pitching in which resulted in a street brawl, a blackeye and a fine of 5/-. The violence was not confined to the customers. In 1864 James Sheppard landlord of the Canteen Tavern just up the road saw someone going to Sherry's with two spirit containers belonging to him. He went to get them back upon which Sherry hit him with a large stick causing severe bruising to his arm, a witness confirmed that Sherry had ordered Sheppard to leave and the magistrates were sorry that the case had come to court but fined Sherry 1/- for the use of a stick. There were a number of other reports of a similar nature -and these were just the ones that appeared in court. The inn was advertised to be let by owners Devenish in 1868 and described as containing, a bar, bar parlour, two sitting rooms, seven bedrooms, kitchen, cellar, and offices, with a good skittle alley attached.

There was a bizarre incident in 1910 when a soldier rushed into the bar drew a bayonet from underneath his coat and made a lunge at Abia Sims the landlord. Apparently, the soldier, Thompson, had attacked Sims before but no motive was ever mentioned in court. Sims drew a revolver from behind the bar and threatened to blow the man's brains out if he did not leave and he was eventually bundled out of the pub. In court what could have been a very serious incident indeed was treated very lightly with Thompson bound over to keep the peace and to find sureties for his future good behaviour. In the same year Sims mother-in-law was in court to recover a debt of £8 that she had lent

The Military Arms in 2017

him and judgement was entered in her favour. In August of 1919 the Military Arms was one of several Devenish pubs who had their landlords returned to them after being away on active service. In 1934 landlord Lieut. John Mozart Haylock advertised for a pianist, (entertainer preferred) to accompany his 'Minstrels' opening on Monday night.

When the pub closed Devenish rented the property to the Royal Naval Association for a peppercorn rent and opened as the Anchor Club which ran for about 17 years. Derelict and boarded up, in 2000 the builders moved in and discovered the original name Military Arms Inn hidden behind rendering, this has now been restored and the building is a private house.

THE MILTON ARMS
Petticoat Lane & New Street (renamed 21 St Alban's Row)

THE FORMER MILTON Arms is undoubtedly one of the oldest surviving buildings in the town dating from the late 16th or early 17th century but when it first became a public house is not known, in fact surprisingly little is known about its history at all. There was an application by Thomas Longman before the magistrates in October 1834 as under the terms of the 1830 Beer Act his house was required to close at nine in the evening whereas for some reason premises nearby were licensed under a different system by magistrates and were allowed to stay open until eleven. The act did give magistrates the discretion to alter this and that was the basis of Longman's appeal which was successful. By the census of 1841 the building was occupied by James Holloway a 44-year-old painter and his wife Eleanor and by the 1851 census their occupations are the same but the building is named as the Milton Arms, another ten years and Eleanor is now a 46-year-old widow and retailer of beer which had probably been her role since the start. In 1864 the freehold was put up for auction and described as 'formally a public house with an extensive yard, garden, buildings and premises adjoining fronting towards New Street and formerly in the occupation of Mrs Holloway'.

The Milton soon reopened as a pub and the next landlord was Kingman Cook a former omnibus driver who in his application for a spirits licence explained that he had kept the Victoria Tap for many years which was licensed to sell spirits. The Milton had eleven rooms including seven bedrooms and had formerly been a licensed house for upwards of 20 years but due to the illness of the former proprietor it had lapsed, the application was refused and Cook moved on to be replaced by another cab driver Richard Chubb and his wife

The Milton Arms in 2024

Elizabeth in about 1868. Chubb had convictions for soliciting for passengers without his badge displayed and touting for business which was not allowed and had been fined 5/-. In yet another application for a spirits licence, the police alleged that the house was frequented by prostitutes adding, 'in fact this was a case where a prostitute lived there', this remark was neither challenged nor explained and so we are none the wiser as to what was meant. Chubb and his wife seem to have had a rather strange relationship, so much so that in February 1869 he took her to court charged with threatening his life. She had apparently attacked him with a chopper and a knife but had not actually made contact. He said that he didn't want to bring the prosecution, in fact he said that he had 'as good a wife as any man in the world – apart from her violence and just wanted her to live peaceably with him'. The business was doing very well and within five to six years instead of having to pay £30 a year for rent the Milton Arms could be his own but if she continued to make such rows they would have no bread to eat as all their customers would be driven away. In reply Elizabeth described her husband as violent and said that she could not live with him. The magistrates bound her over to keep the peace for six months herself in the sum of £20 and another surety for a similar amount to which she said defiantly that she could not find and the law must take its course. She was taken to the cells but released the following morning when a surety was found, her husband not wishing to see her in prison. They were still together in the census of 1871 but Mr Chubb was to provide the local population with far more entertainment.

In March of 1874 a young greengrocer named Charles Denning summoned Chubb, 'a rather dark sturdy looking man' for using abusive language towards him. Chubb had an attractive young lady named Sophia Gollop acting as a housekeeper at the pub and Denning was engaged to her. Chubb was insanely jealous and very protective of her claiming that Denning was not good enough for her, although the exact nature of their relationship can only be guessed at. When Sophia, her sister, and Denning went out for a walk together he followed them trying to engage Denning in a fight and constantly hurling insults at him, shaking his fist in his face and trying to provoke him into a breach of the peace. The plot thickened when it emerged that it was Sophia's unnamed uncle who actually owned the Milton Arms and he had made it over to her which perhaps went along way to explaining Chubb's attitude in proclaiming that Denning should not have her or the licence! The case was resolved with Chubb being bound over to keep the peace for three months with 8/6d costs and on 1 July 1874 Charles Denning married Annie Alice Sophia Gallop.

The Dennings had gained possession of the pub and Chubb was now lodging with a neighbour since his wife had 'run away and left him' but he retained the use of the pub stables for which he paid rent. In November, the lease being up Denning came around and ordered him to leave that evening. Chubb claimed that he had a horse that was ill and could not remove it whereupon Denning knocked him down and kicked and pummelled him for about ten minutes telling him that if he didn't leave his rent would be doubled. Chubb took Denning to court for assault once more and despite the extreme violence the bench had had enough of the pair of them and they were both ordered to keep the peace for three months in their own recognisance of £10. But things were not over yet. Denning owed Chubb £43 for fixtures and fittings in the pub and an order was made for this to be paid in £2 instalments which Denning could not do forcing him to liquidate his grocer's business and the tenancy of the pub which Groves & Co. advertised for rent in August 1876. Chubb had his revenge, remarried, and returned to working has a cab driver and groom but died in the workhouse at the age of 70 in 1903.

In January of 1877 the tenancy of the Milton was transferred to a Frederick Woods despite police objections on the grounds that his wife had once been sentenced to six months hard labour for receiving stolen horsehair. The Dennings took over the Albion Inn at Chapelhay which they kept for many years and their story is continued in that entry. By 1881 the house was being run by Joseph and Sarah Farthing both aged 29 and he was described as a cider merchant. He applied five times for a spirits licence saying that the house was one of the oldest in Weymouth with eight rooms, stabling for eight horses and a considerable yard with premises behind. He had been there about three years and the rent was a little less then £30 per year, the public preferred Groves beer to Devenish and were disappointed that they could not get spirits. The application had to be withdrawn due to inadequate paperwork and in July 1889 Farthing put all his furniture and fittings into auction as he was giving up the pub. The final landlord was Thomas Howard who was there when the Milton closed its doors in 1896 and had himself and the licence moved to the Old Borough Arms, Chickerell Road then under construction by John Groves the brewers. The building was restored in 1980 and is now a shop.

THE NAG'S HEAD
New Street, Melcombe Regis

THE NAG'S HEAD is a fine example of Victorian pub architecture which deserves a more prominent position but is tucked away down a narrow side street. There are mentions of a Nag's Head in the town going back to around 1753 but there is nothing to tie them to this site which is first mentioned in census of 1851 as 14 New Street in the occupation of William Whicker beer house keeper and whitesmith. His application for a spirits licence was refused in 1854 on the grounds that it was too close to the Cutter and the Victoria despite being a 'very extensive house'. A licence was granted under the new landlord James Taylor two years later. Taylor had moved up from the Victoria Tap just down the road and gave way to Thomas Whittle in 1861. In February 1884 the pub was subject to a raid by a customs inspector looking for illegal weights and measures during which many unstamped cups were taken away and landlord George Munden appeared in court along with nine others. In the end they were all dismissed with a caution and a more complete account is included in the Royal Oak entry.

In 1898 at the annual licensing session Laban Sandbrook then steward of the Dorset Yacht club applied for a full licence for a restaurant he was building at 71 St Mary Street and if agreed he would surrender the licence on the Nag's Head. The magistrates agreed on condition that the new restaurant would have no bar, not open on Sundays and that the Nag's Head be closed. In the census of 1901 Sandbrook's new premises are shown as a restaurant and coffee house

The Nag's Head 2024

with his family in residence. The date 1898 still appears in large numbers on the front of the building and the Nag's Head was no more.

THE NELSON INN
North Quay, Weymouth

THE NELSON INN was situated on North Quay on the Weymouth side not far from the Weymouth Arms and the New Inn along High Street, later Trinity Street, and is first mentioned by name in 1867 when landlord was John Randall who was involved in a bit of a misunderstanding over some boots which had found their way via various intermediaries from the army barracks to the pub. The magistrates were unimpressed by his rather convoluted explanation and he was fined three times the value of the boots plus 40/-. During the same summer Randall was summoned for an assault by customer Michael Caldewell who was distressed at seeing a woman named Jane Canning 'towards whom he had some claim to affection', in the company of some soldiers and tried to, 'get her away' upon which he claimed that the landlord and others assaulted him. The bench dismissed the case but not the next one shortly after when Randall was fined £12/10/-for selling spirits without a licence. When not up in court he was happy to agree to some entertainment at the house and when Thomas Thompson a one-legged tailor turned up in January 1870 and asked if he could sing a song Randall was pleased to oblige resulting in a woman being hit over the head with his crutch followed by the landlord being treated the same way and Thompson being fined £1/-.

A few weeks later Randall had gone and Daniel Vosper was in charge and tried once again to obtain a spirits licence for the house claiming that he had 13 rooms seven of which were bedrooms plus attic, but a conviction for selling spirits without a licence three years before counted against him and it was refused. The situation in the bar hadn't improved much either with one of the local prostitutes engaging in a stand-up fight with Vosper which involved a poker and a cast-iron spittoon. Attempts to raise the tone of the place were made in 1880 by the owners John Groves & Co who installed Sergeant John Daniels a man who had spent 16 years in India and China and was of impeccable character being both honest and sober, a widower supported by his son-in-law who promised that all the prostitutes would be a thing of the past. What could possibly go wrong? At the annual general licensing meeting of August 1883, it was reported that as many complaints were coming in as before with reports of 'drunken prostitutes and men carrying jars of beer on a Sunday afternoon at closing time seen coming out of the house'. Daniels was replaced soon after and on 30 September 1885 the Nelson closed for good which provoked comment in a provincial paper,

Daniel Vosper's Advertisement from 1870

A Change for the Better. One of the greatest moral and social improvements which has taken place for many years in Weymouth has been the conversion of a public house known as the Nelson Inn into the Gordon Club and Coffee Tavern.

The club was named after General Gordon of Khartoum who had died a hero the previous year and prompted by Richard Howard the mayor. During its first year he established a men only reading room for the benefit of the artisan class until the building was sold in 1906.

THE NEW BRIDGE HOTEL
Little George Street Commercial Road, Melcombe Regis

THE NEW BRIDGE Tavern, later Hotel was built, as one might expect, to service travellers across the new Westham or Backwater Bridge which opened in 1859. Its first occupants were Edwin and Elizabeth Langford from Hampshire and their two children. They were soon replaced by William Fuszard whose application for a spirits licence was refused as the property 'had only recently been built and once the extensive repairs to the Backwater Bridge were completed it would no doubt to be a great thoroughfare for persons coming from the country who would will pass by the house, but now was not the time'. Surprisingly, for such a fine new building the house run through several licensees in a short period including Leah Stone Baggs whose family had interests in several pubs around the town, she was there for the census of 1871 and held responsible for giving the house a 'bad name'. During the licensing session of September 1871, the licence was ordered to be 'stood over' as the house was nothing more than a common brothel.

Henry John Roper, a potter by trade, applied for a spirits licence in 1875, describing his house as having seven bedrooms, a club room, bar, smoking room, parlour and kitchen. He and his wife had been there for three years and had kept the Baltic previously without any complaints. The freeholder owned a great deal of property in the area having invested money believing that he could make the whole neighbourhood valuable and sought after, catering for a large number of visitors. They had many people from Birmingham and recently there had been 27 lodgers staying there, the licence was granted. There was an unfortunate argument between Mrs Roper and the wife of a customer who stormed into the pub demanding that her husband be served no more drink as he was already drunk. Mrs Roper replied that she would serve whoever she liked upon which the woman grabbed her husband's beer and threw it on the floor. The legal argument revolved around whether he was drunk or not when he had been served. Mrs Roper claimed that when he entered the house he had asked for 'A half pint of beer Mrs Roper please' the magistrates did not believe that a drunken man would use the word 'please' and dismissed the case. Hannah White moved from the Somerset Hotel at the beginning of 1878 and was there until her death in 1894. Meanwhile, in 1884 Henry Roper was summoned for assaulting and beating his wife Harriet after 26 years of marriage she accused him of threatening to murder her, kicking her to the ground and hitting her in the face so hard that she had to be fed with a spoon for three weeks. In reply Roper claimed that his wife got so drunk and aggravated him so much that he did not know what he was about, adding that if a woman stayed away from her husband 13 nights out of 15 it was enough to make him do what he otherwise would not do. Mrs Roper who had an independent business offered to pay her husband £1 per week if granted a judicial separation to which he readily agreed but he was still fined £4 including costs for aggravated assault.

Arthur Scott aged 30 and licensee during 1916 was granted an exemption from military service until August 31and expressed himself willing to serve in the armed forces if a suitable corps could be found. He was landlord between

The New Bridge Hotel 1987

1915 and 1935. In 1927 the owners Groves & Co. carried out extensive renovations to the building in keeping with the rest of the area and leisure facilities which were increasing rapidly including tennis courts and a bowling green. The house continued to serve until 2003 when it was demolished and replaced with flats and shops.

THE NEW COOPERS' ARMS
Maiden Street, Melcombe Regis

WHY A BEER house with this name should open up so close to the original and long-standing Coopers' Arms is not known. The first record is from 1836 when a Matthew Roberts is shown as a tenant and Charles Payne as the owner. Roberts is there for the 1841 census, a stable keeper aged 51 with his wife Elizabeth. By 1844 the house had passed to James Wareham and his wife Marina, he seems to have died shortly after leaving his widow in charge.

In August of 1848 a post boy, 36-year-old George Davis, was having some angry words with a coal carrier named Bolt, the exact details are not known but there was apparently an argument over some aspect of the races. Bolt gave Davis a smack in the face upon which landlady Maria Wareham took Davis by the shoulders and pushed him out of the back door but he returned shortly after with a shoemaker's knife in his hand and rushed at Bolt, called him by an 'opprobrious epithet' and plunged the knife into his side penetrating the liver. Davis was immediately taken into custody and Bolt to the infirmary. Bolt survived and Davis stood trial at the assizes in Dorchester the following March charged with 'stabbing with intent to murder' he was sentenced to death but later commuted to 15 years transportation but in fact he didn't go that far and served his time in Millbank Prison.

Marina Wareham seemed more than capable of running the busy pub and when not throwing out potential murderers she seems to have been quite shameless in serving customers outside of permitted hours. When taken to court in 1852 the magistrates comments were, 'nine months had not elapsed since the defendant was summoned for a similar offence but as she very adroitly contrived to let the parties out of the house by the back door she escaped the fine'. There was no doubt of her guilt but it could not be satisfactorily proved, and they feared that it was her constant practice to keep her home open at illegal hours and in an endeavour to teach her to pursue a better course in future she would be fined 20/-. It didn't teach her anything of the sort of course

The New Coopers' Arms 2025

and she continued in her old ways. It seems likely that she married a John Bunn as a Marina Bunn of the right age appears in the census of 1871. John had died earlier in the year leaving her widowed once more.

By the census of 1881 William Hill a gardener was the landlord and his son James took over in about 1890. Like a number of other publicans James was also involved in the cab trade almost killing himself at one point grabbing the reins of a horse and cart that had bolted bringing it to a standstill but injuring his leg in the process. He also seems to have been quite free with his opinions and was summoned a couple of times for using abusive language which was usually settled with an apology unlike his overcharging on a trip to Upway for which he was fined 10/-. James also kept a very vicious dog and was summoned for not keeping it under proper control as it attacked other dogs and passers-by. In the end and despite some very unParliamentary language he was let off after paying expenses of 8/6d and was still landlord in 1926.

In celebration of New Year's Day 1941 three young soldiers managed to 'liberate' a nine-gallon barrel of beer that was being delivered to Mrs Beatrice Honnor landlady of the Coopers. Despite saying that they didn't mean to steal it and that it was just a lark they managed to get it to an air raid shelter on the seafront and fill their glasses. The lads had served well in France and claimed that they could not remember anything about the barrel because they were drunk. They were ordered to pay for the cost of the beer between them and bound over for 15 months.

THE NEW INN
North Quay, High Street, Weymouth

THIS BEER HOUSE was on North Quay, in what was then High Street, Weymouth opposite the Weymouth Arms. The first known landlord was George Parker in 1854 the brother of Sophia Carter who had held the Anchor beer house with her now divorced husband Robert. Their early career can be traced in the Anchor entry. George doubled as a potato merchant and during his tenure suffered the usual round of drunks broken windows and police visits one of which, in 1860, involved Parker appearing in court charged with 'obstructing the police in the execution of their duty'. According to the evidence Parker caught Superintendent Lidbury moving from room to room in his house and when questioned he would not say why he was there or what he wanted, and despite being repeatedly asked to either explain himself or leave he refused. In his defence Parker said that the police were in the habit of frequently visiting public houses, so much so that it was complained of by landlords as it was calculated to injure their trade. It emerged later that the police were looking for a deserter from one of the ships but the magistrates had heard enough and dismissed the case with a warning that in future not cooperating with the police might tell against him on licensing day.

In 1865 Parker and two other landlords got together to appeal against the repeated rejection of their applications for a spirit licenses but withdrew shortly before the hearing which involved them having to pay court costs. Parker lost a lot of money when his 50 ton schooner the *Alice* bringing a cargo of buckwheat and vetches sank in a gale in 1867 but was not insured. He died the following year and his widow Mary left the pub to become a laundress. His sister Sophia took over but was taken to court for selling gin without a licence in August 1868, and was fined £12/10/-, she may well have lost her licence because she next appears under her maiden name of Parker in London as licensee of the Stirling Castle, 50 London Wall, All Hallows on the Wall before remarrying sometime later.

Next up at the pub was John Jeanes who took the place on in his mid 60s having been at

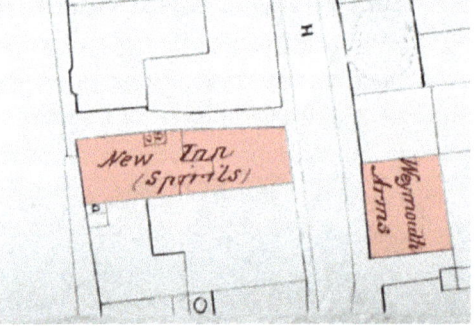

The New Inn. Pierce Arthur 1857

the Crown Tap in St Nicholas Street since 1854 he died in 1883 at the age of 80. From around 1872 the pub is shown as owned by Mrs Sarah Ann Newman and managed at some point by brewers Devenish & Co an arrangement which continued until it closed.

In 1880 the brewery advertised the house for rent with a double entrance in High Street and the Quay. An army pensioner, Alexander Miller Sharpe was next in charge, he was there for about three years but seems to have fallen foul of the brewery who removed him and replaced him with one of their own employees which displeased the magistrates mightily as a tenant had to live on the premises and the employee, John Nixon did not. In 1883 a proper licensee William Stagg was in place but the New Inn closed for good on 30 September 1885.

THE NEW MUSIC HALL TAVERN
St Nicholas Street, Melcombe Regis.

IF THERE WAS a competition for the pub with the most names this tavern would win it hands down having been known as The Concert Hall Public House, The Concert Hall Tavern, The Music Hall Tavern, The New

Victorian Tavern Scene

Concert Hall Public House, The New Concert Tavern, The New Music Hall and possibly others. It opened in 1865 in a disused Congregational Chapel under the direction and ownership of Captain Joseph Cosens a director of the Portland Steam Packet Company who was granted a 12-month theatrical licence. The house was owned by Groves the brewers and Levi Bartlett was landlord in 1867 when summoned for keeping his house open at 12.40 am. Three men were seen at the bar with three glasses, one was full of beer and the other part full. Bartlett claimed that they were lodgers and connected with the theatre, a stranger had entered at the same time as them but no beer was drawn for him. The bench decided that there was really no case against the defendant and the summons was dismissed.

The house was caught up in the great weights and measures raid of February 1884 when landlord William Siddons and a number of others were summoned to the Borough Petty Sessions for having unstamped, illegal, and deficient cups in their possession. After hearing detailed evidence of two of the many cases brought before them the magistrates retired for about a quarter of an hour and returned to let them off with a caution and a warning that publicans must in future have proper stamped cups in their possession. (see Royal Oak entry for more details).

The leasehold of the former New Concert Hall Tavern, 25 St Nicholas Street was sold at auction in November 1903 and after a number of uses was demolished and now forms part of a car park.

THE NEW ROOMS INN
Cove Row, Weymouth

Believed to have been built in the 1850s the first known landlord of the New Rooms was William Mattias Hart, beer retailer aged 40 from Bridport with his wife Mary who appear on the 1861 census having moved from the Old Rooms a matter of yards away due to disagreements with the new owner. His application for a spirits licence was refused despite the fact that the new building had been recently fitted up at considerable expense now having 13 rooms and an extra storey added. The main opposition was from his previous house, and Joseph Mabey at the Old Rooms, given his previous good record he was disappointed that the licence did not go with him. In another application in 1869 it was stated that Hart had held a licence for a good number of years and had built, furnished, and opened the New Rooms himself having been 16 years in the trade. A further application in 1870 brought results at

The New Rooms Inn 2017

last despite a rather pathetic attempt to claim that he should be disqualified as he was also a carpenter and builder and that this had not appeared on his application. This despite the fact that a large percentage of publicans pursued other occupations and that Hart had given up the trade some years ago. He died in 1871 and the house was advertised to let by the Hope Brewery.

During 1878 a local paper picked up a fine example of British eccentricity, two young fellows, a baker and a fisherman, set out from London in a cockleshell boat about 12 feet long, and entirely open for about three quarters of her length, the bow part being just covered with a yard or two of canvas. They had no compass, or other instruments, they just crept along, as they said, by the 'smell of the land.' 'A few days ago', reports a local paper, 'they were at Eastbourne, and thence they coasted to Portsmouth in one day. Their next voyage was to Swanage, and from Swanage it was one day's sail to Weymouth, where they arrived about seven or eight o'clock on Saturday night, and moored their boat in the Cove finding refreshment and rest at William White's New Rooms Inn. They are next bound for Falmouth, where, it is said, one of them belongs; but the weather was too rough on Monday morning for sail, and they took a run over to Portland. In order to avoid the perils of the Bill, they intend to drag their frail boat across the Chesil Beach and re-launch her in the West Bay'. William White had taken over from Hart's widow in 1873 and was there until 1886 but the longest serving landlord was Joseph Condon from 1904 until 1937 who at a given way to Henry and Evelyn Crickmore by the 1939 register.

In recent times, surprise was expressed that the house had no handpumps along the bar by a correspondent in the *Dorset Echo* which prompted this interesting reply,

'A pub without pumps (beer engines) was not at all unusual, in fact many pubs in older buildings did not have either a suitable cellar or places for the pipework. It was not until the arrival of gas pressurised kegs that a 'tap' on the bar became almost universal. Full barrels as well as kegs were kept on a rack behind the bar and beer was drawn off rather than pumped. Barrels on lower rack, kegs on top rack. The technique for stowing the barrels was: roll the barrel from the beer store, place it with the bung downwards and the side bung towards you, tip the barrel against the rack and then lift and slide into the (wooden) rack, tap the barrel by knocking a spigot tap into the bung hole displacing the bung and ease the side bung (now at the top) to let air in, a drip cup was then hung on the tap. The first glass drawn was considered ullage but often still quite palatable – cellar man's perks. Even the White Hart had this system in place up until the 1960s which was why Daphne Bench always had a well-built barman on hand to help her.

THE NOTHE TAVERN / ROYAL CANTEEN
Barrack Road, The Nothe, Weymouth

THE CANTEEN, as it was first known, was built very close to the Red Barracks which dates back to 1803. Facilities appear to have been lacking as in 1833 an enterprising private in the First Dragons, John Hulme, was caught selling beer, spirits, and tobacco without a licence in the barracks as there was no canteen. His reward for providing this public service was a heavy fine of £120 but later greatly reduced due to his good character in the regiment. It may have taken a decade or more but eventually somebody cottoned onto the fact that a public house near so many thirsty customers might be a good idea.

Its precise origins have yet to be discovered but in August of 1855 landlady Mrs Elizabeth Brinsley applied for a spirits licence on the grounds that the house had existed for many years and that the present proprietor had lived there for the past three years without complaint and it had always been conducted respectably despite being constantly resorted to by soldiers. The house was close to the barracks and satisfactory to the commanding officer, with a large back garden, with much having been spent on improvements a few years ago. The application was refused but granted the following year in the name of Mr R Brinsley presumably husband to Elizabeth who advertised the Royal Canteen for rent in October of 1856.

The good reputation was not going to last. The following year an old soldier was accused of stealing a 'monkey jacket' from the incoming landlord John Dwyer. In his defence he said that he was very drunk and that 'one of the girls, of which there were '*30 or 40* in the basement' put it on him for a joke and he had staggered off with it – and one of the girls. Surprisingly the jury acquitted him.

On Easter Monday of 1858 Police Sergeant George Brine and PC Barrett visited the Canteen as part of their rounds to ensure that all was peaceful and quiet. As soon as they entered they were surrounded by the 30 or 40 soldiers present who started to abuse them. Brine sent the constable to the barracks to tell them what was happening and noticed that his truncheon had been taken from his pocket, he bravely barred the door and demanded its return. 'The soldiers then commenced an indiscriminate attack on him, cups, glasses, the fender and candlesticks were hurled at him forcing him to retreat to the barracks followed by the riotous soldiers and when in the yard one of them struck him a severe blow over the eye with his belt causing the blood to flow.' One of the soldiers had been so badly injured in the scuffle that he was taken to hospital blaming his injuries on Brine but as he had lost his truncheon early in the proceedings it's difficult to see how this could have been the case. The militiamen accused Brine of being drunk which given his record of sobriety and steadiness seems unlikely. 'It is to be regretted that a very hostile feeling exists on the part of the militia towards the police which appears to have arisen solely from the determination of the constabulary to repress the disorderly conduct of which the soldiers have exhibited in so many instances during the time they have been here. The very cowardly and dangerous practice which they adopt of fighting with their belts ought certainly to be prevented and if this mode of aggression is persisted in, no man should be permitted to wear his belt when out on leave'.

In a strange turn of events Sergeant Brine was taken to court by Lieutenant Colonel Crompton of the 2nd West York Militia charged with

The Nothe Tavern 2017

drunkenness while on duty and assaulting two privates. He is alleged to have kicked up a disturbance with the soldiers and taken off his coat to fight, one of the witnesses said that the inn door was barred and that he had to knock out one of the panels to get out. Brine tried to clear the pub but the landlord had permission to stay open all night. Another witness said that Brine struck him in the face with a pint pot and he hid in the kitchen until taken to the hospital. Brine was not attacked until he hit the witness it was claimed. A number of soldiers were called as witnesses and all testified as to Brine being drunk. The defence case was of course that Brine was perfectly sober which was supported by Superintendent Lidbury. And so the evidence flowed back and forth, soldiers against policeman and continued for five days until Brine was informed that, 'the magistrates have given this case the most attentive consideration and the decision is that the charge against you be dismissed'.

When it came to the original charges one of the soldiers was fined 5/- for the assault on Brine but the situation was far from diffused. Lidbury reported having seen a party of militia passing by the police station and making use of the most disgusting language with some reports of them having bayonets up their sleeves. Colonel Crompton apologised for any wrongdoing on behalf of his men saying that this was the first posting which had resulted in complaints. The mayor felt differently and feared a greater disturbance, calling on the men of the town to come forward and be sworn in as special constables and about 60 did so. He also directed that the inns and public houses close their doors in the evening and everything passed off without further incident with the militia departing on the 1 o'clock train the following day. Throughout the whole proceedings there was no mention of the landlord Jack Shepherd or who was going to pay for the incredible mess that was left behind.

In September of 1864 landlord James Sheppard took over the Rose and Crown in Crescent Street and the owners Eldridge, Mason, & Co advertised the pub for rent. In April 1877 the police were still on the trail of the evil doer and when PC Delament heard loud voices coming from the bowling alley he investigated and discovered seven men singing their hearts out. In his defence landlord Benjamin Pearce said that he did not want to turn the men out for fear of upsetting his customers but he was still fined 40/- despite there being no beer about. Two years later the pub was advertised for rent again to be taken by Henry Strange, his wife Victoria and their six children and it was during their tenure the name was changed from the Royal Canteen to the Nothe Tavern. Following him in 1882 was William Moody who had been in the Dorset militia for several years.

In June of 1904 Mr Crickmay, the local architect, produced plans for the rebuilding of the pub which the magistrates considered to be 'premature' but we can assume that building went ahead fairly soon after, producing the building that we see today.

THE OLD ROOMS INN
Cove Row, Weymouth

THE ORIGINAL 'OLD Rooms' is not the large sprawling red brick building we see today but an imposing and now dilapidated property built of Portland stone and tucked down Trinity Street to the right of the photograph and backing onto the present building. It is believed to date from the 1600s and was possibly built for Thomas Giear a wealthy merchant who was an MP and mayor at the time. It became an inn called the Navy Tavern in its early days and by 1766 a large extension had been added to what had become the town's first assembly room where the well off and fashionable could meet and socialise. In July of that year balls were advertised to take place 'at the new built assembly room on every Wednesday throughout the season with a

The Old Rooms Inn 2017

good band of music'. Despite its undoubted charms within, the rooms were situated on a working quay with all the noise smells and inconvenience that must have meant. The romanticisation of the working man was decades away in the Victorian era but the last thing that the rich and fashionable would want to see at this time. The trend was for golden sands wide-open skies and the increasingly appreciated deep blue sea. During 1771 it was rumoured in the press that, 'there is the intention of building, by subscription a large and elegant set of assembly rooms and an hotel adjoining of eight rooms on a floor with stabling for 60 horses and 20 carriages', this building was later to become the Royal Hotel. The fashionable scene was moving across the river and away from the smelly port. The Old Rooms had carried that name since at least 1777 not because they were old in years but because they were redundant and just to confuse things even more there is no connection with the New Rooms next door which did not appear until the 1850s.

In 1777 the tenant, Mr Thomas Good, had all his fixtures and fittings sold by Isaac Cook auctioneer, upholsterer and undertaker at his rooms in Bennet Street, Bath. Good announced that he had taken a grand and commodious building to be known as 'The Hotel and New Rooms' and 'to be immediately fitted up' and states that, 'the Old Rooms and Tavern which he now occupies, will, on his removal, be entirely shut up.' In 1780 the Old Assembly Room Tavern and Coffee Rooms are advertised to be let with the proviso that, 'if a proper tenant does not offer before the season they will be operated by the proprietor'. It seems that he was unlucky as a new advertisement appeared in June announcing that proprietor Thomas Delamotte intends to open the Old Rooms 'which had been clandestinely shut up for two years by his late tenant' on Thursday, the 9th of June 'for the reception of company' and by August tickets to the balls were obtainable from Mr Delamotte's Circulating Library. Delamotte died in 1782 at the age of 74 and in May the 'Old Rooms, Tavern and Coffee House' was put up for auction, 'consisting of an assembly room nearly 60 feet long and 25 feet wide with a marble chimneypiece, a cardroom, three chambers and four garrets, a coffee room, billiard room, two large parlours, a spacious kitchen, scullery, two bathrooms, a servant's lobby, excellent brick arched wine a vault, two cellars, larder, yard freshwater cistern and many other conveniences, the whole in exceedingly good repair. The premises are held for a term of 1,000 years of which 962 remain unexpired.'

In 1788 what was now called the Old Rooms and Navy Tavern was advertised by William Lodder as a going concern, whether this paid off initially is not known but his tenure seems to have come to an end in 1793. In 1798 the property is back in the auction rooms, 'now occupied as a barracks for soldiers under the Barrack Master General at the yearly rent of 6d.' The land tax returns for 1801 show the Old Rooms in the possession of William Bower.

The Revd John Skinner, curmudgeonly vicar of Camerton and pioneer archaeologist was not very impressed with Weymouth describing it as 'very bare and barren' when he passed through in 1804. However, he brightened up a bit when, 'In the evening at the Rooms, there was a pleasing variety of animated beauties which amply repaid for all disappointments as to other prospects. I had the felicity of dancing with Miss Daubigny, and spent a very agreeable evening'.

Tragedy occurred in December of 1822. The landlord was 39-year-old former mariner Munday Dyer assisted by his wife Jane. They had two sons at the time one named Munday after his father aged 7 and an older boy of about 12. They were playing together in the cellar when they discovered a pistol lying on a shelf which had been left behind by one of the seamen from the revenue service. Playing with it between them both boys snapped it several times not knowing it to be loaded until the elder boy shot Munday through the heart with fatal results .The coroner brought in a verdict of accidental death.

An interesting report from 1824 states that while taking down an ancient building near the Old Rooms a very curious signboard of great antiquity was discovered. This had once belonged to a public house kept by a mariner and on one side was a representation of the Devil tempting Eve with an apple which she refuses and on the other side a painting in which she appears to accept it.

In November 1829 the pub was one of the nine public houses auctioned with the late William Bower's Dorchester Fordington Brewery estate. (see The Bear entry for more details .)

In about 1835 the inn was run by a man named Winter who died in 1837 leaving his widow Jane with a pub and two children to look after at the age of 27. In 1839 one of her lodgers was a Captain Charles Butt owner of some shares in steam packets. They became attracted to each other and were engaged to be married. In September she had the misfortune to yield to his solicitations on the assurance that she should become his wife which resulted in the birth of a daughter the following June. Butt, having borrowed £5 from her left denying that there ever was an agreement to marry and saying that she was violent and immoral which witnesses denied. Some short time after he left he married a woman alleged to be worth £10,000. Judgement was found in her favour and she was awarded £100. By 1858 the pub was in the hands of Devenish & Co who advertised for tenders needed for rebuilding the premises to the specifications of local architects Crickmay and a large part of the red brick building we see today would date from that time.

The Original Old Rooms Inn

The inn fell victim to con-man John Knaresborough in December of 1859 who had just come from fleecing the landlord at the Globe. Describing himself as a coal merchant, he approached landlord William Hart for a bed saying that he had a large shipment of coal coming in and that he had been recommended by prominent local businessman and ship owner Charles Beale. After eating and drinking his fill the police arrived to arrest him for obtaining board and lodging at the Globe using a similar story. Although charged with these activities the jury acquitted him on the grounds that what he owed was just a common debt and therefore a civil matter.

1869 saw a tremendous storm with tons of water pouring onto the promenade about a foot above the harbour wall and at the Old Rooms a wave smashed against the front door and burst it open making a complete breach of the lower portions of the house with much property being injured or destroyed in consequence, Hope Square was so flooded that a good sized boat might have sailed about in it. In 1883 Devenish advertised the pub for rent and again in 1890 'as a consequence of illness' when it fell to John Mabey and family. There followed a succession of landlords without much incident until 1940 when a Mr Rook took it upon himself to smash one of the pub windows as he believed it was showing a light during blackout. Landlord Thomas Stevens claimed that there was no light showing at all and Rook was fined £7/10/- plus £12/10/-for the repair of the window. Today the pub is owned by Greene King and still maintains the old traditions of good food and service.

THE PARK ESTATE INN
Lennox Street, Melcombe Regis

THE PARK ESTATE Inn, now 22 Lennox Street, was built by brewers Devenish & Co as part of the new Park Estate development owned by the Conservative Land Society. The story of the area is examined further in the Waterloo Stores entry. Around £2,000 had been spent on this property which contained a bar, tap room, kitchen, back kitchen, and on the first floor there was a club room and four bedrooms. Construction was completed in the early 1870s and first occupied by Walter Holt a brewer's clerk employed by Devenish who was staying there paying £35 pa while arrangements were being made to open the house officially. Holt had occupied the White Hart for three or four months, the Stag Inn and other houses on behalf of the brewery, this activity was known as being a 'warming pan' – preparing the ground for its eventual tenant. In August of 1874 a licence was applied for to take the place of the Portland Arms which would then cease to be licensed premises. The magistrates agreed to this arrangement and the licence was granted. Walter Holt's story is told in the Stag entry.

The first 'proper' landlords were George Hedges a baker and publican and his wife Mary Ann both in their 20s and without children, they are listed in the census of 1871. At first everything went well. Mr Hedges was even able to claim possession of a hen which in a single year had laid 11 double yolk eggs, one triple yolk egg and on one occasion she had laid one egg inside another, the smaller about as large as a partridge egg. Everything was fine until the

The Park Estate Inn 2023

end of October 1876 when there was a knock on the door. It was a soldier named John Burke and he wanted to see his wife – Mary Ann. Apparently the two had married in January 1865 when she was just 17 shortly after which he disappeared never contacting her or sending her a penny, leaving her with nothing. She was told several times by his comrades returning from abroad that he was dead and in 1870 she remarried under her maiden name of Clements. Her new husband was of course George Hedges who said when the matter came to trial that they had lived most happily together for the past seven years. Burke, the first husband, was alleged to be in Malta and therefore not able to give evidence. The marriage to Hedges had taken place in a nonconformist chapel and doubt was cast on whether this was even properly registered for marriages. For some reason the case was causing the judge great irritation and he declared that the matter should never have been brought to trial asking the jury if they believed that the 1865 marriage had even taken place. Responding to his tone the foreman of the jury said that it was open to question and the case was thrown out. The couple should have gone home and put the whole matter behind them – and maybe they did for a while but in March of 1878 all the household effects from the inn, furniture, cups, glasses and sundry other effects were put up for auction 'at short notice' by Mr G Hedges and the pair disappear from the record. The business passed to Mark Drew another baker and now publican who by the 1881 census was aged 38 with his wife Maria and four-year-old son George. He run the pub until his death in 1913 when the licence passed to his widow and then to their son George otherwise a musician. The inn was still serving in 1958.

THE PARK HOTEL
Grange Road, Radipole, Melcombe Regis

THE ORIGINAL PARK Hotel was operational since at least 1837 when an inquest was held on the body of a new-born infant that was discovered on the beach at nearby Greenhill. It had stood in Dorchester Road in the Radipole district, 'near the old turnpike' which is probably why it was in that location and it still looks quite isolated on the 1864 map. In 1848 the landlady was a Mrs Street who employed a young shoemaker. It seems this lad had promised to marry a Miss Burrows and when he didn't appear she stormed up to the hotel to find out why and got involved in a fight with Mrs Street who took her to court resulting in a 5/- fine. Edward Robinson was granted a spirits licence in 1853 doubtless helped on by its isolated situation add lack of facilities nearby.

In 1868 the hotel is put up for rent by Eldridge, Mason & Co comprising stable, coach house and a large garden and in 1871 it was occupied by Philip Hawkins a 31-year-old guard on the Great Western Railway presumably leaving the house to be run by his wife Mary Ann during the day. From the O/S map the site resembles a smallholding more than a hotel and by 1874 serious questions are being asked about the state of the surrounding grounds described as like a swamp filled with pits, hollows and mud. Hawkins claimed that he was losing £50 per year because of the state of the surrounding ground and the council was urged to get on with the required building and drainage work. By 1878 it had been decided that the old hotel would have to go as part of the development of the site. The then landlord Joseph Howard applied to the magistrates for a full licence for the replacement hotel the plans of which were being finalised for submission to the justices. The new house was being built at a cost of £1,500 and the removal of the old one would be of great public benefit. Upon approving the plans the magistrates granted a provisional licence to take affect when the old premises were pulled down which happened during August of 1878.

The new Park Hotel was erected in Grange Road during the following year on land leased to Alfred Edwin Pope the brewer from Sir Frederick Johnstone MP at £20 per annum. The new building was designed by prolific

The Park Hotel (website)

local architect George Crickmay on behalf of Eldridge Pope & Co and put out to tender. The result was a very fine building and Joseph Howard continued as landlord.

An unusual inquest took place at the hotel in January 1893 when the body of William Howe, a cook, was found frozen solid in his own home after having been missed by his friends who broke in and found his body. It seems that he had had an apoplectic seizure and had broken his neck in a fall. Landlord William Hale was summoned for selling outside of the permitted hours during September 1895 as most publicans were at some point in their careers. In this case nothing could be proven and the house was described as one of the best kept in town. In October of 1895 watercress vendor Felix Summers got so drunk that having smashed several windows in the pub it took four men to hold him down and for the police to get the 'nips' on his left arm upon which he refused to get up and had to have his legs tied together so that he could be carried off. He received a month's hard labour. The loving couple who stayed at the hotel from June to July 1909 were in fact Maggie Northam a tea buyer and her lover James Newbolt. The pair had eloped but after a short time she changed her mind and asked her husband to take her back. He refused, got a divorce and packed her off to her mothers.

Brewers Eldridge Pope purchased the freehold land for £870 on 31st January 1921 and despite been damaged by enemy action on 27/28 May 1944 The Park, as it is now known, still flourishes today.

THE PHOENIX INN
Great George Street, Melcombe Regis

THE FIRST MENTION of the beer house in Great George Street comes from 1868 when Henry Gough described as an accountant, beer seller, and grocer faced a bankruptcy hearing with debts of £96/7/8d and no assets. He was discharged in September and in August 1870 his wife Elizabeth applied for a spirits licence saying that she ran the business as her husband was in a poor state of health for some reason she admitted that she was not often asked for spirits and the bench, while sympathising with her plight refused the application. The Goughs are listed as being at the Phoenix until 1874.

From 1898 the history of the house is largely the history of the Frampton family. William Frampton aged 29 his wife Sarah and their four children took up residence in that year and apart from having to strongarm the odd drunk, business seems to have been good if uneventful. In 1911 their 17-year-old

The Former Phoenix Inn

son Albert joined the Royal Navy as a wireless operator and was killed in 1914 aboard HMS *Pegasus*. He had been intended for the teaching profession but was so keen on the navy that he joined as soon as he was able. By 1922 George was a widower and due to a conversation overheard between a taxi driver and a punter he was summoned for a contravention of the Intoxicating Liquor Laws accused of permitting his licensed premises to be used for the purposes of betting. Two taxi drivers were brought forward as witnesses, one of them when being interviewed by the police, was asked to sign a blank page in the officer's notebook which he did and consequently, as nothing had been read over to him, he did not know what he had signed but apparently it involved taking betting slips from the pub to bet on horses. The prosecution case fell apart as all the witnesses claimed that George had nothing to do with betting and the magistrates perhaps reluctantly agreed that there was not sufficient evidence to convict.

In 1923 the property was conveyed to Devenish & Co. for £250 despite which it was subject to an attack by the local temperance movement ever eager to close down a public house, who considered the Phoenix to be unnecessary as there were only 12 houses in Great George Street and many other pubs nearby. It was pointed out by the defence that the Phoenix was the closest to Arcadia one of the most popular halls in the town which held a variety of meetings and entertainments, Frampton explained that he had held the pub for 25 years without serious complaint and if it was closed it would have no way of earning a livelihood and the licence was allowed to continue. A new lease was agreed in 1932 between the owners and William Frampton whereby he paid them an annual rent of £40 on condition that he keep the house and all its fittings, glassware etc in good order and not to sublet. He was still there for the 1939 register aged 70 years.

THE PLUME OF FEATHERS
Little George Street, Melcombe Regis

THE PLUME WAS first heard of in 1873 when the wife of landlord George Turnbull produced a baby girl. Very little has been discovered about the history of the house which was next door but one to the Prince Albert in Little George Street renamed Westham Road in 1922.

In February 1901 28-year-old William James Talbot Pitman son of the then landlord George Pitman was one of a number of men who answered the call by the Dorset Imperial Yeomanry for volunteers for military service in South Africa. Whether he was selected to go is uncertain but by the census of 1901

The Plume of Feathers 1911 (Weymouth Museum)

pub is being run by Charles Northover a 46-year-old builder and stonemason and owned by Eldridge Pope & Co. In March of 1908 the house was selected by the authorities for closure. It had shown a decline in takings recently and was very close to the Prince Albert and the Bridge Inn both larger than the Plume. It was described as having no back entrance but two front entrances with a smoking room beside the bar on the ground floor and seven bedrooms of which four were for lodgers The house had been very well conducted by Northover and largely resorted to by bluejackets for sleeping purposes but it had not been constructed as an inn and was very inferior physically to the others in the road. The average number of casks supplied to the house was 57 a year and bottled beer an average of 349 dozen. The normal takings for tobacco and minerals were about £60 and for food and lodgings between £70 and £80. It was the only house in the street to serve Eldridge Pope & Co's ales but despite a number of people speaking up for it and claiming that it was wanted by the working man the committee decided that it should be closed. The licence was extinguished on 14 December 1908 but the Northover family were still listed in the rates as living there in 1919 as a private house.

THE PORTERS' ARMS
St Mary Street, Melcombe Regis

On 12 August 1850, 23-year-old Robert Carter a mariner from Chickerell married 21-year-old Sophia Parker. On the marriage certificate his father's name and occupation are left blank and she is the daughter of Edward Parker a currier from High Street, Weymouth. Together they took on the Porters' Arms beer house in Edmund Street but despite such a promising start at a young age it seems that their relationship was abusive from the start with Robert subjecting to her to extreme cruelty from the first month of their marriage including beatings, an attack with a knife and constant obscene language. By 1854 they had moved onto the Anchor beer house and their sad story is continued in that entry.

Daniel Dober aged 50 and his wife Susan moved to the pub with their three children during 1861 having had the Market House Inn opposite the Guildhall for a short time. Daniel was a cooper by trade and soon applied for a spirits licence but the police gave the house a 'very indifferent character', presumably the legacy of Robert Carter and it was refused as it was again in 1864 despite claims of it being of a 'commodious nature' with the tramway about to open which would give rise to greater demand. In opposition it was said that to grant a licence would be committing an injustice to the owners of the private properties adjoining and there were already eight licensed houses in the vicinity. In an unusual change of roles landlady Susan Dober was taken to court for assault by a female itinerant organ player called Montedoneo. Dober had apparently called her bad names before throwing water over her and in rebuttal Mrs Dober claimed that she was drunk and had used vile language but was nonetheless convicted and fined 1/- plus costs. The battle for a spirits licence continued into 1870 this time the house was described as containing eleven rooms and was 'frequented by a large number of strangers and foreign sailors', and this time it was successful.

A 'collision' between the military and civilians took place a during November 1871 causing a great commotion. Three artillery men and a private belonging to the 7th, all more or less inebriated, came down St Mary Street between six and seven o'clock singing and making a noise before going into the Porters' Arms, where there were some Portland men. One of the artillery men 'fell against' a person named Anthony, who, in self-defence, put his hands up to fend him off. The soldier then struck him a violent blow in the mouth, causing blood to flow freely. The other Portlanders took part and a general battle spilled out into the street, where a regular stand-up fight took place, and the men were covered with blood. An artilleryman was hit a blow which almost stunned him. The melee lasted for about ten minutes, and, although being close to the police station, the constables were out on duty, and the combatants had it all their own way for some time. A crowd of 300 or 400 persons congregated; and

Site of the Porters' Arms in 2024

Sergeant Brine and PC McMahon somehow managed to separate the men, and took them to the station. Hardly one of their features was discernible for blood, and their clothing was ripped and bespattered with it. An artillery man, named Head, pretended to have fits, and was so violent that it required six or seven men to overpower him. A very strong picquet arrived, and took the military offenders back to barracks but once the names of the civilians had been taken they were allowed to go.

In May of 1875 in what could have been rather embarrassing situation Jane Dober was charged with being in possession of a pair of military trousers. Gunner Higgins had apparently left the Nothe barracks wearing two pairs of trousers, the second pair belonging to bombardier Ryan which he intended to sell. Once it was realised that the item was missing enquiries were made at the Porters' Arms where Mrs Dober was found to be in possession and said that she had been asked to look after them for 15 minutes while the defendant went into town. The trousers were valued at 14/- and the Dober family had been at the pub since 1861 without any trouble but despite this the mayor said that he had no option but to convict and she was fined £2/3/6d, three times the value of the trousers.

Susan Dober continued after the death of her husband in 1874 at the age of 65 and was there until her own death at the age of 87 in 1898. In 1900 the Porters' Arms was subject to a bit of horse trading. A deal was struck whereby the licence be transferred to premises known as Cook's Restaurant (later the Weymouth Restaurant) in Augusta Place, Esplanade. The Porters' Arms had a full licence and Cook's only a six day beer licence. The pub was leased by Eldridge Pope & Co. and the argument was that the new restaurant would occupy a position favourable for a first class establishment which would need a full licence. The new building would be of three stories with up to nine bedrooms and cater mainly for those arriving by steamer with a dining room capable of supplying 150 persons. The architect was John Edward Crickmay and about £2,500 would be expended if the licence was granted. It was stated that for every glass of whiskey drunk at the Porters' Arms 1,000 would be drunk at the new place, people do not like to get drunk at the Porters' as it was too close to the police station but the removal of a licence was certainly something to be taken advantage of. However, the inn premises consisted only of the ground and first floor, the floor above was not connected to the pub and was let out separately for storage. The freeholders were the town corporation who would be giving away a valuable piece of land if the plan was to go ahead and get nothing in return, it was also the case that the lease was to expire in 11 years after which it would revert the to the corporation. At the licensing hearing during March 1903 it was stated that there were 12 fully licensed houses within 100 yards of the pub and that it was unnecessary. The rent was £25pa with no stabling but four bedrooms were available for the use of the public, there was no back entrance and it was occupied by husband, wife and two children, the magistrates decreed that not sufficient trade was done to earn a livelihood. Earnest appeals were made on behalf of the Porters' and the other six, the Shipwrights Arms, the Steam Packet Inn, the Three Tuns, the Yacht, the Baltic and the Royal Hotel Tap that they should be allowed to trade until their licences expired in October and the bench agreed that they would grant the concession with the exception of the Yacht Inn and the Royal Hotel Tap which would be closed forthwith. In all probability the Porters' Arms was or became one of the gabled buildings to the right with the horse and cart outside it.

The original Guildhall before 1838.

THE PORTLAND ARMS
Maiden Street, Melcombe Regis

ROBERT FLEW, BREWER and occupier of the Portland Arms, Maiden Street died in 1798 and his property including the Portland was put up for auction held under a lease by Sir William Pulteney. Between about 1816 and 1824 William Sly from the family that had many interests in the town's pubs was running the place and holding auctions of various boats and ships.

The former Portland Arms 2024

Samuel Moore was owner occupier in 1840 and was fined the large sum of £5 for keeping a disorderly house. In 1842 the question of Moore's entitlement to vote in a local election was discussed. Apparently, it was dependent upon him occupying the pub which he no longer did, having left before June 1841 claiming that he had taken the house for his nephew. This was not enough to qualify him for a vote as he had no personal interest in the premises at the time of the election and his vote was disallowed.

In 1852 the landlord was a Benjamin Case Larcombe a tailor 'employing four hands' and in March of 1854 William Whicker of the Nag's Head went for a drink in the Portland but Larcombe refused to serve him with a glass of brandy and water saying, 'I have not forgotten about the knives and forks!', guided him towards the door and pushed him out claiming that he would not serve him because he had 'had enough'. Whicher accused him of 'assaulting and forcibly ejecting him,' to which Larcombe accused Whicker of using every low and abusive term he could think of and of attacking the character of his house. The magistrates dismissed both cases basically telling them to grow up and charged them 2/- each in costs. Larcombe's next encounter with the law was not quite so trivial. In July 1858 he appeared at the Dorset Quarter Sessions charged with receiving, one electroplated teapot, one dozen large black handled knives and forks, six china chimney ornaments, one telescope, and one tobacco jar, all the property of Samuel Simmonds and recently stolen from his house by Samuel Lucey, his nephew who was also the son of Simmonds recently deceased housekeeper. Lucey was in custody charged with having stolen a six-barrel revolver from the house and was the main prosecution witness claiming that Larcombe was very keen on possessing the gun plus anything else that he could steal as he would know where to place it. Acting upon Lucey's statement, the police under Superintendent Lidbury, raided the Portland and Mrs Larcombe handed over the items described when asked. In response to questioning she said that Lucey had brought the items to her house hoping she would buy them as he needed the money to buy some gilt in his profession as a gilder. Lucey's testimony was very confused and contradictory followed by some excellent character witnesses for Larcombe which resulted in his acquittal.

An unusual case in 1863 involved a cutler named Robert Bennett who went around to various people selling bars of soap which would have been fine except that it wasn't soap at all but some fake substance that he had cooked up in the copper at the Portland where he lived and did not, 'answer the soap purpose at all'. In court Bennett challenged anyone to prove that it wasn't soap and stood by his product, 'let them put it in hot water and it will rise as nice a lather as possible'. The judge was not in favour of the product being tested in his court and left the matter in the hands of the jury who decided to convict. Bennett and his wife who had assisted him in the manufacture received six months hard labour each.

In August 1874 Devenish & Co. applied to close the pub and transfer the licence to new premises to be called the Park Estate Inn under the 50th section of the licensing act which provided that licences may be removed from one part of a licensing district to another in the same district where the wants of the public may require it. The Portland Arms belonged to Sir Frederick Johnston and was held on a lease by Mr William Hurdle, the licensee was Benjamin Ireland, the order was agreed and confirmed and the Portland Arms was soon to be no more but just before it closed in May 1875 landlords Benjamin and Jane Ireland, publicans, where arrested and charged with feloniously receiving off Sarah Fickus, a 50-year-old laundress, two aprons, one sheet, one tablecloth, the property of Richard Rolls.' Marianne and Charles Talbot of the Fisherman's Arms were similarly charged. The matter came to trial but in the end, it could not be proven that the recipients knew that the items were stolen and the jury acquitted them but with grave reservations from the judge. Frickus received 12 months hard labour followed by a two-year supervision order.

THE PORTLAND RAILWAY HOTEL
King Street. and Commercial Road Melcombe Regis

THE PORTLAND WAS built in 1864 and its first known landlord was Matthew Dix Roberts, a twine and net maker who had moved up from the Bridport Arms to take on this new 13 roomed property beside the railway line. He applied for a spirits licence in 1867 which was refused. Repeated applications by various landlords were brought in front of the magistrates but in almost every case opposition from existing businesses was too strong and they were refused. Roberts retired from the pub scene and continued with his

The Portland Railway Hotel c1900

nets. The next landlord was William Hodder from Yeovil and his wife Elizabeth who transferred the Portland to Emanuel Gear in 1877. His wife Leonora died in 1886 and he put all his household furniture and effects up for auction in June as he was leaving the business and by the census of 1891 he was a 57-year-old widower living in the workhouse at Weymouth with his occupation given as gardener. In 1893 the Rose and Crown in Crescent Street was closed and its full licence transferred to the Portland. The following year the licence passed to Alfred Rogers and his family who were there until 1930s. In more recent years the Portland was divided into self-catering holiday flats before being converted into permanent accommodation.

THE PRINCE ALBERT INN/ FINNS
Great Little George Street, Melcombe Regis

Built in the early 1850s in anticipation of the new railway station landlord Job Russell applied for a spirits licence in 1853 which was strongly opposed by the licensee of the Star Hotel in nearby Park Street, John Elmes on the grounds that his licence had been successfully opposed for 15 years and that the granting of another nearby would 'do him personally a great injury' upon which the bench stopped the case and refused the application. The pub had to wait until 1857 before one was granted to John Jones victualler and musician from Westminster with his wife Charlotte.

By 1871 the house was being run by Charles Crocker and his family. He was soon fined £1/- for selling during prohibited hours and the following year, the family suffered 'an extraordinary escape from instant death' when Mary Crocker sent her four children to play on the sands putting them in the charge of the oldest boy who was only seven and he led the party up to the cliffs at Bincleaves to see the regatta at Portland. The baby dropped her hat over the edge of the cliffs and while trying to retrieve it the two boys fell over after it. They were rescued bleeding and insensible and at first it was thought that they had both died but they recovered and had it not been for their timely rescue the two younger children would probably have gone over the edge as well.

In April 1873 a soldier named Mark Kitcher arrived at the house at 10.30 pm. He sat quietly drinking until closing time when he was asked to leave at which point he knocked landlord Crocker to the floor, seemingly without provocation upon which a fight ensued and Mary Crocker was hit in the eye with a stick while Charles had his leg broken putting him out of action for over a month. When arrested it emerged that he had also been fighting down the road at the Baltic Inn assaulting another customer and arguing over who was to pay for the quart of beer that they had just ordered and on that occasion as well the landlord and his wife had been seriously assaulted. In court he claimed that he had no recollection of what had occurred, 'more than a baby unborn' and for this drunken rampage he was awarded six months hard labour. In 1883 the then landlord Thomas Le Warne was one of the victims of Charles Lamborne who toured the west country extracting money from businesses on the promise that they would appear in a directory that he was producing, the full story is told in the Clifton entry. In October of 1874 Mrs Jeffery's shop was robbed of some money including a sovereign and some silver. Christopher Nelson a hawker was challenged by the owner as he left the premises but gave her a violent blow in the face and escaped eventually being traced to the Prince Arthur. He was searched but nothing was found until for some reason they looked up the chimney and recovered the money. Nelson was sentenced to eight months hard labour.

By far the longest licensees to serve behind the bar were George Albert Pashen 42 and his wife Amy who took over in 1900. George from Bincombe in Dorset had been a porter at the Royal Hotel in the 1880s. Amy died in 1916 and Albert carried on until retirement in 1922. In around 1930 the Albert was greatly enlarged. The 1864 O/S map shows the premises occupying one plot facing Little George Street and stretching back along Great George Street. The rebuild took in the property next door and expanded along the road producing the rather fine mock Tudor building that we have today.

In recent times (2000) the pub has been renamed Finns promoting itself as a music venue. A visitor during 2012 sets the scene,

'…a dimly light and slightly grubby interior with lots of music posters on the walls. There is also a lot of American memorabilia and the jukebox was playing

The Prince Albert 2017

random songs which included the Doors and Nirvana. I doubt that there are any modern dance CD's in their collection. There are a couple of plasma screens that were showing muted Olympic coverage and there is a pool table and three dartboards that are found either side of this U shaped pub. There is also a stage area to the left where the bands set up. The barmaid was friendly enough, but the few other punters in attendance weren't the friendliest bunch. I think that they were wondering why a nosy bloke wearing white Reebok Classics had walked in to their pub!'

THE PRINCE OF WALES TAVERN
Park Street, Melcombe Regis

THE PRINCE OPENED in about 1863 having been converted from two small houses at 11/12 Park Street by brewers Eldridge and Mason, and in 1865 landlord Henry Dibben who had been born in the town was recorded as having occupied the pub for two years. He had once been an inspector at the south-western railway station and an ostler at Luce's hotel. He applied for a spirits licence stating that the premises were of a commodious character consisting of ten rooms and close to the station. In opposition to his request it was said that the house had only recently opened as a beer shop and that the applicant would have to reside for a considerable period before his application could be considered. By 1874 Dibben had moved to the Bridport Arms.

In October of that year landlord James Chutter was summoned for selling beer outside of permitted hours but no sale had been proven to have taken place. There was a new act to be introduced on the following day which meant that proof of sale was unnecessary but as his was not yet in force the officer's action was premature and so the case was dismissed. In January 1875 the house was up for auction as part of the settlement in the case of Tizard v Tizard. Details have proved very hard to find but John Tizard was a solicitor and partner in Eldridge Pope & Co the owners of the Prince and when he died various discrepancies meant that some properties had to be sold including the Prince and the Steam Packet Inn. In the late 1880s the pub was run by local lad Charles Stone a builder and carpenter by trade with his wife Charlotte. They stayed until just after the 1901 census when he left the pub and went back to the building trade. In April of 1918 the Prince held a meeting of the South Dorset Licence Holders Trade Protection Association hosted by landlord George Austin

The house was put up for sale by auction in 1924 and described as 'a fully licensed premises the Prince of Wales Hotel now held by Eldridge Pope & Co

The Prince of Wales 2016

along with shop and premises adjoining held by Mr Coleman under a lease which expires in 1933. The property contains a large bar, parlour, large living room, scullery, two yards with greenhouse, sitting room, five bedrooms and box room, and a large double yard. To be sold at the Crown Hotel on the 16 September 1924.' In the census of 1911 the pub was being run by Alfred and Beatrice Coombs who had previously been licensees at the Portland Roads Inn on the Isle of Portland but they moved to Wales to continue his trade as a ship's carpenter. The Prince closed in 2018 and is now residential accommodation.

THE QUEEN'S HOTEL
corner of King Street and Park Street, Melcombe Regis

THE OLD ALBERT Hotel was renamed the Queen's Hotel shortly after 1862 when it was advertised to let by Eldridge, Mason and Co. and the licence passed to George Board listed as a victualler living in King Street on the Jury List for 1864. The following February he was a victim of prolific swindler Henry Taylor who although only 18 posed as an inspector for the railways and talked a number of people in the town and beyond into cashing cheques for him before being tracked down and arrested at the Queen's where he was staying. He pleaded guilty at the assizes was sent to prison for nine months with hard labour. Board was involved in the municipal elections of 1867 for Melcombe Regis and the pub was used for meetings during that time, he had put his own name forward initially but withdrew at an early hour. Nonetheless, politics continued at the Queen's when in September of 1868 there was a meeting of the, 'anti-compacters' which was probably less exciting than it sounds and the following resolution was carried,

> That this meeting is of the opinion that the compact existing between the Conservative and Liberal candidates and the leaders of the two parties is an insult to the intelligence and manhood of the electorate of this town, and pledges itself to adopt every legitimate means to secure the return of an independent candidate.

You probably had to have been there.

On Wednesday 6 June 1877 landlords Henry and Sarah Cook travelled to Bath to visit the Bath and West Show, a yearly agricultural exhibition then celebrating its 100th anniversary. Hundreds of tourists alighted from the 10.47 am train coming from the Weymouth and Salisbury area. The day-trippers surged onto the narrow foot bridge, the tollhouse was nearest to the showground on the Widcombe side, the opposite end to the station meaning that the mass

The Queen's Hotel 2024

of people paid to get off the bridge rather than onto it. In normal times the flow would probably have a been equal in both directions. This unprecedented event led to large queues of people waiting on the bridge while their half pennies were collected by the single toll keeper assisted by his daughter. The bridge was overloaded and suddenly the middle gave way with a great crack plunging between 100 and 200 people some thirty feet into the river below; some landed on the stone pavement or the quay wall which ran alongside the river, others clung desperately to the collapsing timber frame. There were eight immediate deaths and over fifty injuries. It appears that the Widcombe end

The Widcombe Bridge Disaster 1877

was the first to give way and that bridge section rested for a few seconds on the tow path which runs underneath the bridge allowing valuable time for a few people to escape. Henry was seen helping his wife amongst the rubble, both were hurt but able to walk and taken to the Royal United Hospital. Henry said that when they reached the toll house he was asked to pay a toll which he was not expecting and turned to a friend to borrow the money but before he could turn back again he felt the bridge oscillate twice and all he remembers was being on the tow path with his wife in the water, he managed to pull her out but she was suffering from severe contusions.

In September 1880 Cook had £270 stolen from his bedroom in cash, gold and cheques, worth an incredible £40,000 in equivalent purchasing power today. Two frequenters of the race track who had been sleeping there were suspected and arrested but although they had some money on them it could not be traced back to the robbery which, coupled with police warnings of a

London gang of burglars arriving in the area, led to their acquittal and a remark from the judge that there are four banks in town and it was foolish to keep so much on the premises. An interesting equestrian event occurred two years later during a visit of the Yeomanry when a corporal of the Sherborne troop rode his horse up the front steps of the Queen's through the hall and around the coffee room intending to return via the same route but was persuaded to dismount much against his inclination. Sadly, there are no further details.

Hotel boots, 17-year-old Alfred Hall tried to hang himself in the stables which he had threatened to do for some time saying that was tired of life and had something on his mind. He was discovered hanging from a beam about two feet from the ground and was only just rescued in time. He continued saying that intended to kill himself to which the magistrate responded that 'this was one of the most serious charges that could be brought against any man. He was just as guilty in trying to take away his own life as if he had tried to take that of another man, in fact it was an attempt to murder and the most serious offence'. He was committed for trial but his eventual sentence does not seem to have been recorded.

In July of 1900 Robert Henry Griffin and his wife Sarah Ann took over but tragedy struck in the early part of 1902 when Griffin was thrown from his horse whilst on a ride to Wareham. The horse was rearing and bucking along the way and Griffin controlled it well for a while but was eventually thrown and landed on his head and was killed instantly. Griffin was a farmer and prominent Mason who before taking on the Queen's had been Mayor of Tamworth and ran the Kepple's Head in Portsmouth. WH Critchell who had for many years worked at the Paddington Station Master's Office took up the reins before his retirement in 1927. In 1938-39 the handsome old building that had housed the Albert and the original Queen's was demolished and rebuilt by brewers Eldridge Pope in a style totally out of character with its surroundings in anticipation of the railway station being revitalised with a corresponding increase in custom. The proposed works didn't happen, but the pub survived until 2013 and is now an office.

THE RAILWAY DOCK HOTEL
Rodwell Avenue, Weymouth

T<small>HE</small> R<small>AILWAY</small> D<small>OCK</small> building was designed by Crickmay & Co who also designed the Globe on land purchased for the scheme by the brewers Devenish. Work began in 1893 and was completed in 1902. It took its name

The Railway Dock in Retirement

from a new harbour that the Great Western Railway was intending to build at Newton's Cove. The GWR's service to the Channel Islands had outgrown the limited facilities at Weymouth Harbour which was used mainly for pleasure traffic and it proved impossible to adapt it to the railways increasing requirements. One scheme to alleviate the problem was to build new berths abutting Newton's Cove adjoining the Admiralty Breakwater covering 70 acres. This would not only save paying harbour fees to the Weymouth Corporation but attract additional trade. Not surprisingly the council objected, but their opposition to the Parliamentary Bill of 1898 promoting the scheme was ineffective. The proposed railway connection to the docks was to run parallel to Underbarn Walk, through two tunnels of 598 yards and 1121 yards respectively and then round the west of the town to join up with the main line south of Upwey Junction. Cost estimates continued to increase and it became necessary to scale things back with a branch line joining the Portland line near Rodwell Station. The existing line would be doubled from Rodwell to Weymouth. In 1902 the licence for the Castle Inn Horsford Street was successfully transferred to the new building and the firm's first licensee was a George Seaford after which James Underwood took over.

In 1903 it was announced that work on the new dock scheme would start immediately but by 1914 the dream was over when GWR sold all the land to the Admiralty. Had it been built, it would have solved problems of space and congestion which beset Weymouth Harbour during its operation as a commercial port. This was particularly noticeable when Weymouth was ruled out as a container port through lack of space and infrastructure. It would also have ruined a beautiful piece of coastline enjoyed by many to this day.

In the summer of 1936 long-term resident of the Railway Dock, former Sergeant Major William Farmer was outraged when he saw six small boys stealing apples from the pub garden, so much so that he grabbed one boy of six years and hit him on the leg with a dog whip leaving a deep mark about four inches long. His mother brought the case to court but owing to the high character of the defendant they decided to dismiss the summons on payment of costs. James Underwood had died in 1920 and was followed by his wife Blanche, the house stayed in the same family for almost 70 years before being closed in 1981 and demolished in June 1989.

THE RAILWAY HOTEL
Park Street, Melcombe Regis

THIS PARK STREET pub is another that owes its existence to a close proximity to the railway station and was built by John James Ham Longman in about 1849. By the census of 1851 it is being run by George and Sarah Moors. George died in 1853 and the licence passed to Thomas Foot a tailor who was granted his spirits licence in 1858 but was in trouble soon after when PC Harvey turned up at his door just after midnight to find about a dozen people plus cards and a cribbage board – undoubted signs of people enjoying themselves. George's daughter attended court as he was not well. When asked if she knew what time it was she replied optimistically 'a little after 11.00' whereas in fact it was approaching 12.30 and she claimed that those present were all lodgers. The matter was further complicated by George being drunk and at first refusing to allow the police entry. Despite a robust defence the bench found them guilty and it being the first offence the fine was mitigated to £1 for refusing admittance to the police and 5/- for keeping the house open.

Thomas Foot retired in his mid 70s and all his furniture and effects from bedsteads to tin beer warmers were put up for sale on the premises in February of 1863 during which time it was described as 'brick built and slated with water laid on and sewage carried by drains into the Backwater'. On Boxing Day of the same year the new landlord William Oliver who had held the licence for the Dolphin across the road, was surprised when one of his regular customers, 35-year-old watchmaker Frederick White rushed into the pub at about 10 pm 'all of a fright' and looking like a wild man claiming that James

Hatton landlord of the Sun where he lodged, was after him with a gun. Oliver eventually calmed him down and he left but shortly afterwards he was found drowned in the Backwater. The inquest was held at the White Hart during which Hatton denied that there was any animas between them and the jury brought in the only verdict they could of 'found drowned'. In 1868 Oliver

The Railway Hotel in 2024

moved once again to take over the New Arrival, later renamed the Duke of Albany. There followed a succession of short-lived landlords and in 1886 Devenish became the owners and installed Uriah Davidge who remained until 1897 when the house was closed and became a shop its licence transferred to the Railway Arch Tavern in Chickerell Lane which is outside of our area.

THE RAILWAY TAVERN
Commercial Road / Wesley Street. Melcombe Regis

THE RAILWAY TAVERN was first mentioned in the local paper of December 1854 when there was a complaint to the local council about the metal sign outside, 'screeching day and night' and the matter was referred to the board of health. William Vining the landlord in 1856 was convicted of the usual offence of selling beer outside of permitted hours on a Sunday and was fined 10/-plus costs as it was his first offence. Elizabeth Kenton took over from around the end of 1857 her family having originated at Oakhill in Somerset. By the census of 1861 the Railway had passed to her son Job, who also worked as a railway guard, and his wife Hannah. The house had been granted a spirits licence in 1858 but due to the strange and complex licensing laws this had been transferred to the Prince of Wales in Park Street thought by some to be an 'inferior house' and in 1870 it was necessary to reapply. The premises were described as consisting of a bar, bar parlour with room behind, very large clubroom, three bedrooms and a large attic and a licence was granted once more. Landlord Brown was pulled up for serving after midnight on a Sunday and tried the usual dodge that the three people there were lodgers, and in response to a complaint that he admitted prostitutes, he said that he did not allow them to sit down and warned them off as much as he could.

Sidney Cornelius Foot was summoned in 1872 for being open during prohibited hours on a Sunday despite him claiming that they had only come for some tobacco. Apparently, it was common practice to post lookouts to

The Railway Tavern 2024

warn of approaching police officers when serving after hours but on this occasion, it was raining so hard that there was nobody there. Foot was fined a total of £2/7/- and 'threw the money down in a great rage declaring it to be worse than highway robbery.' The Stroud family ran the pub throughout the 1870s and were there when the freehold was put up for auction by Woodhouse & Co brewers along with many other properties including the Rising Sun in Prospect Place. They were licensees until at least the census of 1891 and widow Margaret Stroud continued into her 60s but it was not to last. This quiet unassuming and largely trouble-free pub the only serious complaint against which was a charge of permitting gambling in 1899, was recommended for closure in 1910. Brewers Eldridge Pope were the owners and the landlord was Robert Joseph Bascombe Nunn who had been there for seven years and 'made a good living'. His house consisted of eleven rooms, namely one kitchen, one wash house, on the ground floor, one sitting room and four bedrooms on the first floor, and three bedrooms plus a box room on the second floor or attic. There are also two bars, one public and one private, business turnover was about £37 per month. The situation was very pleasant to certain visitors as it was facing the Backwater and its views.

The magistrate's reasons for refusing to renew the licence was the usual one that there were a number of other houses in the area and this one was simply not needed, there were nine fully licensed houses and two beer houses within 300 yards of each other and in Commercial Road there were 22 houses of which three were licensed premises. Nunn claimed that he had a house that was well-managed and well built which could put up as many as 24 sailors a night and that his trade in beer and mineral water was £40 the previous month with a large floating population consisting of sailors, residents, and visitors whom he computed to be not less than 50,000. Magistrate Sykes commented that 'Weymouth may have a large 'floating population' but it does not 'float' towards the Railway Tavern but towards the seafront or other directions', and with that the pub was ordered to be closed for good.

THE RANELAGH HOTEL
Ranelagh Road, Melcombe Regis

THE RANELAGH was first mentioned in August of 1870 when Stephen Brown applied for a spirits licence for the newly built hotel which formed part of a large block of buildings that had been erected on land known as the Park Estate at a cost of between £2,000 and £3,000, the estate is examined in

The Ranelagh Hotel 2024

more detail in the Waterloo Stores entry. The hotel consisted of 22 rooms, nine bedrooms, four sitting rooms, a large clubroom, smoking room with stabling and coach houses and stood opposite the arrival platform of the railway station. Strong objections were made on the grounds that Mr Brown was not a 'real' tenant and did not actually live there but was just put forward by the brewery Groves & Co. to obtain a licence. He countered this by saying that he did sleep there sometimes and had some furniture there apart from which there was no law against anyone occupying two houses. The application was granted and as suspected the house was up to let by December.

The first real tenant was Harriet Woodland a widow of 70, daughter Hannah, who acted as a barmaid, and son John a 'fly driver' on the 1871 census who was an enthusiastic officer of the Ancient Order of Foresters and was running the pub by 1875. Mother Harriet lived for a respectable 91 years. In February 1877 the brewery put the hotel up for rent but it was not until 1892 that its most long-lasting licensee appeared. Arthur John Rodway and family ran the hotel for 36 years, Arthur dying at the age of 84 in 1929 having retired sometime before when his son George Frederick Rodway took over. He was chairman of the South Dorset Licensed Victuallers Association for many years and much respected by all. The Ranelagh closed in January 1968 and became home to the local Conservative Club.

THE RED LION
33 Hope Street, Weymouth.

IN 1781 PERMISSION was given for local residents to fill-in a water inlet known as Hope Cove, described as very offensive at low tide, at their own expense. Once this had been achieved it formed the basis for today's Hope Square. There are various references to pubs called the Lion or the Red Lion including one for 'The Lion' in Hope Street from 1823 when it was owned or run by Christopher Calcon but their locations are uncertain. We are on firmer ground from 1840 when Thomas Downie was landlord of an unnamed pub in the square and in the census of the following year it is being run by his widow Mary described as an 'innkeeper'. She married a seaman, James Hartnell and the licence passed into his name. The first mention of the Red Lion in Hope

The Red Lion 2017

Square comes from 1842. Hartnell gave up the pub in around 1848 when he returned to the sea becoming a master mariner. The census of 1851 shows the licensee as Edward Newman from Portland and his wife Jane. In 1855 the pub was taken over by Richard Attwooll a stonemason who died in 1865 to be replaced by his son William a boat builder.

In 1878 the old building was demolished and rebuilt giving us the pleasant red brick structure that we see today. The Attwooll family were still there and remained until 1901 when Richard fell into a sort of coma and died 'after a hearty breakfast' at the age of 64. There followed a succession of landlords but the pub continued quietly and successfully and is still running well today a magnet for tourists and locals alike.

THE REST AND WELCOME
Boot Lane, Weymouth

THE FIRST MENTION of this beer house comes in 1859 when it is granted a spirits licence. Most applications contain arguments back and forth and very often useful descriptions of the premises but this report just says granted to Thomas Board who was a shoemaker by trade and lived on the premises with his wife Maria both aged 43. In 1863 he was caught with two earthenware cups that were deficient in size which was of course news to him as he had been using them as shaving mugs not for drawing beer but despite this ingenious defence he was fined 5/-plus costs.

In January 1877 a search warrant was issued and the pub raided. Board was asked if he had any foreign manufactured tobacco in his house to which he replied that he had not, adding, ' I have not a cigar in the house'. The officer searched the premises in the presence of his wife and two officers. In the chiffonier in the parlour leading from the grocer's shop the officer found a box of cigars. Board claimed to know nothing about them as did his wife, they were found to weigh a total of 1lb 3oz and in the same room they found three packages of Cavendish tobacco weighing over 10 lb and again they denied all knowledge, a further 8lb of the same contraband tobacco was found in an outhouse. The value plus duty on the entirety came to £5/16/6d and the magistrates are entitled to fine three times the value of the goods which came to £17/9/6d. Upon a promise to the police officer that, 'he could put his hand on him at any time' Board was not taken into custody immediately. When he appeared in court it was explained to him that the burden of proof lay with the person with whom the tobacco had been found. Still protesting his innocence

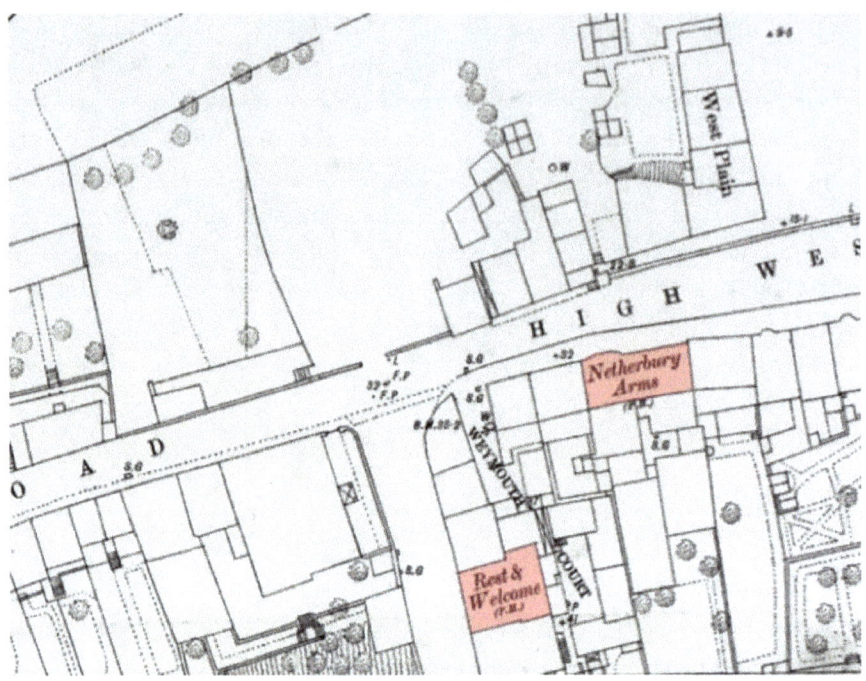

The Rest and Welcome on the 1864 O/S Map

Board said 'I stand here as an innocent man, believe me had I known it was there I should not have been so ready to open the door. I rather offered to open the door and I said 'You can search anywhere'. Despite his protestations without proof of having paid the tax the magistrate's hands were tied and he was fined £18/6/6d which included costs. In 1893 without a particular reason being given owners Groves the brewers had agreed to the licence for the Rest and Welcome be given up and the local corporation paid £300 in compensation. The pub was demolished in 1894 to make way for the Edward's Alms Houses which survive today.

THE RISING SUN INN
Prospect Place Chapelhay, Weymouth

THERE IS A 'W Fowler' possibly widower mentioned in the book recording those eligible to vote during the 1760s shown as running the Rising Sun ale house in High Street Weymouth but no further mention of the name has been found during the next hundred years and so it is quite possible that there is no connection between this pub and the one that followed. In the 1871

The Rising Sun 1942

census Sarah Ann Tuggey 58-year-old widow of a brick burner Richard Tuggey from Hampshire is shown as head of the family with her son Charles Batt Tuggey a seaman. They have no known connection to the licensed trade but living on the same premises is George Hounsell cordwainer and his family who is shown as innkeeper from 1872 and probably before. He suffered the obligatory summons for selling outside of permitted hours and was threatened with a further penalty for not bringing his certificate to court with him but in the end he was fined just a £1 including costs. Interestingly the magistrate said that they would not endorse his licence because that would be really injuring somebody else as it was no punishment to the defendant to have his licence endorsed but injured the reputation of the property.

The Sun was owned by John Gillingham until it was sold at auction on 15 March 1882 to Groves the brewers. In its last incarnation the pub had been created by combining two properties numbers 5 and 6 Prospect Place into one the redbrick facade in keeping with that period as above. The Hounsells were there until 1884 when the Edwards family from Ireland took over and continued until 1918. The Rising Sun continued its quiet existence until 1956 when it was purchased from Groves Brewery and demolished to provide housing.

THE RODWELL TAVERN / HOTEL
Rodwell Road, Weymouth

This house first appears as the Rodwell Tavern when Arron Charles Buckell is refused a spirits licence in August of 1860. The census of a year later describes him as aged 32 and a 'temporary Chelsea pensioner and victualler ' from Wallingford in Berkshire living on the premises with his wife Mary and two young children. They left the same year and the owners Eldridge, Mason & Co advertised the pub for rent which was taken up by Alfred Neale formerly of the Railway Tavern in Commercial Street who was successful in his application for a spirits licence in consequence of the licence of the Eagle Tavern having been lost when it was demolished for 'public purposes' and the proprietors made it one of the conditions of selling the property that the licence should be transferred to another of their houses. Neale died in 1874 the licence passing to his widow before being taken up by John Bishop JP a former mayor of Dorchester retiring to the seaside at the age of 74 with Emily his bride of three months. He died of apoplexy in June and Emily stuck it out until September of 1877 when she decided to leave and put all her household furniture and effects up for auction.

The Rodwell Hotel 2017

The brewery advertised the house for rent once more and up stepped James Collingwood 41 and his wife Susan late of the Dolphin Inn Park Street, they were there until 1890 when James Coombs from Bristol took over. He held the position of Bugle-Major in the 1st Volunteer Battalion Dorset Regiment which didn't prevent him from being seriously beaten up by three gunners who turned up after hours one day demanding drink and as he tried to close the door on them he got beaten around the head but as they were of previous good character they were only fined 13/- each. In 1910 Coombs was elected treasurer of the 'South Dorset Licence Holders Trade and Protection Association and Benevolent Fund'. He and his family were there until the mid 1920s. Around Christmas time 1939 a little old lady in her 80s popped into the pub to buy a bottle of gin which she paid for with a £50 note. Both she and the landlord Cyril Matthews mistook the note for £5 and once he realised he made strenuous efforts to find her. When she was eventually tracked down it emerged that the money was part of the proceeds a house sale and the matter was soon sorted out. Her relatives did not comment on what happened to the gin. The pub continued to trade until 2018 when it was closed and converted into flats.

THE ROSE & CROWN
Crescent Street, Melcombe Regis

THE ROSE AND Crown was certainly going by 1838 as an application for a spirits licence in 1858 described landlord John Canning as having 'been in possession for 20 years'. Despite repeated refusals, in August of 1859 Canning applied again but was once more opposed by local vested interests on the grounds that the notices were incorrect not being in accordance with the Act of Parliament which required it to be stated that the house was used as an ale house, beer house, or victualling house, and that Canning was incorrectly spelt as 'Caning' but the magistrates for once saw through these rather pathetic objections and concluded that the spirit of the law had been complied with and granted the application.

Canning died in 1864 to be replaced by James Lidford Sheppard previously landlord of the Canteen who was seriously attacked by two soldiers stationed at Portland who smashed him repeatedly about the head and face and stole his gold Albert chain. Despite what he thought was a positive identification the suspect was able to prove that he was in the guardhouse at the time and so the perpetrator was never caught. The cat and mouse game of catching publicans serving out of hours and their efforts to avoid capture are sometimes quite remarkable.

Rose & Crown 2024

Charles Lanning Pavey landlord during 1878 was hauled before the court for being in breach of the Beer House Act. PC Prior saw two men leave the house at 8.10 am having been watching it since 7.30 the pub lookout, whose job it was to warn of any approaching police officers, was a girl of about seven years old who was presumably not up to the job. Pavey claimed that the men were there to buy some fish which was displayed in the window along with apples and other groceries. One of the men ran off and the other claimed that he had just come to pick up a pair of bloaters. Apparently Pavey had been convicted of assaulting the constable during the raid and the 'out of hours' case was brought forward simply to show that police had a right to enter public houses when they thought proper and to be treated with respect. It didn't work as shortly afterwards Pavey saw PC Prior outside his premises once more, grabbed him by the collar and using foul language accused Prior of having him summoned. Pavey was bound over to keep the peace for three months in the sum of £10 which seems remarkably lenient.

The lease on the pub expired in October 1893 and its entire contents, trade fixtures etc put up for auction and the premises permanently closed with its licence being transferred to the Portland Railway Hotel.

THE ROYAL ENGINEER INN
Prospect Place, Chapelhay, Weymouth

THE ENGINEER BEER house was first mentioned in an application for a spirits licence by John Hearn Hoskins originally from Beaminster in August of 1860. The house was described as providing a large amount of sleeping accommodation and was the best kept house in the neighbourhood. The objections were that Mr Hoskins was about to leave which would mean a further application in a few months and that it was situated in 'a respectable row of houses with three other licensed houses hard by' and so the application was refused. In the 1861 census the pub is described as The Engineer's Arms and under the control of George Cox Forse. In another application for a spirits licence during 1865 the property was described as two houses converted into one which was able to make up a large number of beds and was very much resorted to by country people attending the market. The main objection was that the house was not well conducted. A Mr Pothecary remarked that he had two houses in the same row and his tenants complained of the way in which it was run – a great many police cases came from that house he claimed and the licence was refused.

Next door to the Engineer lived George Dowell who was brought before the court in November of 1866 by George Forse for repeatedly banging on his wall 'with sledgehammer like force'. He claimed that 'the females who resort there are not of the highest moral character' and it was agreed that only a slight partition divided the two houses and the knocking had been carrying on for over 16 months. According to Mrs Forse, Dowell told her that he did it 'for the purposes of annoyance' as he wanted the house closed. Last Sunday, he continued, there were over 30 people in the house during divine service, he was a carpenter and exercising his trade in his own house which accounted for the banging and insisted that the Engineer should be closed. During the investigation it emerged that the house had a resident violinist named Thomas Paull who was wont to strike up a tune when people arrived. Magistrates concluded that reputation of the house was irrelevant for this hearing, and that there was not sufficient evidence to prove that the defendant had done anything to lead to a breach of the peace and the case was dismissed.

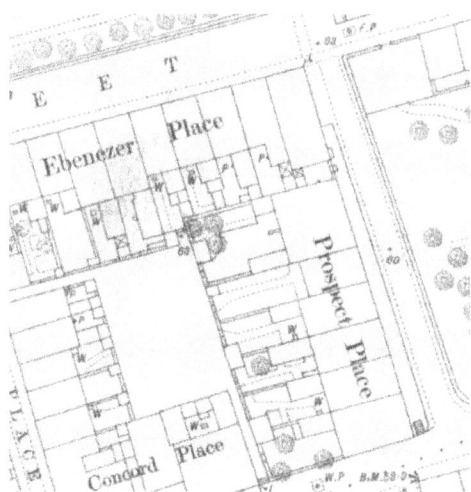

Prospect Place site of the Royal Engineer in 1864

Trouble was never far away, and a few months later information was received that there were stolen goods at the pub. Upon visiting, the police found three soldiers and two bundles, in one of which were three pairs of military trousers, a lieutenant's tunic and an officer's shell jacket. The other one contained more clothing and items of silver all stolen from the Verne Barracks and when questioned one of the men replied that, 'Some fellow gave them to me.' They were all sent for trial but the outcome does not seem to have survived. A rather amusing exchange occurred during 1869. Thomas and Mary Fulljames, the landlords made another application for a licence with Thomas, who had been steward on board a ship declaring that he was determined to conduct the house in respectable manner. Magistrate Ayling remarked 'Fulljames you are not sober now!, Yes I am sir! he replied but the licence was refused. The Royal Engineer closed before 1871 and the area has been completely redeveloped.

THE ROYAL HOTEL / STACIE'S HOTEL
Gloucester Row, Esplanade Melcombe Regis

In the *Gloucester Journal* of 21st January 1771 the following announcement appeared,

> We hear from Weymouth, that there is an intention of building by subscription, a large and elegant set of Assembly Rooms, and an hotel adjoining consisting of eight rooms on a floor with stabling for 60 horses and the coach houses for 20 carriages.

The land for this expensive venture was leased from Weymouth Corporation by a speculative developer from Bath named Andrew Sproule during 1770 and was initially known as The Hotel and Assembly Rooms or simply The Hotel. Way out from the centre of town at the time, it was a bold move to turn away from the harbour and the centre of the town's commerce and face the sea. During August 1772 it was advertised to let as almost finished,

> To be let, together or separately. All the new buildings consisting of an hotel containing four servants halls, four cellars, eight parlours, eight dining rooms, nine rooms in the attic story, and nine garrets. Adjoining this and communicating to it is the long room, 70 feet long by 39 in the bow windows, under the long room, a large coffee room, a billiard room and two shops. Adjoining to the long room, a card room, and a lady's withdrawing room, with five garrets over them, under the cardroom, are two large parlours, a kitchen

The Royal Hotel 2024

and tap room, with other cellars and wine vaults, at the back of the building, separated by a large yard, stabling for 60 horses, and coach houses for 20 carriages behind the brewhouse. The rent not to commence until midsummer 1773. Full particulars enquire of Gabriel Steward or Andrew Sproule Esq. at Weymouth, or Mr Roberts the attorney at law in Bath.

NB the Hotel is now finished, except papering, and a tenant may enter upon it immediately to prepare for the next season.

Originally known as Stacie's Hotel after its first manager it was soon occupied by a Joseph Maidment who moved from the Antelope in Dorchester in June of 1776. He didn't stay long, if at all, as the Hotel was up for rent again in March, in fact things didn't seem to be going to well for him in general as in 1778 all his household furniture at his 'late house, the Mansion House in Market Street Weymouth' was also put up for auction. The Hotel itself seemed to be failing despite its grandeur and 'all mod cons' its contents were up for auction in July 1780 and again in 1783 when the tenant William Flack was declared bankrupt – 'the whole of the goods were entirely new about 18 months ago'. Mr Stacie seems to have had enough of tenants and the following May inserts a notice in the local press,

> Stacie respectfully informs the nobility and gentry, that the ASSEMBLY ROOMS and GRAND HOTEL at Weymouth are fitted up in an elegant manner and are now open for reception of company with the best accommodation. The BALLS will begin immediately and continue until November with horns and clarinets every evening on card nights.

His appeal was followed by,

> STACIE being informed, that from a confederacy among the drivers, the company who honour Weymouth with their preference are taken to other houses, begs they will be positive in ordering the boys to drive to the HOTEL where they may depend upon great attention and superior accommodation.

The original Royal Hotel 1772-1891

The Hotel was not part of the general route and daily schedule of what he called the 'post-horse work' which may have been a problem from the start. As it was not one of the regular stop off and pick up establishments the drivers just ignored it, perhaps he didn't pay them and the other hotels did. In what must have boosted Stacie's confidence and self-esteem the Duke of Gloucester, George III's younger brother, built himself a lodge next door in 1780 which was used by the King himself from 1789 'where retirement is a principal object with all regal state and ceremony is dispensed with', and by 1791 Stacie's Hotel had become the Royal Hotel. Stacie & Co were still running the business in 1803 – and still complaining about the lack of visits from the cabbies despite the huge boost of having His Majesty visiting the town just about every summer between 1789 and 1805.

By 1810 the post coach Royal Express included the hotel in its itinerary from Weymouth to London and the establishment thrived on extravagant balls, dinners, concerts and general high-class entertainment and although King George no longer visited the town the hotel continued to be patronised by other members of the family like Princess Charlotte who was there in 1814 when a ball took place in her honour at what had become, 'Russell's Royal Hotel and Assembly Rooms' after its new owner William Russell. By January 1829 things seem to have hit another rocky patch and the Royal was put up to be let by tender, all furniture was to be included and business continued as usual, a brief announcement in May said that Russell had left the hotel. Next in line was Susanna Bayly Carter a single woman who announced her arrival and occupation of the hotel with her sister in July of 1830 who had also moved from the Antelope in Dorchester where she had been since at least 1794, showing an enduring link between the two etsablishments. They undertook a serious refurbishment and so the merry round of entertaining and catering for the fashionable, rich and famous continued – including providing rooms for the King of Saxony in 1844. By the time she left in the late 1840s Susanna was in her mid 60s, her sister having disappeared from the record fairly early on.

By the census of 1851 38-year-old local bachelor Thomas Dorney Luce had taken over with his maiden aunt Harriet. Luce had previously run the family hotel that was to become the Victoria Inn, Augusta Place after the death of his mother Jane Luce in 1840. Thomas was born into the trade and spent his entire life in it with hardly a blemish apart from the time that he was charged by the Inland Revenue for exceeding the number of journeys to the railway station and back allowed by his bus licence and was fined on that occasion. He was in a bit of trouble in 1872 when taken to court by the executors of Walter Williams who claimed that he owed £129/8/4d for the hire of coaches that he had run for some years between Bath and Weymouth and which remained unpaid. The case was described as 'of the most tedious description which lasted about six hours and was as uninteresting as it was long'. It seems that Mr Townsend at the Bath end of their coaching operation who normally paid the charges had become bankrupt and upon the death of Mr Williams who supplied the carriages, the relatives sought to get what they could from Luce but the jury found in his favour and the claim was dismissed. Highly respected, Luce had served in a number of civic capacities throughout his career and ran the hotel until 1878 when he moved a few doors along to the Gloucester Hotel which he had owned since 1859 and where he died in 1886.

Rundown and out of fashion, in the early 1880s the Corporation landowners decided that something new and exciting was required and schemes were being hatched for a new development on the site possibly including a pier but everything was delayed by legal argument over a right of way, disputes over the proposals and where the money was to come from. Tenders were invited from various firms during 1890 and somewhat prematurely the old building was demolished in 1891. Two years later the Weymouth Grand Hotel Company Limited was chosen to build on behalf of local brewers Devenish & Co. The hotel company fell into liquidation and the Corporation repossessed the site which had left an ugly hole in the Esplanade for some years whilst the wrangling went on over what was being described as 'this mournful business'. Eventually, a syndicate emerged with a proposed initial outlay of £20,000 and work began at last under the direction of architect Charles Orlando Law and the magnificent piece of Victoriana that we see today was finished in 1899 to receive its first tenant, businessmen and wine merchant Thomas Hodges Vinnicombe. He, wife Lizzie and seven children moved into the hotel and were there for the 1901 census but it seems that his business acumen did not match that of a hotelier and by 1905 having left Weymouth to try his hand at a hotel in Tenby, Wales the business failed as did his attempt at dealing shares in South Africa and he was declared bankrupt. The business continues today as one of the town's premier hotels.

THE ROYAL HOTEL TAP
Gloucester Row Mews, Melcombe Regis

As with many large hotels the Royal had what could be described as a 'public house' at its rear to service its workers, draymen and ordinary members of the public not worthy of using the front entrance. There are indications of its existence as far back as 1816 when a Henry Woodward, builder and victualler was in charge of stables and premises known as the Royal Hotel Commercial Hall in Gloucester Road Mews at the back of the Royal which had been going since the 1770s. The first definite mention comes in 1834 when William Weston Rogers, victualler and ferryman formerly of the Royal Hotel Tap, goes bankrupt.

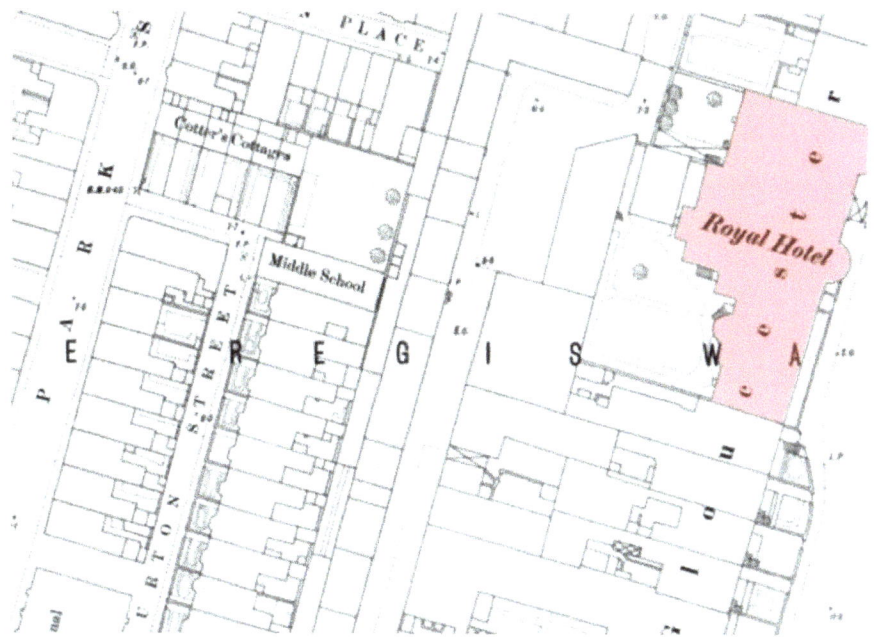

The Royal Hotel with the Tap occupying one of the buildings at the rear

His place was taken by the Soper family until 1847 when landlord John Soper died and the ultimate owner Miss Carter of the Royal Hotel let it to William Hardy who died in 1852. The following year an inquest was held at the Tap on the body of Patrick Gordon who had been discovered at his lodgings in Edmund Street 'the corpse presenting a most ghastly and horrible appearance with the head almost separated from the body. He was discovered lying in bed covered in blood by the landlady who asked 'Oh Mr Gordon what have you done during the night?!' At which the deceased made a gurgling sound attempting to speak but could not. Shortly after he said that he had begun by sitting in a chair with a razor and then used a knife. He refused all forms of help and eventually died of exhaustion and general shock to the system. His daughter said that he had been generally depressed since his wife left and the jury brought in a verdict of temporary insanity.

By the 1871 census Thomas Prist Le Warne, 41, a coachman from Cornwall was landlord and presumably running the stables. In 1896 it was announced that with the rebuilding of the Royal Hotel the Tap and adjacent buildings were to be demolished and replaced by a 36ft wide road into Clifton Place thus converting 'a very unsightly and slummy place in the very centre of town into a pleasant street which will afford protections from the east winds in winter '. In 1903 the Tap was ordered to be closed immediately.

THE ROYAL OAK
1 Custom House Quay, Melcombe Regis

The Royal Oak's situation on the Quay would mark it out as one of the town's older establishments right in the centre of a working harbour. In the Land Tax returns for 1813 William Bower a banker and alderman who owned a number of pubs in the town is listed as the proprietor and Henry Clark the occupier. By 1823 Simon Fowler has replaced Clark and in 1829 following the death of Bower the house is auctioned as part of his holdings along with the Fordington Brewery in Dorchester, the details of this are examined in the 'Bear' entry. Simon Fowler possibly, Captain Fowler, was there until around 1841, shortly after Solomon Sly took over and was treated to a 'tastefully laid out supper with upwards of 50 respectable tradesmen and friends attending'.

The Royal Oak 2017

1854 saw a brave defence against the charge of selling out of hours. Mrs Austwick who had recently taken over the pub was accused of selling beer outside of permitted hours on a Sunday and could reasonably be expected to be unaware that she was breaking the law by selling *before* divine service, in this case between nine and ten in the morning. The licence doesn't prohibit before or after but only *during* divine service she claimed. Nice try but the magistrates were not convinced and fined her 40/- including costs upon which she declared that she did not feel inclined to pay it. The bench gave her a fortnight and she left, 'wondering what people had licenses for…'

During 1858 the Oak was described as 'of very ancient date, rooms small and low, front portion of the house was gabled and windows latticed. Pulled down recently and a new brick house erected on the site bearing the name of the former and used as an inn '.

A bit of fun was to be had during November of 1869. William Richards of Oxford claimed that he could walk 50 miles in 12 hours – ten of them backwards! This prodigious feat was divided into segments of 6 ¼ miles from the Royal Oak and back. He performed in front of a huge crowd before passing the hat around and by all accounts did very nicely.

David Prodger and his wife Eliza had been landlords since 1876 and in February of 1884 they were summoned to the Borough Petty Sessions for having unstamped, illegal, and deficient cups in their possession which was an offence under the act of 1878, along with nine other publicans from, the Ship Inn, the George, Sailors Return, Concert Hall Tavern, Bird in Hand, Nag's Head, Steam Packet Inn, Yacht Inn, and the Eagle Tavern. Rather than go into each case individually the magistrates decided to take the Royal Oak and the George as test cases. Samuel Bull, inspector of weights and measures for the past 15 years, gave evidence that on the 4th of February he visited the Royal Oak and seized four pint cups, three being an eighth of a gill deficient and others by a quarter of a gill; five half pints, two being one eighth of a gill deficient; 16 unstamped quarts; 21pints and three half pints. In defence it was argued that there was 'not a tittle of evidence to show that the cups had ever been used as measures'. Counsel for the defence was highly critical of the inspector's actions saying that he should have said to the publicans, 'You have certain cups in your position which are unstamped, and you must have them gone, if at the end of a fortnight I find them still unstamped the penalty must be enforced'. Instead of which he had merely grabbed every cup in sight in one case taking more than 70 and putting the publicans to great inconvenience. He had done nothing to prove that these cups were used as measures. They were not, and there were pewter measures kept for that purpose.' In front of the magistrates was a table containing a jumble of over 300 cups with no indication of which had come from which house. The magistrates retired for about a quarter of an hour and returned to dismiss all the cases but let it be known that publicans must in future have proper stamped cups in their possession. It can be assumed, and in most cases quite rightly, that under-measure cups were there to cheat the customer but this was not always the case. The law stated that beer could only be dispensed in certain measured vessels at a certain price but sometimes the customer did not have enough money to pay for a full measure and cups would be kept to measure out quantities that he could afford, helpful, but still illegal.

In 1889 William Hines moved from the George next door. The family had been subject to a terrible accident in 1879 when two of his sons were playing with a gun which went off and killed William junior as reported in that entry. Hines was there until 1898 before giving way to George Jacquett whose wife was involved in a serious car accident during 1921 travelling back from Exeter suffering from concussion and facial injuries. In August of 1919 the Royal Oak was one of several Devenish pubs who had their landlords returned to them after being away on active service. The pub continues today, serving locals and a growing flock of tourists with food and drink along the Quay.

THE SAILORS HOME INN
Chapelhay Street, Weymouth

THE SAILOR'S HOME does not appear on the census of 1861 and is first found in 1867 as one of a row of cottages divided by Chapel Row, in St Nicholas Street on the Weymouth side. Landlord William Sealey plead guilty to having cups short of the legal measure in his possession, each being one gill deficient and he was fined 5/-. In 1868 landlady Elizabeth Sealey was also fined 5/- plus costs when the house was found to be open outside of permitted hours as when PC Meech entered the premises he, 'found there drinking, two marines, two prostitutes, and a woman named Burden.'

In 1890 the house was put up for rent by owners Job Legg of the Old Brewery Bridport and taken by Francis Murray, licensed victualler, otherwise a 'stationary engine driver' who was there until 1906 when Charles Holland from Piddletown took over and applied unsuccessfully for a spirits licence stating that his house had six bedrooms and could take 15 lodgers. By 1909 the house was owned by John Groves & Son and the rent was £18 plus rates with a turnover of £40 or £50 per month. The house was described as a brick and tile building very old-fashioned and consisting of 'three rooms and two bars on the

After a Hard Day's Work

ground floor, four rooms on the first floor and two attics, one private room, one scullery, one tap room or smoking room-a very small room situated at the end of the bar, the jug and bottle is on the right as one enters the outside door and the public bar as one enters the inner door'. The jug and bottle is 7'3" x 3'1" x 7'x4" high, the bar is 13 'x 3'x9' x 7'5" high, the taproom is about 11' long x 7' 11"and about 7' high. The entrance to the back yard is very small and contains a WC for the use of customers. There is one room on the first floor containing two full-size beds and one single bed sleeping five persons, the second bedroom contains one full size bed sleeping two persons and the third bedroom contained one full size bed also sleeping two persons, the fourth bedroom is occupied by the landlord his wife and child. The first attic room contained new mattresses but was awaiting bedsteads, the second small attic contained one bedstead and three mattresses. Altogether there was room for 13 lodgers. Police Inspector Day said it was the worst licensed premises he had ever visited without elaboration, whereas those in favour of its retention described it as a small comfortable place where people could have a quiet drink. Mr Holland appeared in person wearing the South Africa medal with five clasps and stated that his customers do not require a spirits licence and that his trade was mainly supplying dinner, supper and beer, in one year between January and February he had accommodated 132 men while his wife cooked the meals. In 1908 they had sold 77,272 pints and the house has been existence for some 60 years. Holland stated that although a bricklayer by trade he was unlikely to find work if the pub was to close. The magistrates agreed on the renewal of the licence and the Holland family were there for almost 40 years until the pub was destroyed during an air raid during the war and the then landlady Olive Winifred Rowe was awarded compensation under the Licensing Compensation Act of 1910.

THE SAILORS RETURN
St Nicholas Street, Melcombe Regis

THE SAILOR'S RETURN first appears in 1840 being run by James Ferry a 32 year-old blacksmith and wheelwright from Burton Bradstock with his wife Sarah and four children, he was granted his spirits licence in 1857. In August of 1864 Sarah Ferry dropped dead in the kitchen and James was left to carry on alone with the help of his family. In 1872, along with his fellow publicans he made an application to the Licensing Board to be able to remain open until 12 midnight claiming that because of the late arrival of the boat trains and the 'inconvenience to which members of the friendly societies who held their meetings at the inn were subjected to, being obliged to quit the houses before they had transacted all their business' they were in unfair competition with those club houses who didn't come under such strict licensing laws'. Their plea fell on deaf ears and as was probably expected the bench stuck firmly to the letter of the law. Also during his tenure he was fined 10/- for having deficient measures in his house about which of course he knew nothing. By 1874 James had left the pub and had moved further down the street with his son.

By 1884 the landlord was James Fuszard who was involved in the great deficient cups raid of 1884 when ten pubs were raided and their landlords summoned to the Borough Petty Sessions for having unstamped, illegal, and deficient cups in their possession an offence under the act of 1878, in the end all cases were dismissed with serious warnings. The full story is told in the Royal Oak entry. There was trouble with a couple of drunks in 1893. John Reed and Mary Stanley were seen drunk on the bridge and when moved on went to the Sailors demanding more drink. Landlord Fuszard attempted to throw them out but was threatened by Reed who said he would 'put my stick cross your nut' should he touch Stanley. When they appeared in court she was find 20/- and Reed only 5/- as it was his first offence. There was a further charge for Stanley who when in the cells had asked for a cup of water, she threw the water away and spent the rest of the evening banging the cup against the door and using bad language, she was fined an additional 1/-for damage to the cup.

The Sailor's Return 2017

In August 1917 landlord Richard Chaddock was summoned under the Defence of the Realm Act for failing to exhibit in each public room of his licensed premises a copy of the regulations with reference to the liquor control order. Chaddock stated that the copy of the order in the bar and got torn but he had notices up in other rooms. The Clerk of the Court expressed incredulity that the regulations required that every public room had to be covered, 'what about the Gloucester Hotel?' he asked, 'every lavatory? billiard room? dining room?' It was agreed that Mr Chaddock had always conducted the house well and as this was the first case in the town and new to everyone it would be dismissed on payment of costs. A similar charge against Robert Loveridge of the Wellington Arms was treated in the same way once he explained that the sign was taken down because the room was being painted. The bench pointed out that should the regulations be contravened in future they would be dealt with more seriously now that publicans were aware.

Richard Chaddock died in 1918 and the licence was taken over by his widow Mary Jane who was summoned before the magistrates in November 1920 for not following exactly the very complex rules regarding prices on various types of brandy according to strength and origin along with notices supposedly explaining this to the customers. This was part of a case which included five pubs the Fountain Hotel, the Victoria the Sun, and the Clifton. Having pleaded guilty, she was fined 2gns plus costs, a far lesser sum than some of the others.

The Sailors Return continues today in fine form providing an excellent early breakfast to seamen of all nationalities and even the passing historian....

THE SHIP INN
Maiden Street, (Custom Quay) Melcombe Regis

THE EARLIEST MENTION we have for the Ship is 1840 when it was being run by a James Tizard and by the end of the decade it had passed to 50 year old James Caundle from Radipole. Caundle had been landlord of the Bear Inn St Mary Street from around 1837 and had moved to the Ship by 1848 when a rather sad story emerges, best quoted verbatim from the *Dorset County Chronicle* for 11 May of that year,

> Elizabeth Caundle wife of John Caundle late of the Black Bear Inn, was brought to the station house by her husband, who refused to take her away again. Caundle has troubled the police so frequently with his wife, who is an abandoned character, that they refused to take charge of her and handed her over to the relieving officer'

Elizabeth died the following year.

In 1868 Caundle advertised a large quantity of potatoes for sale and upon receiving a favourable reply from a Mr Barnes he sent him 20 tons by rail for which he received a promissory note and upon going to London in pursuit of his money he found at least 20 other cases of a similar nature and Barnes under arrest. Caundle left the pub the same year when his place was taken by another member of the Tizard family who in his application for a spirits licence in 1870 stated that he had been an engineer in the Channel Islands Company for ten years and that the Ship had been kept as a beerhouse for 30 years. It was owned by brewers Hall & Woodhouse and had nine furnished rooms but the bench decided that neither the landlord or the house was deserving of a licence. The delightfully named Reuben Fudge who took over in 1875 was summoned for the usual crime of serving out of hours but he had been cautioned before and his house was blamed for much of the drunkenness on the Quay, he was fined 5/-. Fudge died in 1878 and was followed by his widow Mary Ann who was there until 1883.

In February of 1884 landlord George Cross and a number of others were summoned to the Borough Petty Sessions for having unstamped, illegal, and deficient cups in their possession about 40 of which came from the Ship. Cross's was one of two used as a test case brought against nine others. In court all the cups were mixed up on the table and it could not be told which came from which house. In the end all the cases were dismissed with warnings. A more complete account is included in the Royal Oak entry.

During 1892 landlord James Henry Crisp was summoned for an attack on James Williams, a barber of Park Street, in the Portland Railway Hotel. It seems that the animosity was of long standing but the cause is unknown and despite having his victim on the floor in front of witnesses and destroying part of his clothing the case was dismissed with both parties to pay their costs.

The Ship in 2012 before the render

Serious proposals were put forward in 1900 for the demolition of the pub and the transference of the licence to another house, to be called the Melbury Arms at 14 Prospect Terrace and for the corporation to buy out owners Hall and Woodhouse for £855. The plan was to include the redevelopment of the huge warehouse which backed onto the Guildhall. Landlord George Henry Frampton was not to receive compensation should the scheme go ahead but it seems that the idea was dropped.

In March of 1907 the tenant was Sydney Charles Lucas and the Ship was still owned by Hall and Woodhouse as it is today and whose only other house in the town was the Portland Railway Tavern. Trade had almost tripled in the last four years and the house now contained six bedrooms which could accommodate 25 persons, and was mostly used by those working on the Quay more in the nature of a lodging house then a public house, the magistrates approved plans for renovations to the building but the licence was still refused. In February of 1912 two sailors had an argument over football which resulted in a bit of pushing and shoving during which William Johnson was pushed over hitting his head on stone floor resulting in his death. His assailant Henry Jarvis was charged with manslaughter but the case judged to be an accident and the matter was dismissed at the assize court.

The Ship continues today a haven for tourists and locals alike.

THE SHIPWRIGHT'S ARMS
Salem Place Chapelhay, Weymouth

THE SHIPWRIGHTS ARMS was a Victorian beer house which is believed to have first received its licence in about 1855 but the first definite mention comes in 1865 with an application for a spirts licence by landlord Thomas Vallance which was turned down as many were at the time. Vallance was summoned for serving out of hours when PC Mitchell happened to be passing by and heard some men discussing playing cards for half a sovereign followed by 'be quiet here's a policeman coming!' Upon being questioned Mrs Vallance claimed that the men were either lodgers or nephews a defence which the bench must have heard 100 times before. They were fined 10/- with 9/10d costs. Another application for a licence was made in the following year during which it was stated that the house was owned by Vallance who had spent a lot of money on the premises in an improving area despite which the application was again denied. In August 1869 the landlord for the previous two months had been George Honeyborne and was described as having 12 rooms three of which were bedrooms and very well constructed.

Landlord John Baggs was hauled before the court in November 1874 for assaulting his wife Martha who claimed that her husband had been absent for a while and returned in a drunken state. When she asked him where he had been he hit her several times then took a poker and smashed all the ornaments on the mantelpiece. She claimed that he had been in the habit of beating her for the past twelve years. Baggs was fined £5 and bound over to keep the peace for six months on the sum of £50, they left the pub soon after.

By 1875 John Spencer Bleathman a cab proprietor had taken over. He had been before the courts a few years before for mistreating one of his animals and using obscene language towards an RSPCA inspector, a charge dismissed on payment of costs, he was there with wife Henrietta until 1892. Uriah and Emily Davidge took on the tenancy in June 1898, Uriah died in 1902 and Emily carried on. A report to the magistrates during March 1903, following an examination by the police, described the house as having only one bar, and despite having five or six bedrooms only two were available for public use, there was no stabling, two exits and the premises were occupied by one person and a servant. Emily explained that they paid £17 a year for the pub and that she had been with Devenish for 20 years and was previously at the Railway Hotel. The magistrates decided that the pub should be closed along with six others, the Steam Packet Inn, the Three Tuns, the Yacht, the Porters' Arms, the Baltic and the Royal Hotel Tap. Appeals were made that they should be allowed to trade until their licenses expired in October, the bench agreed to grant the concession with the exception of the Yacht Inn and the Royal Hotel Tap which would be closed forthwith. The building was put up for auction on 25 November 1903 as a leasehold dwelling house otherwise 4 and 5 Salem Place. The property was bombed during the war along with the Albion and vast swathes of the area and redeveloped after the war.

OBSCENE LANGUAGE.—*John Spencer Bleathman*, cab proprietor, Weymouth, was summoned by Richard Warr, Inspector of the R.S.P.C.A., for using obscene language in St. Thomas Street on the 3rd inst. Mr. Malin appeared for the defence. Prosecutor said while in St. Thomas Street on the day named he saw defendant driving a horse attached to an open carriage. Seeing that the horse was slightly lame on the off-fore leg he said that he had had a complaint about the horse and if it became worse the defendant must not work it. Defendant became very excited and said the horse was not lame. Prosecutor walked away, whereupon defendant turned his horse round, followed him, and him a ——monkey, and declared with an oath that he would not be annoyed by a——like him. He had never had such language used towards him before in all his 23 years of experience as an officer of the R.S.P.C.A P.S. Barratt said defendant told him that he lost his temper and called the prosecutor a——monkey. The Bench dismissed the case on payment of the costs by defendant.

Rude Landlord 1870

THE SOMERSET HOTEL
King Street, Melcombe Regis

THE FIRST MENTION of the Somerset comes from August 1859 when Edwin Dunn was granted a spirits licence but he left the premises before the census of 1861 and moved to the Victoria Hotel. The pub was advertised to let by the owners Eldridge, Mason & Co. brewers from Dorchester. The house faced directly onto the end of the line at the railway station and faced annihilation the following August when the brakes failed on a Great Western Railway train which smashed the barriers to splinters and careered right into the road heading straight for the pub but managed to stop in time and there were no serious injuries. In May of 1864 Mrs Harriet Woodland a 64-year-old widow from Yetminster took control with daughter Hannah and son John, the pub continued in various combinations of the family until 1898. Hannah married a Charles White who took over the licence from 1874 until 1878

The Somerset Hotel 2017

when they moved to the New Bridge Inn but not before rubbing the police up the wrong way when caught with four people at the bar after hours. Two were prostitutes who claimed to be 'excursionists' saying that they had just got off the train which made them travellers and entitled to be served. Mrs White pointed out that other houses were open at the same time and asked why they were being singled out to which the mayor set the fine at £2 saying that he could increase it to £10 and endorse their licence if they continued with such remarks.

There was a very sad case in 1876 when Mary Powell was charged with being drunk and disorderly outside the pub. It was said that she had many fine and remarkable achievements but had fallen shockingly low, 'she is now elderly and much disfigured in appearance, her face being shockingly bloated and repulsive.' She was shocked to hear herself described as a prostitute saying that if that was the case she would have worn better clothes. She claimed to be a teacher and begged in a hysterical manner to be allowed to go without a fine – prison would be heaven to her, she claimed, but feared the distress of her friends knowing. She went into maudlin lamentations that she was not able to take beer without policemen being after her. Men could get drunk without being locked up but she could not. The bench said that there was no point in being lenient with her and fined her 20/- upon which she was led off to the cells crying and lamenting her fate.

In 1881 tenders were invited for general repairs and restoration which probably accounts for the red brick finish that we see today and the pub passed into the hands of Harriet's son John Woodland who ruled until his death in 1882 when it passed to his widow Mary Ann. She escaped a fine the following year when at a licensing hearing it was said that there had been complaints about the way in which she ran her house, which included encouraging rowdy lads there on a Sunday, luckily the summons was taken out under the wrong section of the act which enabled her to get away with a caution. In recent years the property traded as the Somerset House Hotel specialising in home-made pies but this seems to have failed and the business has now closed.

THE STAG INN
Corner of Lennox Street & Walpole Street, Melcombe Regis

THE FIRST DEFINITE mention of the Stag is in 1875 when 59-year-old former cooper and brewer's clerk for Devenish & Co. Walter Holt took on the licence. Along with his previous profession Holt had been known as

The Stag Inn 2025

a 'warming pan' a trusted servant of the brewery who occupied their newly built or empty properties while waiting for licence applications to go through or permanent tenants to be chosen. He had 'babysat' the White Hart for about three months, the Park Inn Tavern and others during his career while maintaining his family home in Hope Street. The practice was stopped when applicants for licences had to appear in person before the magistrates. At his age it was time to settle down with his second wife Eliza and run a pub of his own. The following year he had to show his property qualifications so that he could register to vote but for some reason he had put down 'Walpole Terrace' as his residence rather than Walpole Street and those who decide these matters took great glee striking him from the register only to have it reinstated on appeal.

1881 saw the case of the stolen manure when Holt took a Charles Jolliffe to court for having removed a pile of muck that he had bought from Sanger's Circus. Jolliffe claimed that he was the official scavenger for the town and it was his duty to remove all refuse. The magistrates told them to go away and sort it out between themselves as it was a civil matter and not a criminal one.

Walter Holt ran his pub until his retirement in 1894 at the age of 74, his long experience with Devenish standing him in good stead with little to trouble the courts or the press. Henry Foot took over and put himself up for election as one of the four Guardians of the Poor representing the Melcombe Regis North Ward. During 1915-19 Henry J Adams was landlord but went off to war leaving his wife Elizabeth in charge, all was restored in 1919 when he was discharged and the pair continued to run the pub into the 1930s and by the 1939 register it was being run by John and Gladys Trevor at 29 Lennox Street. It remained a shop until very recently when it was converted into a private house.

THE STAR AND GARTER HOTEL
Crescent Street, Melcombe Regis

THIS HOUSE WAS opened in 1864, or shortly before by Job Abbott originally from Fifehead Magdalen the son of an agricultural labourer. He shortly after applied for a spirits licence and was described by the bench as not an 'untried man' as he had previously conducted a licensed house in a very respectable manner and at the present time he was a government mail contractor. He says that he had given the house the name of the Star and Garter after that famed hotel in Richmond as he intended to conduct it in the same exemplary manner. In referring to the petition in favour of his licence which he had handed in the paucity of signatures was mentioned to which he

The Star & Garter (Weymouth Museum)

replied that it was the quality not quantity that mattered but the application was refused it being claimed, on the usual grounds, that there was no need for another licensed house in the area.

Abbott had moved on by 1870 to become a provision dealer in St Mary Street and Henry Foot was next in line, his licence application was more successful and he described his house as having eleven rooms plus stabling for four horses. He had accommodated some of the Yeomanry earlier in the year and they had been disappointed that he did not sell spirits. Foot was also a builder and gave up the pub in favour of James Broomfield in November of 1876 to pursue his former trade. One evening Irishman Mark Higgins turned up at the pub drunk and began singing and throwing his stick around. When told that singing was not allowed he threw a pint cup with all his might and broke two soda water glasses. In court Higgins remarked that if he had known he was going to be locked up he would have thrown another as he wouldn't be locked up for nothing.

In 1903 plans were submitted and approved by architects Crickmay & Son for altering and enlarging the premises and as can be seen today pub is a combination of two buildings from this time. In 1986 the Star was bought by the brewers Gibbs Mew and is now a chemist's shop.

THE STAR INN
Hartford Terrace, Park Street, Melcombe Regis

IN MARCH OF 1854 the *Southern Times* newspaper contained an advertisement for the sale of the freehold, by private contract, of the Star Inn with 80 years remaining on a 100-year lease granted by the Corporation of Weymouth. The premises were described as comprising on the first floor, 'a commodious bar, two parlours, a shop, (easily converted into and admirably adapted for the retail spirit trade), kitchen, scullery and outhouses. The upper floors comprise eight good sized bedrooms and a sitting room commanding extensive and uninterrupted views. A recreative ground is attached with a two stall stable, coach-house and capacious cellaring adjoining. The furniture and fixtures to be taken at the valuation. Satisfactory reasons can be given for the present owner parting with the property and business', continued the brief article. The tenant in question was John Elmes shown in the census of 1841 as a 34-year-old tailor with his wife Jane and three children. Three years later he is described as a beer seller and it was of course not unusual for publicans to have another trade while his wife ran the bar. He spoke in opposition to

126 The Star Inn in 2017

an application for a licence in Great George Street which he claimed would do him personally a great injury and would confer no public good. Fiercely protecting his own interests, he explained to the bench at the hearing in 1853 that he had built the house at a time when there was a pressing need for the sale of spirits but had been refused for 15 years despite a large and respectable body of persons supporting his application before it was granted. The magistrates stopped the hearing and the licence was refused.

The following year the Star was put up for sale by private contract with 80 years left on the lease and the Corporation still having the freehold. The new landlords were Mr Thomas Preedy and his wife Eliza. The Preedy family appear to have been involved in the John Bull coaching business from Weymouth to Frome and the death of a Thomas Preedy, proprietor is recorded at Hartford Terrace for August 1858 after which Eliza Preedy became landlady. The only other notable event is in 1861 when a stepson of Eliza successfully sued a customer to whom he had lent money betting on skittles and received a judgement of £6/18/- .

Richard Handy moved to the Fountain Hotel in 1874 to be replaced by George Wadsworth but the pub was back on the market again in 1878 now being let by brewers Devenish & Co with immediate possession and boasting an excellent 'bowling saloon' as well as being very close to the railway station. Builder William Lovelace took over and was there until 1898. Clifford Hardy a naval pensioner who must have had the longest tenure of all was first recorded in the 1901 census and still there in 1931 but had given way to William Dredge and his wife Beatrice by the register of 1939.

THE STEAM PACKET INN
St Thomas Street, South Quay, Melcombe Regis

THE STEAM PACKET Inn opened in around 1852 and in 1855 James Tizard who had been there for three years made his last of many applications to sell spirits. The house was described as 'respectably conducted' and the nearest alternative was the Turk's Head some distance away and due to increasing traffic from the Channel Island steamers his application was granted as it would 'raise the character of the house, take it away from the reputation of a low beerhouse and induce a better class of persons to frequent it.' A short while later the master of the *Emperor of Bridgewater* fell off a ladder while attempting to board the ship cracked his head on the side and died. When asked about his condition at the inquest he was said to be 'drinky' apparently a state between 'half drunk' and 'incapable of looking after one's self,' a state in which he could not maintain his equilibrium. The inquest was held at the Steam Packet and a verdict of accidental death was brought in, he left a wife and four children.

In January of 1875 the Steam Packet was put up for auction as part of a dispute over the property of the late John Tizard. What few details there are can be found under the Prince of Wales entry. In 1882 landlord John Connolly was charged with harbouring 10lb of foreign manufactured tobacco, he pleaded guilty and was fined £5 including costs. It seems that he left shortly after as Ambrose Charles Orchard a former a prison guard and licensee of the New Arrival moved in a few weeks later. While there are no complaints about the way in which he ran the house, neighbours complained about he and his wife 'cursing and swearing all night long' which he denied completely but was cautioned nonetheless. He wasn't there long but long enough to be one of those raided in the Great Short Measures Case of February 1884 in which a number of landlords were taken to court for having illegal measuring cups in their possession. (see Royal Oak entry for further details). The following July bailiffs were sent to evict Orchard and his family from the pub, details do not seem to have survived but one of his regular customers was fined 5/- for obstructing the bailiff as he tried to carry out his orders.

German citizen Joseph Duchscherer took over immediately, after

The Steam Packet Inn as Floods 2012

describing himself as a musician, putting many adverts in the local paper to recruit various instrumentalists to take part in the town band, he was there until 1896 when he left to run a grocery shop. Nicholas George Baggs and his wife Alice were next in line until he left in 1900 to join the Imperial Yeomanry at the age of 31 leaving Alice in control. He survived and they went on to run the St Peter's Finger Inn in Poole during 1906 at the age of 38. In March 1903 the pub was one of seven houses selected for permanent closure being described at the time as having six bedrooms for the use of the public, with three front entrances one of which led to the bar, one was unused and the other serviced the jug and a bottle. Robert William Austin who had been there for 18 months and thought it very hard that he should have his licence taken away as apart from other expenses the house had cost him £101 to enter. Earnest appeals were made on behalf of the Steam Packet and the other six, the Shipwrights Arms, the Three Tuns, the Yacht, the Porters' Arms, the Baltic and the Royal Hotel Tap that they should be allowed to trade until their licenses expired in October the bench agreed to grant the concession with the exception of the Yacht Inn and the Royal Hotel Tap which would be closed forthwith. A couple of years later tenders were invited for wiring the premises formerly known as the Steam Packet Inn for the purposes of 'electrical lighting' and it has since been run as a restaurant.

THE SUN / TIDES INN
King Street, Melcombe Regis

THOMAS NEWBOLT APPLIED for a spirits licence in August of 1859 but was rejected on the flimsy grounds that his paperwork was a few days late. James Hatton was also refused the following year as it was claimed that there were enough licensed houses in the area already. By around 1862 the Sun was being run by Joseph Keeley and family. Joseph was a native of the town who also worked as a blacksmith and had a workshop adjoining the pub with a large quantity of horsehair stored in the loft above. A bricklayer named William Legg was seen entering the shop with an empty bag and leaving it with a full one which, strangely enough, when examined was found to be full of horsehair which he claimed had come from somewhere else but unfortunately for him a quantity of tar had been spilt over it, Legg's hands were covered in it and his fate was sealed. In 1870 the application for a spirits licence was finally granted.

In September of 1876 Keeley was summoned by Thomas Kellaway of the Half Moon a few yards away for threatening behaviour. Unfortunately, they were persuaded to settle their differences in private 'to the disappointment of an expectant audience who had assembled in the court' and so we shall never know what it was about. Each party to pay their own costs. A couple of years later some Irish lads stationed at the Nothe decided to extend St Patrick's Day with a celebratory pub crawl part of which included knocking one of their number through the window of the Sun and striking Joe Keeley with a stick.

The whole event had at one point involved about 200 people. Some of the perpetrators were discovered back at the barracks and already in the guardroom for being drunk including a man named Smith who had broken the window estimated at 4/-. Despite claiming that it was all the fault of St Patrick's Day two of the revellers including Smith were given three months with hard labour and a number of others two months.

Aside from selling outside of permitted hours, selling drink to the already inebriated and serving short measures from illegal cups, another hazard that faced the landlord was possession of contraband tobacco, particularly a brand known as Sweet Cavendish or Negrohead. This contained an additive which was contrary to the Manufactured Tobacco Act of 1863. Among those arrested was the now widowed Ellen Keeley found in possession of three ounces and despite the inspectors pulling the house apart they could find no more. Son Thomas Keeley who now ran the house for his mother said that the tobacco was given to him to smoke to which the magistrate responded that he had no right to have it on him in the first place adding that in his position he could not be ignorant of the law but he was treated lightly with a 1/- fine. The full

The Sun Inn 2024

story is told in the Globe entry.

Landlady Ellen Keeley died in 1894 at the age of 76 and son Thomas took over officially, in 1903 it was agreed that the old pub be demolished and rebuilt to plans submitted by architects Crickmay & Son which is the building we see today. In 1914 the licence passed from the Keeley family to William Groves and his wife Mary who were to have their own problems. In November 1920 along with four other licensees, the Fountain Hotel, the Victoria, the Sailors' Return and the Clifton they were charged with 'selling whiskey at a price that exceeded the maximum' in breach of the incredibly complex, 'Spirits (Prices and Description Order) 1920' which set standardised prices and detailed descriptions for all spirits sold in the country, essentially controlling the market and ensuring consistency in quality and pricing across different brands, or that was the theory anyway. The Bench imposed a fine of £5 with costs which when all the cases were added together came to £120/2/-. The pub changed its name from the Sun Inn to the Tides Inn during 2014 and is now a noted a music venue.

THE SWAN INN
St Thomas Street, Melcombe Regis

The Swan in the 1930s

The revitalised Swan 2024

THE EARLY YEARS of the Swan are obscure. There was a Job Rupell and his wife Rachel who ran an unnamed pub on the site, 41 St George Street in the census of 1851 and a William Samways ten years later when the Swan is named for the first time. Number 41 is shown as 'uninhabited' in the 1871 census return and so possibly it was being refurbished or between tenants. William Norris, beerhouse keeper took over in about 1873 and applied in vain a for spirits licence with Henry Reynolds and George Heathorn of the Melcombe Regis Brewery next door, described as the owners. In the 1881 census Norris is shown as living at 41 aged 49 with his wife Jane and described as a brewers assistant, he has gone by 1888. It seems probable that the Swan was initially just a small pub attached to the brewery and at one point it was owned by the Grove Brewery before being taken over by Devenish. The last landlords were Bob and Mary Willis who were there for 19 years until its closure and demolition in 1975. The site was rebuilt as Centre News followed by John Menzies and then converted to a Wetherspoons pub which opened its doors in 1999.

THE TERMINUS HOTEL
Queen Street, Melcombe Regis

THE TERMINUS WAS first mentioned in 1859 and was one of the first buildings in Queen Street opening within two years of the railway station a matter of yards away as did several other houses in the area. George Gandy was granted a spirits licence in August which passed to Job Abbott in time for the 1861 census and then to livery stable keeper William Hardy snr. Hardy died in 1874 and the licence passed to Susan Barnes who had apparently been there since about 1862 but in what capacity is unclear.

In January of 1884 three cab drivers were summoned for assaulting Barnes. There seems to have been a large amount of animosity between the parties. Some of the witnesses insisted upon calling her 'Miss' Barnes and Mrs Jane Hardy refused to, 'stand by the side of such a thing' and her husband Richard Hardy got very excited and shouted, 'I will not allow my wife to stand by the side of a prostitute; my wife is respectable!' He kept disrupting the court and the mayor ordered him to be taken down to the cells until the case was over. In evidence Barnes said that she had closed up for the night when John Palmer, Frederick Northover, John Coleman and Jane Hardy pushed their way in demanding to be served. In the bar at the time was her daughter, also Susan, playing the piano, Albert Golding, school teacher, Charles Howard a parcels' clerk on the railway and a Miss Linter. Having gained entry a battle raged both inside and outside the pub with many of the windows being smashed. The defence case was that they had all been served after hours many, many times but were refused on this occasion, Barnes refused to serve Northover which began an argument that escalated. There was obviously far more to it than met the eye and just to add a bit of spice to the mix, Susan Barnes jnr's full name was, Susan Sarah *Hardy* Barnes and on her marriage certificate the father was given as William Hardy hotel proprietor... Northover and Palmer were fined 40/- each.

Barnes career did not end well, in October 1888 she was made bankrupt but did not attend her public examination which showed her to have liabilities of £180/9/3d and assets of £29/5/- the official receiver stated that in his opinion 'she has shown great indifference to the condition of her affairs'.

In 1899 landlord Henry Lang was convicted of permitting drunkenness on the premises and it seems that he had refused to evict an incredibly intoxicated man when asked to by a police constable, an unusual event as Lang had been there for over eight years without complaint, in fact the event was so unusual that the magistrates argued amongst themselves in open court

The Terminus as the Giant Pot

before the mayor inflicted the heavy fine of £5 plus costs. In 1902 it was the turn of Mrs Martha Lang to appear in court but this time as a witness. Mr and Mrs Bridle were arrested for keeping a disorderly house or brothel at the back of the Terminus in Queen's Court with soldiers, sailors and civilians coming and going at all times of the night putting off trade for both Mrs Lang and a Mr Tell who run a restaurant next door. The couple received three months imprisonment upon conviction. The next licensee, Thomas Field gave evidence in support of an application to renew his licence in 1907 explaining that he had been a tenant for the past two years and that the house was almost entirely dependent upon railway people except when the fleet was in when there was a very large increase. There were no refreshment rooms at the station and so he always kept sandwiches, bread and cheese etc ready and was doing a large trade every day. From April 1905 to April 1906 takings had reached £967 and the following year £1,098. During 1906 191 barrels of beer were sold representing

55,152 pints and 194 gallons of spirits representing 29,568 three pennyworths and by estimation the number of customers during that period was 84,720. Henry Lang the previous landlord had been there for 14 years and had only given up owing to poor health. The property was owned by a Mrs Norton and let to Devenish & Co and despite arguments put forward for its closure, the magistrates agreed unanimously that the licence should be renewed. In August of 1919 the Terminus was one of several Devenish pubs who had their husbands return to them after being away on active service. In recent times the pub had been subject to the indignity of being called, 'The Giant Pot' followed by the Handmade Pie and Ale House. At the time of writing it is closed and awaiting its next adventure.

THE THREE TUNS PUBLIC HOUSE
Maiden Street, Melcombe Regis

THE THREE TUNS is one of the town's older houses, possibly going back to the 1730s but the first definite mention is from Pigot's Directory of 1823 when it is named and shown as on the east side of Maiden Street at the junction of Governor's Lane and in the occupation of Joseph Pitman who played host to the annual dinners of the Poor Man's Friendly Society from at least 1826. In 1830 the land tax returns show a William Pitman as the occupier and William Bower as the owner. Bower died in 1829 and his estate was put up for auction along with a number of other properties including his Fordington Brewery in Dorchester, the details of this transaction are recorded in the entry for the Bear. Joseph died of a brain fever in 1837 having moved to run the Black Swan in Frome, sometime previously he was 43 and left a widow and six children.

From the census of 1841 Robert and Honor Buckland had taken over but both died very young, Honor in 1842 at the age of 26 and Robert in 1846 aged 34. John and Harriet Mitchell had the house in the 1851 census with two children and 13 lodgers on the night including five travelling German musicians. In 1852 Harriet found herself in possession of a number of boxes left behind by a John Gould who had been staying there for some weeks 'with a woman who passed as his wife' the couple left 'in her debt' but nothing was said about the boxes being left in pledge. Shortly after, a detective named Edward Langley arrived enquiring after the boxes which when opened were found to contain a large quantity of silk and clothing stolen from Henry Case who kept a shop at Milborne Styleham and worth over £100. There had been a number

The former Three Tuns Inn

of people involved in the robbery who also faced other charges of a similar nature involving a shop in Maiden Newton. All were convicted; two received 14 years transportation, three, seven years and two others six months imprisonment with hard labour. The Mitchells held the pub until about 1872 surviving the deaths of John and Harriet before passing briefly on to their daughter Susan, a dressmaker, in 1871.

Richard William Morgan Tredrea aged 44 son of a miner from Ludgvan in Cornwall, was landlord by 1879 and the census of 1881 shows the house containing nine lodgers and a servant including two opticians. His wife Sarah had died in October of 1880 and the house was put up for rent by owners Devenish. Previously, in the 1861 census Tredrea is shown as a herbalist with the family lodging at the Portland Arms before moving to the Albion beer house in Cheap Street, Frome. By 1891 he had remarried and resumed his career as a herbalist in Sturminster.

In March of 1903 Weymouth magistrates decided to close down seven public houses in the town and the Three Tuns was one of them, Earnest appeals were made on behalf of the pub and the other six, the Shipwrights Arms, the Yacht, the Steam Packet Inn, the Porters' Arms, the Baltic and the Royal Hotel Tap that they should be allowed to trade until their licenses expired in October, the bench agreed to grant the concession with the exception of the Yacht Inn and the Royal Hotel Tap which would be closed immediately. The pub closed in October of that year when the licence expired. Its final description was, 'stabling for eight horses and eight bedrooms for the public, five on the ground floor and upstairs a sitting room and eleven bedrooms, he paid £4 a year in rent but could not say what the takings were, husband, wife and two children reside on the premises. Landlord John Alford did not follow any other occupation and had been in the house for 13½ years without a complaint.

THE TIVOLI GARDENS INN
Franchise Street, Weymouth

THE TIVOLI FIRST appears in the record in the summer of 1860 when an application for a spirits licence is made by James Kirby owner occupier of what was described as a most delightful spot near the barracks with accommodation which included a large number of beds but the application was refused. Kirby was a naval pensioner from Sussex aged 41 who lived with his wife Cecilia. When applying for a licence again in 1862 Kirby said that he intended to lay out some ground for refreshment gardens as there was a 'great dearth of amusements for people' and the licence was necessary due to the large number of people that came here. The opposition ridiculed the idea saying that even if gardens were laid out it would be 'impossible for a stranger to find his way thither.' In refusing the application it was said that Kirby was not 'a man of straw' but had a great stake in the business which would be respectably conducted but it was believed that he would never see a return on his money so little demand would there be for spirituous liquors. He let himself down a bit in 1866 when he was summoned for being drunk and riotous in High Street, shaking his fist in a constables face, he was fined 10/-plus costs. Kirby owned and ran the house himself until 1872 when he installed George Ryall a 49-year-old engine driver at the brewery and Jane his wife for ten years until he regained his licence and moved back in himself. He died in 1886 when he collapsed in his kitchen of a heart attack at the age of 67.

Irishman Thomas Brennan took over next and in 1896 his careless actions lead to an act of heroism. Having taken a party of sailors and others for a drive out of town in a landau he stopped at the Bridge Inn for refreshments leaving the horse unattended. The animal got spooked by something and tore off down the Dorchester Road towards the town at great speed dragging the carriage behind it 'whilst the horse was dashing at a full gallop past the Gloucester Hotel gunner Lazenvenry succeeded in jumping onto the step of the carriage and climbing over the hood on to the drivers box. He then gripped the reins and applied the brake bringing the runaway to a standstill near Chesterfield Place'. The soldier was loudly cheered and the sum of 25/- was collected for

The Tivoli Gardens Inn 2025

him and his exceptional bravery which involved a very serious threat to his life. Brennan was also careless in the way he ran the pub it seems, renewal of his licence being held over as a 'salutary lesson' during 1897 because of improper conduct, but worse was to come. In May of 1899 he was summoned for being found drunk in his own house during licensed hours which had apparently happened on numerous occasions but this time he was found totally incapable and asleep on the staircase. The police were instructed to visit the house every day and he was fined 10/- plus costs totalling £1/4/- or 14 days imprisonment and as he did not have sufficient money he was, 'removed below' with a warning that if this happened again he would lose his licence.

Surprisingly, Brennan was still there at 1907 but was found drunk on the premises once more when the magistrates carried out a tour of inspection to examine the condition of the lavatories and facilities. After a long trial with several witnesses he was fined £2/3/- and at a later licensing hearing he lost his licence.

In March 1910 the magistrates did their best to close the Tivoli down it having been referred for closure as unnecessary as there were eight fully licensed houses within 315 yards. It was described as the last house in a row of cottages in Franchise Street, a brick building with a cemented front and slate roof, eight rooms and two bars with jug and bottle, one sitting room, one kitchen and a washhouse. The business turnover was about £66 per month with the ground floor containing a saloon bar, public bar and a back entrance onto Trinity Terrace. In defence of its retention it was described as one of the cleanest houses in Weymouth and the new landlord, George Harvell had been in the employ of Messrs' Groves for 23 years and had been there for three years. The bench must have been satisfied as the Tivoli was allowed to remain open which it continued to do until it was finally closed in the 1960s.

THE TURK'S HEAD INN
East Street, Melcombe Regis

THE TURK'S HEAD is one of the town's oldest pubs, mentioned briefly in the 1760s as being run by a T Scriven in East Street 'with garden through to the sands '. In 1822 'the most unfortunate Mrs Hardy of the Turk's Head died at the age of 64 after a painful illness', and when the post-mortem was carried out 'a large tubercular mass of a flashy consistence and a globular form was found adhering to part of the bowel which was found to weigh 8lb and measure 30 inches in circumference. Such a foreign mass has never been known to exist in the human frame in the practice of the oldest surgeon, or is even mentioned in the earliest medical records'. In March of 1828 sealed tenders were invited for the pub which was held on a lease for a term of 99 years along with a large dwellinghouse attached 'an individual would find ample room for the erection of a brewery and thereby render the profits of the business more lucrative'. Presumably that was unsuccessful as the same properties were advertised to be sold by public auction on 18 June. There is no record of who bought it but in 1839 it was offered for sale once more this time with a six – stalled stable, coach house, yard, and offices for the reminder of a term of 21 years.

In the census of 1841 the occupier is Levi Honeyborne aged 45, his wife Ann, and seven children who ran the property very successfully. A Mr Buckland had a stroke of luck in 1847 while working away behind the bar. James Lydford came in, a notorious burglar and criminal who is said to have terrified the area the previous winter. He was on the run having escaped from custody and on his way to the Channel Islands when the boat sprang a leak and had to return to Weymouth. Foolishly entering the pub he was recognised by Buckland who had grown up near him and knew him well. A policeman was summoned and Lydford recaptured. 'the £20 reward offered for his apprehension is very likely

The Turk's Head 2024

to be awarded to Buckland'.

The licence passed to William Pride in about 1859, an enthusiastic member of the 'Ancient Order of Foresters' he formed the court 'Sailor's Hope' and organised celebratory dinners and activities. He had moved on by 1867 when owners Eldridge Mason and Co. put the pub up for rent once more and it was taken by former agricultural labourer Henry Strange from Stratton in Dorset who had left to take over the Nothe Tavern by 1881.

In June of 1872 a 40-year-old tinker named Thomas Jennings fell in with some old friends determined upon a serious drinking session. After consuming a large amount of beer, he ordered a half pint of gin which he seems to have knocked straight back without the knowledge of his friends before ordering another doing the same with that claiming that he could drink all the gin in the house – which he had. Unsurprisingly, within five minutes he was lying on the floor unconscious and despite being taken out to the yard and laid on some straw he soon died. The landlord Edmund James was called to account but had only been there for a month having never run a public house before and it seems that he was very soon out of this one as Eldridge Pope & Co advertised it for rent within weeks.

Thomas Rendall an ex Post Office employee with a pension of £20 a year was granted a licence in 1882 but the house was ordered to be kept under strict supervision as its reputation was not good. A couple of others held the licence briefly until 1889 when George and Annie Chalker were installed until 1905 when the licence was taken by George Henry Taylor a first class petty officer in the Navy.

The Hanks family were there by 1915 and managed to survive an attempt to close the pub down by the local temperance movement fronted by a Baptist minister's wife. The landlady at the time was Helen Hanks who had been there for 14 years and had sleeping accommodation for 30 guests. A couple of witnesses told of the medicinal virtues of its stout and said it was regarded as a convalescent home at which point the licence was reviewed. The Hanks family were still listed as licensees in 1931 and in residence during the 1939 register.

THE UNION ARMS INN
St Leonards Road Wyke Regis, Weymouth

IN 1841 A small terraced house in Union Place in the Chapelhay District was home to John Williams a 50 year old shoemaker and his wife Mary, and by the census of 1861 the pair had been there for at least 20 years and his occupation is now shown as a victualler and publican. He died in 1866 followed by Mary in 1870 paving the way for John Tomkins who seems to have had what could be described as a varied career. The census of 1851 shows him aged 38 and living just down the road at 18 Union Place working as a journeyman butcher, ten years on he is sharing number 18 with a carpenter and described as labourer which rather looks as though things didn't go too well in the butchery trade. By 1871 he has moved into no.15 as a 'brewer's labourer' presumably running the pub with his wife Mary Ann. Another ten years, another census and he is now 68 a publican and cow keeper before breathing his last in August 1891 at the age of 78 passing the licence to his daughter Alice.

In 1901 William Thorne along with landlords Devenish & Co. sought

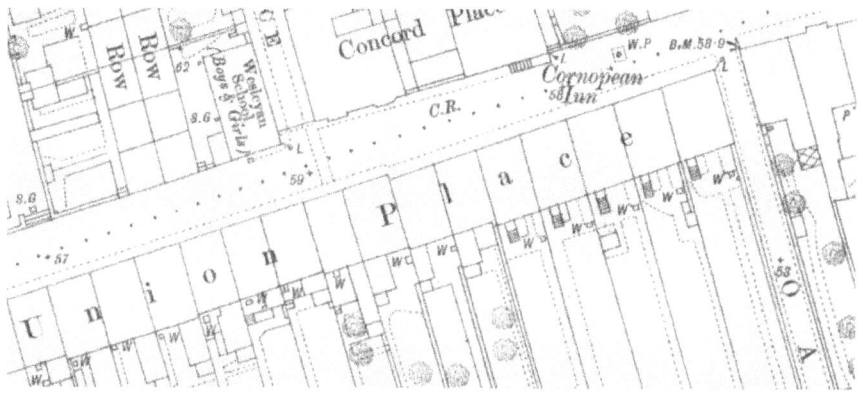

Union Place 1864

permission to close and rebuild the pub a few doors down at the end of the same terrace onto a corner plot now renamed as 33/34 St Leonard's Road. In a spirits application attached to the request they explain that 'At present the pub is a small beer house but if the application were granted £1,000 would be expended fitting out the new premises. The bench refused the application for the corner site but intimated that they would be prepared to consider a reconstruction of the present building.

At a licensing hearing in March 1908 the Union Arms was one of four licensed houses objected to by the police as they believed that there were too many in the area. An architect from Dorchester described the inn as 'a brick and slate building, part of a row of cottages in a narrow road never built for its purpose but converted afterwards into a public house'. The report to the magistrates continued that, 'It was a small beer house carried on in what might be called a 5/- a week cottage and owned by Devenish who had at least 38 licensed houses in Weymouth at that time. The Union had no accommodation for lodgers and was simply a beer shop, the tenant, William Styles paid £26 rent for the house and some adjoining cottages with a business turnover of £32 per month. It contained eleven rooms in total, two downstairs and two upstairs, the licensed part consisted of one bar, one scullery, one front room which was used as a club room, and four bedrooms, three being used for the landlord his wife and children leaving one spare room. William Styles had held the licence for six years since May 9 1902 paying rent quarterly and claimed to be making a good living on a three-monthly tenancy, the house had been licensed for over 50 years without any complaint. The principal portion of his trade was the jug and bottle and he provided bread and biscuits, mutton chops, steaks, chips or anything that might be required. They had a club with a membership of 50-60 people. It was admitted that the area was catered for by the nearby Cornopean, a fully licensed house only 48 paces away and belonging to the same firm, the General Gordon Hotel was 87 paces away and the Albion Inn was also nearby. The police considered that these three houses were sufficient for the area and 'far superior in construction and design'.

Defending his pub, Styles stated that he was giving a choice of beers, other local pubs were supplied by Eldridge Pope or Groves. He was asked if the increase in trade at the house meant that the working classes were spending more money on drink than food and clothing to which he replied that the more money they earned the more could be spent on all three adding that the population is increasing in the neighbourhood, 66 new houses being built since 1901. Witnesses described the house as a quiet respectable place and a great convenience locally. The magistrates agreed to renew the licence for another year after which, 'the licensing atmosphere in the country would be more settled' and adjourned for lunch. It wasn't long before this poor little beer shop was picked on again in March of 1910 when it was pointed out once more that there were seven other houses within 300 yards. In defence it was said that the Union was a place to go when the Cornopean or the Dock became too crowded or noisy. One problem facing those in favour of its closure was that they would be liable to a pay out from the Licensing Compensation Authority at Dorchester and they only had about £3,000 most of which was already earmarked for the closure of four pubs in the town and this house would be entitled to about £1,000, and it was felt that the authorities would not deal with it. It was possibly this argument which swayed the bench, ever keen to deny a licence or close a pub, which persuaded them to let it stand but they insisted upon some structural alterations like blocking up one of the doorways. In August of 1919 the Union Arms was one of several Devenish pubs who had their landlords returned to them after being away on active service. The Union carried on without any further attempts at its closer until it was bombed out of existence during the war and replaced by flats.

THE VICTORIA AND GREAT WESTERN HOTEL
Augusta Place, The Esplanade, Melcombe Regis

IN MAY OF 1812 Samuel Scriven, 'impressed with gratitude for the very liberal support with which he has been honoured in past seasons, begs leave to return his sincere thanks for the same, and has spared no expense in fitting up his house which is now ready for their reception'. This short notice is headed 'Royal Boarding and Lodging House', Esplanade, Weymouth and the establishment was perhaps to have more variations on its name than many others in the town. On the anniversary of Waterloo in 1816 Mr Scriven of the Hotel and Navy Tavern provided a cold supper for up to 80 of the 23rd Light Dragoons. By 1817 it had become Scriven's Hotel and on the occasion of the King's birthday a new mail coach running between Weymouth and Dorchester, carrying mail from London was initiated.

In May of 1820 Daniel Luce took over Scriven's Boarding House at Augusta Place and in doing so thanked the public for their support during his long residence at the King's Head and 'respectfully acquaints them' that he has taken and fitted up what is now Luce's Hotel in a 'superior style.' Scriven himself praises Luce, recommending a continuance of the favours of commercial gentlemen and is now retiring. Before Luce left his old pub he had to organise an auction of all his furniture and fittings as Scriven was taking nothing with him and he was obliged to take the contents with the building. Luce died very shortly after and the business was taken over by his wife Jane who in August of 1824 announced that she had added a new suite of spacious drawing rooms with large and airy bedrooms at great expense. She also involved herself in a mail coach running to Bristol under the name of 'Luce, Pickwick & Co' the Pickwick name was adopted by Dickens for his novel *The Pickwick Papers* of 1836. Jane Luce died in 1840 and the hotel passed to her son Thomas Dorney Luce at the tender age of 25 who had presumably picked up the basics of running a hotel since he could walk and also had the assistance of his aunt Harriet throughout his career.

Luce decided to lease out the hotel in April of 1848 now renamed the 'Royal Victoria and Yacht Club Hotel (Luce's)' and its undoubted charms are listed as, 'Coffee and commercial rooms, seven sitting rooms fronting the sea,

The Victoria Hotel 2025

a spacious assembly room, upwards of 40 bedrooms, coach and other offices, extensive cellarage and the kitchen and domestic offices which cannot be excelled, the whole in the most substantial a state of repair'. Thomas Luce now aged 38, took over the Royal Hotel further along the Esplanade.

Joseph Drew became proprietor in 1854 arguably one of the most important men in the town at the time not least for being the founder and editor of the local newspaper *Southern Times* in 1850 which he edited until 1862. By 1857 he had established a refreshment room and art gallery at the hotel to display his valuable collection of paintings. Drew was also very active in local affairs being both a town councillor in the Conservative interest and a JP; he had the dubious honour of being foreman of the jury when the inquest on the steamship *Great Eastern* whose boiler room blew up in September 1859 with the loss of five crewmen and the bodies of the dead were exhibited at the King's Head. He died in 1883.

A new landlord means a new name and when Mrs Sarah Carter took over the licence in August of 1857 it became the New Victoria Hotel and then the Victoria and Great Western Hotel when taken over by Edwin Dunn the son of a stonemason who also acted as an agent for the Great Western Railway during the 1860s. He ran the hotel as Dunn & Co from about 1861 paying an annual rent of £300 to the Scriven family who had retained the freehold. He had a guest calling himself Edward Cargill Taylor who stayed for about three weeks running up a bill of £21 and when it came to paying suggested that he make out a cheque for £30 and be given the change in cash. Mr Dunn, not quite seeing the advantage of this, contacted the bank to discover that they are never heard of Mr Taylor. He was arrested but said that he had no intention of committing fraud and surprisingly the magistrates agreed and he was released. 'For the benefit of licensed victuallers and others, we may state that the 'gentleman' in question is a short thick set man with a beard and moustache; but it is probable that when next seen these may have taken leave of his visage.' There was more trouble in August of 1867 when a couple of well to do gentlemen stayed the night after attending the races followed by a session on the roulette wheel before retiring to bed at about 3 am. When they woke next morning they found their valuables, watches, chains etc had gone from the room and instituted a civil case against Dunn for the loss of the property. Apparently, the landlord was responsible for any loss of items by residents unless their negligence could be proven, which in this case it was as they admitted not locking the door and reassuring Dunn that it was not his fault when they left. The jury found in Dunn's favour.

There was an interesting civil case in March 1874 when a jury were empanelled to assess the amount of damages due to a Mr George Senior funeral director who had a glass thrown in his face by Mr Hibbs a house decorator after the Weymouth races. An argument broke out to do with the election and various amounts of money which resulted in Hibbs throwing the glass which cut Senior's face and inflicted serious injuries which he claimed prevented him from attending to his business for some three weeks. The criminal case had been settled sometime before with Hibbs admitting the offence. In this case Hibb's barrister went to great lengths to prove that Senior was drunk and therefore partly responsible, he also got Senior to admit that the initial cause of the argument was him hiding a glass of whiskey belonging to one of the party as a joke which backfired and soon started a big row with the barmaid and Dunn the landlord joining in. Legal argument took up two full pages of the newspaper but in the end it took the jury only seven minutes to award damages of just £5 presumably concluding that Senior must take some responsibility for the events.

In October of 1879 Dunn auctioned off all the old furniture and effects from the hotel having just had the house refurbished. This did not seem to be going to well with items being sold very cheaply and so Mrs Dunn, who apparently ran the business side of things, engaged a friend as a 'puffer', someone who takes part in the auction to inflate the prices but without intending to purchase anything, but this didn't go very well either as the pair ended up buying some of their own lots and getting into trouble with the auctioneer.

The Victoria itself was advertised for sale in June of 1881 described as having a 'frontage towards the Esplanade of nearly 53 feet and a depth (extending to New Street) of 106 feet or thereabouts. It has a portico over the entrance, and contains two coffee rooms, office, large commercial room, five private sitting rooms, noble dining or assembly room, luxurious fitted billiard saloon, capital bar, 41 bed and dressing rooms, four storerooms four WCs linen room, capital kitchen, still rooms, larder, luggage room, smoking room and bar, first-rate wine cellar with 46 bins, beer seller, bottle rooms, ice house etc etc. The southern portion of the hotel (comprising a frontage of about 28 feet) is held for the reminder of a term of 1,000 years granted in 1740 under an annual ground rent of £42. Dunn, by now in his mid 50s, had moved to the Fountain once the dust had settled in 1883 after a long residence and possibly he did not like the new terms and conditions which may have applied after the sale. He died at the Fountain in 1896.

Local architects Crickmay & Son were employed to organise the works and repairs to be carried out under the new landlord Charles John Dring from Oxfordshire. Dring was a member of the Royal College of Veterinary Surgeons who in a rather surprising career move had been running the Cutter since 1875 before moving to the Victoria ten years later. During 1891 his guests included a missionary to China and his family, a brass founder and a number of commercial travellers. Dring was also a prime mover in the establishment of the Weymouth and Melcombe Regis Steam Laundry Works Company Limited, obviously a man of many talents he died at the hotel in 1908. Army pensioner Walter George Paul was licensee after Dring and was summoned to appear before the magistrates along with the licensees of the Fountain Hotel, the Sun, the Sailors' Return and the Clifton in November of 1920 for overcharging on beer and spirits. In this case Paul was accused of selling bottles of Bass and Guinness at 1/- when the correct price was 8½d. In his defence he claimed that 1/- was the correct price when served in the coffee room rather than the bar. The magistrates were far from convinced and Paul was fined what seems like an incredible amount of £15 for each item – £60 in total. He continued at the hotel until at least 1939 without further incident. During the 1960s it was renamed the Fairhaven Hotel and then the New Vic. At the time of writing it is on the market awaiting extensive renovation.

THE VICTORIA TAP
New Street, Melcombe Regis

B EHIND EVERY GREAT hotel there was often a small public house known as a 'tap' where its employees and the ordinary working man could go for a pint and a smoke with his mates without disturbing the better class of customer booking rooms and going through the front entrance and so it was for the Victoria Hotel. Its date of opening is not known but a James Chalker is recorded as landlord at the Hotel Tap in 1823 and a John Arburry in 1830.

We are on firmer ground of course with the 1841 census when 38-year-

A Quiet Pint

old James Taylor, his wife Charlotte and family ran the pub until 1845 when they moved out in favour of Kingman Cook another coachman who seemed to be in regular dispute with his fellow drivers, at one point being summoned for threatening to kill one of them and although that case was dismissed he was also charged with exceeding the number of journeys he was allowed to make according to his licence. He retired from the cab trade and he and his wife Mary moved to the Milton Arms in 1864. William and Susan King are shown as publicans at 3 New Street in the census of 1871 but no mention has been found of it after that.

THE WATERLOO STORES
William Street, Melcombe Regis

One of the newer pubs in the area and part of the Park Estate development which needs some explanation. It sits on a very large parcel of land that was once an area of marshland fronting the Backwater which was gradually reclaimed piecemeal from 1834 with the original idea of laying out 50 acres of parkland, to be called the Royal Victoria Park. However, land being very valuable this public amenity never materialised. It became part of a financial scandal when some of the towns civic leaders conspired to obtain the land at a ridiculously low price but were exposed to public scrutiny and after much wrangling the land was sold for £5,000 and part of it was purchased by the Great Western and London Railway company and the South Western Railway Company for the construction of Weymouth railway station which was completed in 1857. The following year the reminder was purchased by the Conservative Land Association for housing, the first property being completed in 1861 with many of its streets being named after Tory politicians of the time. Building was at first piecemeal due to problems with drainage and the laying out of roads. An average plot cost about £60 with a build estimate of £160 per property.

The Waterloo Pub 2018

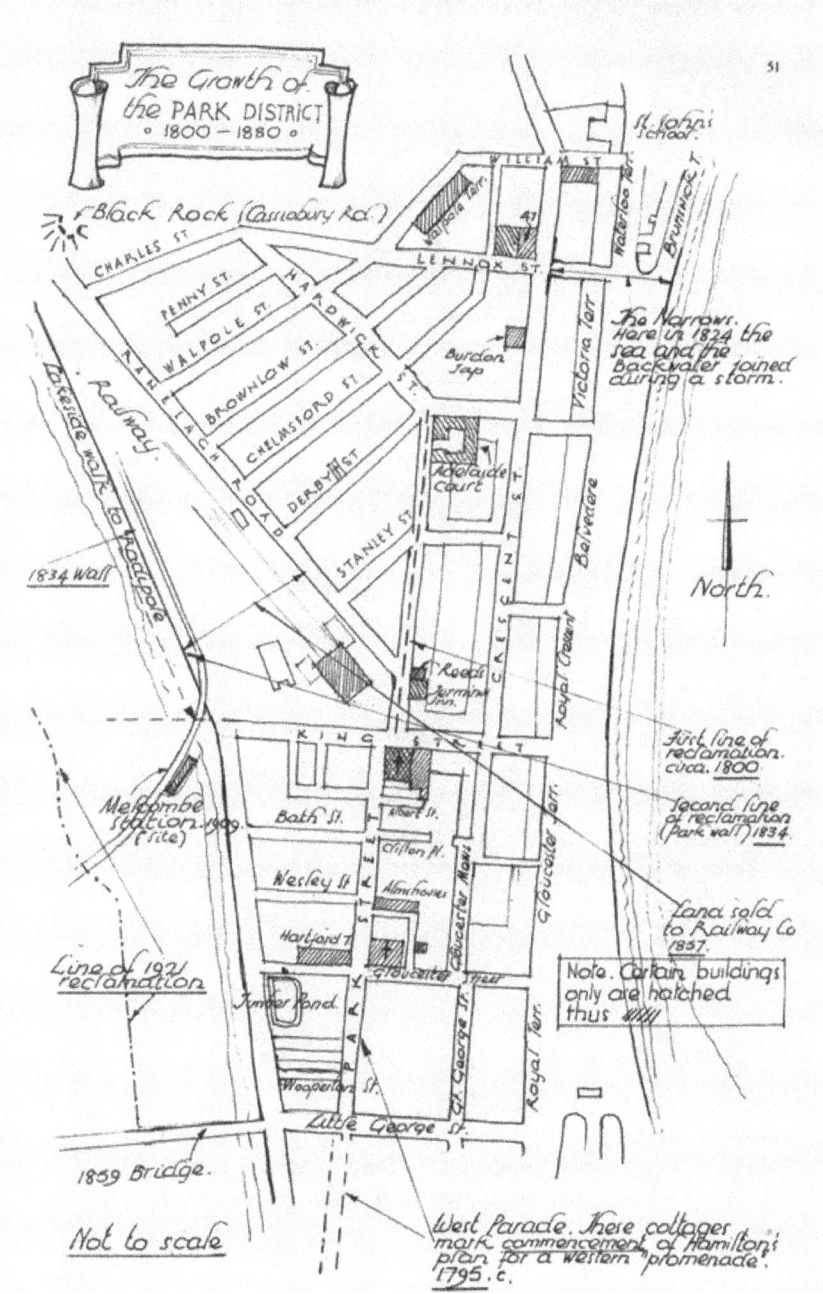

Eric Ricketts plan of the Park District

Plots were set aside for the erection of five public houses the Park Estate Inn c1874 Ranelagh Hotel c1872, Brownlow Tavern c1884, Chelmsford House c.1881 and of course the Waterloo Stores, as it was first known, built by James Penny of Belvedere and completed by 1870. In his application for a spirits licence he describes it as commodious and convenient with six bedrooms above and on the ground floor a store, kitchen and sitting room, with an underground cellar. The licence was granted on the condition that he close the shop section which was agreed and so the Waterloo pub was born, (but the old name stuck).

In 1876 a battalion of 'Dorset Volunteers' set up their summer camp in tents at Lodmoor about a mile and a half from Weymouth town and Waterloo landlord George Smith was in charge of the canteen, a task which he carried out superbly. The following year an advertisement appeared in the local paper 'To be Let. A large marquee and three smaller ones at a moderate charge apply to Mr Smith at the Waterloo'. The licence passed from George Smith to Sidney Tivitoe Stockting, a stone mason, who ran the place in November of 1880 until his death in 1908 when it was taken over by his son Herbert who was there until the 1930s. Today the recently refurbished pub is a much loved local with a strong accent on football.

THE WELCOME HOME
St Nicholas Street, Melcombe Regis

IN THE CENSUS of 1851 James Flower, a married brewer aged 65 is shown living at 69 St Nicolas Street but there is no mention of a public house at this stage. Flower had been in partnership with William Davies as brewers but this had been dissolved in 1813. Flower became an important person in the history of the town having been mayor during the 1830s as well as an alderman and businessman, he died in 1868 at the age of 85. In September 1858 he appeared in person to apply for a spirits licence for his pub the Welcome Home then mentioned by name for the first time saying that his house had dined 20 people and stabled 24 horses and could easily do the same again. His application was granted. The building stretched from St Nicholas Street right the way through to St Thomas Street and consisted of a dwelling house and garden with the fully licensed inn at the St Nicholas Street end. By the census returns of 1861 Flower 75 and his wife Mary 76 are retired and living at the St Thomas Street house now looking rather cramped, at the other end the pub was being run by whitesmith John Gillingham, his wife Eliza and their 18-year-old daughter Sarah. A few years earlier in 1856 the family had suffered a tragic accident when living in Commercial Road by the Backwater. John, Siri Eliza and 12-year-old Sarah had taken a boat probably to do some duck shooting as John

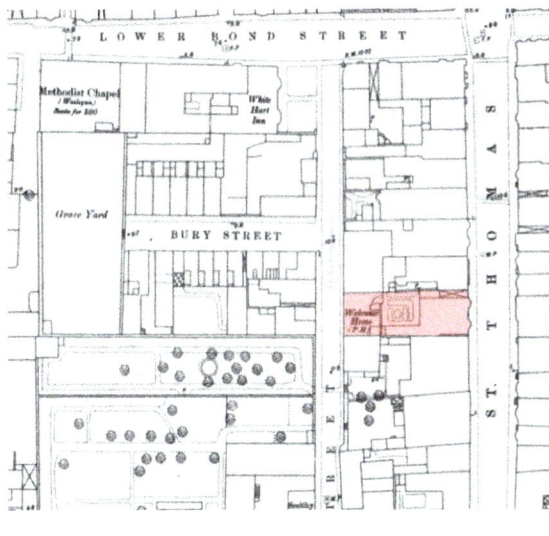
The Welcome Home 1864 O/S Map

had his loaded fowling piece with him. Somehow Sarah's dress caught the gun and discharged its contents into her left shoulder putting her life in imminent danger. She was taken to the infirmary and her arm amputated close to the body with 80 pieces of shot being removed from her side. Her life was despaired of but she survived it went on to marry and produce 13 children.

In July of 1873 the Welcome Home was sold at auction along with the attached residential property in St Thomas Street formerly occupied by widow Flower. The pub half with garden was let to John Groves of the brewing family as a yearly tenant held on a 500-year lease with an annual rent of £13. The pub was up for auction once more in 1881 along with the adjoining house but this was the last time. One of those deals had been struck whereby if the owner agreed to close one of his houses the licence can be transferred to a different one in the same area presumably newer, better or bigger, on this occasion the building was still under construction but nonetheless the Welcome Home was closed in favour of the soon-to-be Brownlow Tavern in Ranelagh Road.

THE WELLINGTON ARMS
St Alban Street. (Petticoat Lane before 1872)

THE WELLINGTON FIRST appeared in about 1850 when it was managed by the brewers which eventually became Eldridge Pope & Co. The first recorded landlord was Robert Foot aged 26 and his wife Selina. The street was known as Petticoat Lane until 1872 when its name was changed to St Alban's Street in honour of The Duke of St Albans. The next landlord, John Drew Philips had the good fortune to be granted a spirits licence in 1857 and was there until his death in 1869 when it passed to his wife Charlotte. Eldridge Pope & Co purchased the freehold in 1879 and installed Londoner Alfred

Seeley and his wife Mary. They were one of the victims of Charles Lambourne the 'sham directory canvasser' who travelled around asking for subscriptions to a new business directory that he was about to publish and Seeley handed over 5/- for an advertisement which of course never appeared. The case appears in more detail in the Clifton entry. Mrs Mary Seeley was seriously assaulted in August 1891 when a 'stranger' tried to intimidate everyone who entered the pub into buying him a beer and when she asked him to go he smacked her in the face giving her a black eye. In court he claimed to be as innocent as a lamb who couldn't remember a thing for which he was awarded 14 days hard labour. The Selleys' were there until 1896 when he went bankrupt with debts of £104/16/10d and the family left the pub to run a lodging house. The Wellington seems to have been a very quiet friendly local with no real trouble having been reported although there was a brief flurry of excitement in October 1922 when the pub was raided and landlord Robert Loveridge was charged with 'unlawfully using his licensed premises in contravention of the Betting Act 1853'. The incident is perhaps best explained by the officer himself,

'PC Head stated that acting on instructions he concealed himself with other constables and kept observation on the Wellington Arms... and gave details of certain persons who entered and left the bottle and a jug department

The Wellington Arms in 2024

including a telegraph boy, newspaper boys, and a postman, 'On one occasion I saw a person hand Loveridge, the proprietor, a slip of paper'. On the next day the witness kept a similar observation and saw a postman hand a slip of paper to someone who counted several pieces of paper which were given to a man in a trilby hat, he also received pieces of paper from Mrs Loveridge.'

Pieces of paper, it would seem, were seen flying about all over the place as was the writing of surreptitious notes in pocketbooks. On the day of the raid pieces of paper with notes were found in a drawer with the names of horses on and a number of racing annuals were also discovered. In his defence Loveridge said that he had held the licence of the Wellington for 16 years and had a clean sheet, he could not help people putting papers in an envelope in his bar and then taking them down to the post office, but to his knowledge no betting occurred on his premises. Evidence was strong enough to convict and Loveridge was fined £10 and seems to have left the pub shortly after.

A visitor during 2009 describes the premises,

> The interior had an open plan L shaped main room (there was a dining room off the corridor leading to the toilets. The pub is small and there are a few tables in what was the dart area (the board is still there). Decor is cream and wood panel with a brick fireplace and there were lots of old photos, watercolours, model ships and other curios like a sewing machine dotted about. The only modern touch was a few twigs with lights on. The food was fine the service friendly but the clientele few. Background music was of a decent level and there was a TV which had sport on.

In 2018 there was a big party to celebrate Martin and Christine Whitehorn having run the pub for 21 years

THE WEYMOUTH ARMS
High Street, Weymouth

THE WEYMOUTH ARMS is believed to have been built in the 1760s as a residential property and converted to a pub certainly by 1852 and probably much earlier when there arose a great dispute between the Prankard family, then running the Weymouth, and the Bonellas' who ran the rival Freemasons Arms across the road. These events are gone into in greater detail in the Freemasons entry. In March 1854 the Weymouth is offered for sale as 'all that commodious and substantially built Messuage or Dwelling House with

The Weymouth Arms 1961 (Weymouth Museum)

spacious stores and workshops, walled garden and premises behind the same situate in High Street Weymouth there in the occupation of Mr John Prankard and known by the name or sign of 'The Weymouth Arms' held on a lease for a term of 1,000 years of which 906 are unexpired at the annual rent of 1/-' .John's parents, John snr. a joiner, and Rebecca are shown as living in the house with sons Samuel 13 and John 20 in the 1841 census and again in 1851 but no pub is mentioned.

There was a very interesting case in October of 1870 when landlady Martha Bailey was summoned for acting as a procuress. 19-year-old Jane Willis gave evidence to say that she came to Weymouth looking for a job as a servant in June and met Mrs Bailey who offered her employment saying that she could 'earn' if she liked as a great many men came to the house. She would pay Bailey 1/6d per week and half of what she got while 'upstairs'. Willis did not object to this arrangement but left because Mrs Bailey said she was not making enough money and she was not paid a wage. Mary Rochett gave evidence to say that she was a general servant for Mrs Bailey but there was no work to do as she and her daughter did it all. Rochett claimed to have paid Bailey 20/-30/- per week as a share of the money she earned upstairs, she and another girl, Emma King left together. Emma had been made pregnant by a soldier who then deserted her before she came to Bailey's. Evidence was then brought to show that the girls had not been quite as innocent as they claimed but the magistrates decided that the case was of too serious a nature for them to decide at once and committed Bailey for trial allowing her bail of £20 in her own reconnaissance and one surety of £10. It seems that she left the pub almost immediately as Eldridge, Mason & Co. advertised it for rent within weeks but no trace of her trial or its outcome has been discovered so possibly the charges were dropped.

Henry Strange was next having moved from the Turk's Head followed in 1878 by John Downton and his wife Maria. There was a bit of a situation on Bank Holiday Monday in 1883 when George Cooper was summoned for being drunk and disorderly as well refusing to leave the premises. Cooper claimed that he was not drunk but merely playing skittles after work and that the case was brought out of spite – he had served seven years in the Weymouth police force. Fined 10/-.

The Downton family ran the pub until 1931 an impressive 53 years, Maria Downton died at the age of 90 in May of 1941 having been retired for some years, had she lived a few more months she would have seen her beloved pub close its doors in November 1940 after suffering blast damage to the back wall. William John Thomas Chalker was the final landlord from 1932 until it was rendered unsafe by the bombing. It was finally demolished in 1961 to be replaced by the new Town Hall which opened in 1971 to be demolished itself to great acclaim in 2024, and at the time of writing the site is another car park.

THE WHITE HART
High Street (Trinity Street), Weymouth

THE WHITE HART was first mentioned in around 1760 when William Cox is shown as occupying the 'White Hart Alehouse High Street Weymouth' in a list of men eligible to vote and in 1773 a grey gelding is advertised for sale at the inn. From the land tax returns of 1815 to 1829 the property is shown in the ownership of William Bower of the Fordington Brewery and a William Cox is named as occupier of a public house and stables without the house being named until 1830. Cox also appears on the Jury List of 1828 as innkeeper. Bower had large property holdings including many pubs and his estate was put up a for auction upon his death in 1829 further details can be found in the Bear entry. Another name mentioned in 1826 is David Miller. But nothing else has been discovered. The White Hart was demolished in 1834

An undated postcard of the Church of the Holy Trinity

to make way for the new Church of the Holy Trinity and in 1873 the name of the road was changed from High Street to Trinity Street.

THE WHITE HART TAVERN
Lower Bond Street, Melcombe Regis

THE WHITE HART is one of the most ancient of the town's pubs with part of the building possibly as old as the 16th century and thought to have been home to Rear Admiral Sir John Brown in 1617. An interesting letter in the *Dorset County Chronicle* for 30 April 1835 concerning Sandsfoot Castle contains the following, ' … October 14, 1662. Colonel Thomas Heane gave his deposition relative to an affray at Weymouth in the alley of the White Hart Tavern, wherein one of the witnesses called him a traitor and said that a penny halter would serve him'. The letter is signed G.A.E and gives no further information on the matter but must be one of the earliest references to the tavern. A plaque affixed to an outside wall suggests that the artist Sir James Thornhill was born in the building in 1675 but nothing has been found to substantiate this. 1780 is our next reference when the White Hart is advertised to let with 'exceedingly good stall-stables for 28 horses, coach houses et cetera with a pump of good fresh water in the yard'. Enquiries are directed to Delamotte's Circulating Library and a land tax return for 1793 shows a Peter

Delamotte as proprietor of a house occupied by James Cass. Delamotte or De La Motte was a postal agent who built his library with the Assembly Rooms over it on the Esplanade becoming an established artist under the patronage of George III. He moved to Oxford in 1798 and the tax returns show Cass as owner occupier until 1813 when Miss Arbuthnot is shown as the owner and Cass as occupying the stables. In the same year Cass moves to the Crown owned by William Bower who is examined in more detail in the entry on the Bear when the pub is auctioned in 1829. The link between Delamotte/Cass and the White Hart is admittedly rather tenuous and more research needs to be done.

In 1837 the house is in the hands of Solomon Sly who advertised it for rent with a covered a skittle alley and a commodious gin shop attached, 'satisfactory reasons will be given for its disposal and immediate possession may be had'. George Mace takes over and rebuilds the skittle alley as well as refitting the interior celebrating, in September 1841, with a substantial supper for 30 people. Another excellent dinner was provided by Edward Muston when in his role of landlord in 1865 he catered for the 47th annual Friendly Benefit Society and a good percentage of it 90 members. In January of 1875 the owners are Devenish & Co and it seems to have had seven landlords between 1874 and 1881, the advertisement of January 1875 being repeated in May of

The White Hart Tavern 2017

1876. Harvey Read who had run the George Inn at Dorchester for 17 years was reluctantly accepted by the magistrates as he had two small convictions during that time and was to be closely supervised. For whatever reason he was there less than a year before being turfed out and by 1882 William Oliver was landlord with his wife Jane, and seven children. He had been at one time a fish agent to the London and South Western Railway and previously the licensee of the Duke of Albany. He died in 1899.

In the middle of the Great War landlord George North was host to a snooker and billiard tournament promoted by the Wounded Soldiers' Entertainment Fund Committee which raised a total of £50. The fund had benefited 6,500 wounded and distributed over 65,000 cigarettes. This grand old pub continues to serve today and is now owned by Greene King.

THE WHITE HORSE HOTEL
St Mary Street, Melcombe Regis

According to the deeds the White Horse was owned by Thomas Gollop the Younger in 1780 who leased it to David Sherry and his wife Sarah for 50 years at an annual rent of 10/- before selling it to them for £270. An advertisement in the *Sherborne Mercury* for 17 November 1783 reads,

> This is to acquaint the public that the WHITE HORSE in Weymouth and Melcombe Regis Regis is to be SOLD by AUCTION on Tuesday 2nd of December next. The said house is in good repair and full stated. For further particulars apply to Mr Daniel Sherrey at the Black Bear Inn.

There is mention of a William Storey from 1790-93 in the Universal British Directory and by the land tax register of 1827 the house is owned by William Bower land owner and brewer and occupied by James Roberts. In 1829 following the death of Bower the pub was auctioned as part of his estate (see the Bear entry). There is a mention the following year when the house plays host to the 12th annual dinner for supporters of the Poor Man's Friendly Society the host is not named, but was possibly a John Plowman. In 1835 the pub is home to the Weymouth Conservative Association holding its meetings and lectures. Joseph Farwell takes over in 1840 and is pretty soon summoned for selling spirits without a licence along with William Gulliver of the Boot, they were both convicted in the mitigated penalty of £50 for each offence. During January of 1860 George Herridge was summoned for an assault on PC

The White Horse Tavern 2024

MacMahon who had attended the pub 'to ascertain if they were not improper characters there', and received a quart cup on the back of the head for his troubles. Herridge claims that it was thrown over his shoulder by another man and called a key witness to prove the point except that in evidence the witness said that he hadn't got a clue who threw it….Fined 19/8d including costs. Farwell ran the pub until his death in 1872 and in 1880 it passed to Charles Clark formally a 'messman' on HMS *Warrior*, an enlisted man on temporary duty in the sailors' or officers' dining quarters whose duties would be to serve the food and clear the tables. He survived for a couple of years before Devenish put the house up for rent once more. Henry John Northover, a Cornishman who moved from the Somerset Hotel in 1909 and was a committee member of the 'South Dorset Licence Holders Trade and Protection Association and Benevolent Fund'. In 1914 he moved to the Railway Arch Hotel outside of our immediate area. In August of 1919 the White Horse was one of several Devenish pubs who had their landlords returned to them after being away on war service. The White Horse closed in 1974 when it became Foster Brothers the clothiers followed by a health food shop.

THE YACHT INN / RED WHITE AND BLUE
Governor's Lane / Stewards Court Melcombe Regis

IN 1851 AN old terraced house in Governor's Lane was occupied by 31-year-old carpenter James Green, his wife Rebecca and two small children. The first mention of public house on the premises comes when Green is mentioned on a register of voters in 1856. During the census of 1861 he is described as a beer house keeper and his applications for a spirits licence were repeatedly refused despite his having 12 rooms available in the house which was his own property. In his favour it was explained that he was well known as being a steward onboard one of the Portland steamers and in that capacity had supplied liquors for many years but his case was not helped by a conviction for selling out of hours. Documents show that he had worked on-board the steamer *Premier* during the 1860s classed as an able seaman, possibly the ships carpenter. Green had an altercation with a PC Apsey during 1863 when the officer turned up after 11 o'clock and demanded that the house be cleared Green said that he would see him damned first and that there was no beer being served, he had just come back from fishing and the people there were too inspect his catch. As there was no evidence of any beer having been served and the house had always

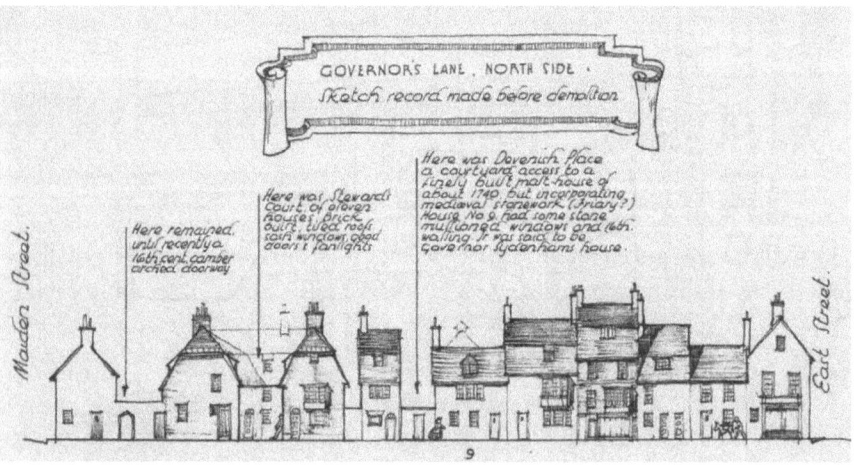

Governor's Lane by Eric Ricketts sketched before demolition

been orderly the magistrates dismissed the case but advised him to 'act more courteously towards the police when in execution of their duty'.

Green retired from the pub shortly after the census of 1871 but retained ownership renting it to a William Vallance who changed its rather bizarre name to The Yacht. Green must have sold the freehold as in March 1883 Devenish & Co advertised the 'fully licensed public house to let 'following the death of the landlord. Landlady, Mrs Williams, was found to be in possession of smuggled tobacco to the value of £1 and knowingly concerned in the evasion of custom duties; she was fined £3/5/-. In February 1884 the Yacht was subject to a raid by an inspector looking for illegal weights and measures during which many unstamped cups were taken away and landlord Samuel Stoodly appeared in court along with nine others. In the end they were all dismissed with a caution and more complete account is included in the Royal Oak entry.

Part of the north side of Governor's Lane (Weymouth Museum)

By March 1903 it was all over. A police report to the magistrates described the premises as 'fully licensed paying a rent of £20 per year, there are five rooms for the public but no stabling and the sanitary arrangements were unsatisfactory consisting of a kind of cupboard, the door of which opened directly into the living room, (at this point the magistrate's clerk remarked that 'instead of finding cups and saucers you find a lavatory! which provoked some laughter), the jug and bottle entrance was inadequate consisting of a trapdoor, and there was no back entrance. The pub was occupied by Frank Dunster, his wife, and one child.' The magistrates ordered the pub to be closed forthwith. Six others, the Shipwrights Arms, the Steam Packet Inn, the Three Tuns, the Baltic the Porter's Arms and the Royal Hotel Tap were given until the following October with exception of the Royal Tap which was also ordered to close immediately. In the 1950s the whole of the north side of the street was demolished for a car park.

Taken shortly before demolition, the photograph shows the 16th century camber arched doorway mentioned by Eric Ricketts in his book, *The Buildings of Old Weymouth* (Part Two). In which case, following his sketch above, the Yacht is possibly the boarded-up building to the right with a glimpse of Stewards Court to its right.

BOOKS

Attwooll, M. *The Bumper Book of Weymouth* Halsgrove 2006
Attwooll, M. *The Second Bumper Book of Weymouth* Dorset Books 2009
Attwooll/Pomeroy *Weymouth Century* Dorset Books 2003
Attwooll/West *Weymouth an Illustrated History* Dovecote Press 1995
Musk, J. *Lesser Known Weymouth* Roving Press 2012
New Weymouth Guide *List of lodging Houses* 1797 Google
Pritchard & Hutchings *Images of England. Weymouth & Portland.* Tempus 2004.
Ricketts, Eric *The Buildings of Old Weymouth Part One. Wyke Regis to South Harbourside 1975*
Ricketts, Eric *The Buildings of Old Weymouth Part Two. Melcombe Regis and Westham 1976*
Urquhart, H. *Weymouth Pub Guide* Weyprint 2012

USEFUL CONTACTS

Campaign for Real Ale West Dorset
Secretary Tony Egerton agegerton@aol.com

Dorset History Centre (Dorset Council)
archives@dorsetcouncil.gov.uk

National Library of Scotland for maps
maps@nls.uk

Somerset and Dorset Family History Society
contact@sdfhs.org

Weymouth Museum
www.weymouthmuseum.org.uk

Dorset Echo
diarmuid.macdonagh@dorsetecho.co.uk

Weymouth Library
weymouthlibrary@dorsetcouncil.gov.uk

Find My Past
findmypast.co.uk

Ancestry
ancestry.co.uk

INDEX OF PEOPLE, PLACES AND PUBS

Abbey, Henry: 140
Abbott, Job: 227, 228, 236
Acock, Charles: 83
Adams, Henry & Elizabeth: 227
Adams, Philip: 115
Albert Hotel, King Street, Melcombe Regis: 1, 2, 190
Albion Inn, Commercial Road, Melcombe Regis: 6-9
Albion Inn, Franchise Street, Weymouth: 9–11, 54, 154, 223, 246
Albion Inn, St Thomas Street, Melcombe Regis: 4-6
Alford, John: 240
Anchor Beer House, St Mary Street, Melcombe Regis: 12-15, 16, 162, 180
Antelope Hotel, Dorchester: 44, 45, 116, 209, 211
Antelope Inn, St Mary Street, Melcombe Regis: 14, 15-17, 116, 135
Apsey, police constable: 264
Arburry, John: 251
Arbuthnot, Elizabeth Long: 129, 261
Arbuthnot, John: 32
Arnold, Richard & Margaret: 20
Arthur, Pierse: 44
Attwool, Richard: 201
Austin, George: 189
Austin, Kenneth Owen: 146
Austin, Robert William: 232
Austwick, Mrs: 215

Babbidge, Gregory: 115
Bagg, Elizabeth: 53, 54-55
Bagg, Herbert: 55
Bagg, William James: 53, 145
Baggs, John & Martha: 155
Baggs, Leah Stone: 158
Baggs, Martha: 144, 145
Baggs, Nicholas George & Alice 231

Bailey, Martha: 258
Bailey, William: 116
Baker, Revd: 90
Baltic Inn, Park Street, Melcombe Regis: 17-19, 79, 158, 183, 187, 223, 232, 239, 266
Banks, Henry William, 122
Bartlett, police constable: 40
Barnes, Susan: 236
Bartlett, James & Mary: 130
Bartlett, Levi: 127, 164
Bascombe, Maria: 14
Batida Bar, see Albion Street, Thomas Street.
Baugh, John & Louisa: 108
Baugh, Thomas & Sarah: 140
Baxter, Robert: 138
Bazzell, George: 24
Bear Hotel, St Mary Street, Melcombe Regis: 20-23, 35, 68, 72, 78, 133, 146, 220, 262
Beard, Edward: 20
Belvedere Inn, High West Street, Weymouth: 1, 23-25, 254
Benjafield, Charles: 117
Bennett, Thomas: 68, 75
Bennett, William & Elizabeth: 55
Besant, William: 126
Bevar, John: 113
Binns, John & Elizabeth: 25
Bird in Hand, St Nicholas Street, Melcombe Regis: 25-28, 78, 215
Bishop, John JP & Emily: 204
Black Dog, St Mary Street, Melcombe Regis: 28-33, 74, 130
Blackburn, Joseph & Mary: 6
Bleathman, John Spencer & Henrietta: 222, 223
Board, George: 190
Board, James White: 8, 80, 123
Board, Joel & Grace: 138
Board, Thomas & Maria: 201
Bond, Susanna: 20

INDEX

269

Bonella, Thomas & Maria: 99-102, 257
Boot Inn, High Street, Weymouth: 22, 34-38, 63, 40, 262
Bower, Thomas Bowyer: 60
Bower, William: 22, 35, 68, 171, 172, 259, 261, 262
Bowes, Nelson: 70
Bowles, Jane & Harriet: 143
Bradshaw, Catherine & George: 97
Brake, family: 145
Bray, Elizabeth: 64
Brennan, Thomas: 240, 241
Bridge Inn, St Thomas Street, Melcombe Regis: 38-40, 103, 180
Bridport Arms, see Duke of Edinburgh.
Brig Inn, High Street, Weymouth: 40-42
Brine, George, police sergeant: 167-168, 182
Brinsley, Robert, Jane, Elizabeth: 124, 167
British Queen, see The Forester's Arms.
Brownlow Tavern, Ranelagh Road, Melcombe Regis: 42-44, 253, 255
Brown, Stephen 198
Brunell, Theodore: 79, 80
Buckell, Aaron Charles & Mary: 204
Buckland, Charles & Eliza: 49
Buckland, Robert & Honor: 238
Bugler, Reginald: 81
Bugler, Robert Francis & Elizabeth: 36
Bunyer, FW & Sarah: 139
Burch, George W: 78
Burdon Hotel, Victoria Terrace Melcombe Regis: 44-46
Burdon Hotel Tap, Victoria Street, Melcombe Regis: 46-47
Burdon, William Wharton: 44
Burgess, James: 42
Burnaby, Margaret: 45-46
Burnell, Martin: 128
Burt, James: 126
Bush, John: 86
Butchers Arms, West Street, Melcombe Regis: 48-49
Butt, Captain Charles: 172
Butt, George: 52, 101
Buxton, Thomas MP: 68, 116, 141

Caddee, John: 21
Caddy, John: 96
Caines, Frederick & Frances: 53
Calcon, Christopher: 200

Canning/Caning, John: 205
Canteen see The Nothe.
Card, Fred: 91
Carter, Henry: 47
Carter, Robert: 12, 16
Carter, Sophia: 162
Carter, Susanna Bayly: 211
Carter, Thomas & Sarah: 248
Case, John & Fanny: 73
Cass, James & Elizabeth: 22, 68, 261
Castle Inn, Horsford Street, Weymouth: 51-53, 194
Caundle, John: 22, 220
Chaddock, Richard & Mary Jane: 219
Chalker, George & Annie: 244
Chalker, James: 251
Chalker, William John Thomas: 259
Chalker, William: 79
Chandler, Mr G: 80
Chapelhay Tavern, Franchise Street, Weymouth: 10, 36, 53-55, 103, 119, 154, 202, 206, 216, 222, 244
Chapman, Jeremiah: 73
Chelmsford House, Hardwick Street, Melcombe Regis: 55-56, 253
Chiles, John & Margaret: 29-30
Chrisp, James Henry: 221
Chubb, Richard & Elizabeth: 152-153
Chutter, James: 189
Cider Press/House, see Albion Inn.
Clapp, Ernest: 27, 118, 143
Clapp, John: 17
Clark, Charles: 263
Clark, John & Elizabeth: 8
Clark, Richard: 71
Clark, Sarah: 141
Clifton Hotel, Queen Street, Melcombe Regis: 56-59, 78, 96, 113, 220, 234, 250
Coal Hole, South Parade, Quay, Melcombe Regis: 59-60
Cockrel, 32
Coleman, Henry: 64, 78, 190
Coleman, William: 65
Collingwood, James & Susan: 205
Collins, Edward & Mabel: 84-85
Collins, John & Maria: 46-47
Collinson, George: 140
Commins, Walter: 69
Cook, Henry & Sarah: 191, 192
Cook, Kingman & Mary: 152, 251

Coombs, Alfred & Beatrice: 190
Coombs, James: 90, 205
Cooper, George 259
Cooper, John: 87, 88, 90
Cooper, police constable: 94
Cooper's Arms, Maiden Street, Melcombe Regis: 60-63
Cornopean Inn, St Leonard's Road, Weymouth: 54, 63-64, 246
Cosens, Captain Joseph: 164
Courtney, William: 29
Cove Inn, Cove Row, Weymouth: 64-66
Cox, Edith: 27
Cox, Edward & Grace: 61
Cox, William: 259
Cozens, Captain: 27
Crickmay, & Co: 23, 49, 93, 124, 169, 172, 176, 182, 193, 228, 234, 250
Crickmore, Henry & Evelyn: 166
Crocker, Charles & Mary: 187
Croom, Henry & Eleanor: 49
Cross Keys, see Jersey Tavern.
Cross, George: 221
Crown Hotel, St Thomas Street, Melcombe Regis: 22, 25, 27, 66-71, 190
Crown Tap, see Bird in Hand.
Curtis, Henry: 18, 19
Curtis, Horace: 37
Curtis, Joseph: 25
Curtis, police constable: 149
Cutter Inn, St Alban's Street, Melcombe Regis: 71-74, 155, 250

Daniels, John, police sergeant: 157
Darley, Benjamin: 18
Davidge, Uriah & Emily: 196, 223
Davies, William Charles & Harriet: 118, 254
Davis, George: 107, 160
Dean, Jeremiah: 91
Defoe, Daniel: 20, 31
Delament, police constable: 169
Delamotte, Thomas: 171, 261
Denning, Charles & Annie: 11, 154
Devenish, & Co. family: 9, 23, 27, 28, 36, 37, 64, 71, 73, 76, 90, 93, 99, 101, 102, 107, 110, 115, 119, 122, 139, 146, 151, 152, 155, 163, 172, 173, 178, 185, 196, 212, 216, 223, 225, 226, 229, 238, 245, 246, 261, 263, 264
Dibben, Henry: 83, 189

Dicker, William: 114
Dober, Daniel & Susan: 144, 180, 182
Dodson, Philip: 44
Dolphin Inn, Park Street, Melcombe Regis: 1, 74-76, 195, 205
Dominy, Eva & Vere: 33
Dove Alehouse, see Black Dog. 18, 31
Downie, Thomas & Mary: 200
Downing, John: 27
Downing, Mr: 124
Downton, John & Maria: 259
Dredge, William & Beatrice: 230
Drew, Joseph: 248
Drew, Mark & Maria: 174
Dring, Charles John: 73, 250
Duchscherer, Joseph: 231
Duke of Albany, Park Street, Melcombe Regis: 76-78, 102, 196, 262
Duke of Cornwall, St Edmund Street, Melcombe Regis: 78-82
Duke of Cumberland, see Duke of Cornwall.
Duke of Edinburgh, St Thomas Street, Melcombe Regis: 82-83
Dumont, Philip: 144
Dunford, Charles Edward: 147, 148
Dunn, Edwin: 69, 96, 224, 248-249
Dunn, Mary: 118, 250
Dunster, Frank: 266
Durling, George: 39
Dyer, John: 136, 171
Dyer, Munday & Jane: 171
Dyer, William & Jane: 136

Eagle Tavern, Lower Bond Street, Melcombe Regis: 84-86
Eagle Tavern, Weymouth: 86-87
Edward Hotel, see Marine Hotel.
Edwards, family: 126, 203
Eldridge Pope, Brewers: 11, 38, 50, 54, 126, 128, 136, 138, 147, 148, 175, 177, 179, 180, 182, 189, 193, 198, 244, 246, 255
Elmes, John & Jane: 187, 228
England, Edwin Taylor: 91
Ewings, John & Margaret: 127

Farthing, Joseph & Sarah: 155
Farwell, Joseph: 50, 162
Felton, Robert: 117, 118
Ferry, James & Sarah: 218
Field, Thomas: 237

INDEX 271

Finns see Prince Albert.
Fisherman's Arms, High Street, Weymouth: 87-90, 185
Fitch, Walter Alfred: 82
Flack, William: 209
Flew, Robert: 183
Flood, Samuel & Mary: 136-137, 138
Flower, James: 254
Foot, Henry: 227, 228
Foot, Robert & Selina: 255
Foot, Sydney Cornelius: 197
Foot, Thomas: 195
Ford, Rob: 78
Forester's Arms, Great George Street, Melcombe Regis: 90-91
Forester's Retreat, St Thomas Street, Melcombe Regis: 91-92
Forse, George Cox & Mary Ann: 118, 119, 120, 207
Forsey, Mrs: 84
Fountain Hotel, King Street, Melcombe Regis: 58, 93-96, 121, 131, 220, 229, 234, 250
Fowler, Elizabeth: 35
Fowler, R: 35
Fowler, Simon: 214
Fowler, William: 71, 214
Fox, St Nicholas Street, Melcombe Regis: 23, 96-99, 107, 119, 138
Frampton, Cyril Horace: 43
Frampton, George Henry: 221
Frampton, William & Sarah: 177, 178
Freemason's Arms, High Street, Weymouth: 99-102, 257
Frickus, Sarah: 88, 89
Friendship Inn, Park Street, Weymouth: 102-103
Frost, Albert: 81
Frost, George: 69
Fudge, Ruben & Mary: 120
Fulljames, James & Mary: 102, 208, 218
Fuszard, Stephen: 41
Fuszard, William: 158

Gandy, George: 236
Gardener, Thomas: 106
Gardener's Arms, see The Castle Inn.
Garnet, Family: 130
Gaulton, Richard: 136
Gear, Emanuel & Leanora: 186

Gear, Thomas: 129
General Gordon, Franchise Street, Weymouth: 103-105, 246
George Inn, Custom House Quay, Melcombe Regis: 105-108, 215
Gibbs, Thomas & Mary Ann: 86
Giear, Thomas, MP: 169
Gillies, Hector: 65, 66
Gillingham, John: 203, 254
Gillingham, William & Eliza: 8
Glanville, Frederick: 73
Glasson, John Richard & Mary: 148-149
Globe Inn, East Street, Melcombe Regis: 22, 60, 107, 108-111, 147, 172, 193, 234
Gloucester Hotel, Gloucester Row, Melcombe Regis: 58, 82, 111-115, 212, 219, 240
Goergslenner, 'Dr': 67
Goff, Mr, 28
Golden Eagle, see Eagle Tavern Melcombe Regis.
Golden Lion, St Edmund Street, Melcombe Regis: 115-118, 130, 135, 141, 143, 145
Good, Thomas: 170
Goodwin, Christopher & Sarah: 82
Goodwin, William Charles: 28
Gough, Henry & Elizabeth: 177
Granville, Henry: 48-49
Green, James & Rebecca: 264-265
Grey, Robert & Virtue: 53
Greyhound, St Nicholas Street, Melcombe Regis: 119-120
Griffin, Robert Henry & Sarah: 193
Groves, John & brewers: 42, 49, 53, 56, 58, 84, 103, 120, 123, 143, 154, 155, 157, 160, 164, 199, 202, 216, 242, 246, 255
Groves, William & Mary: 113, 234
Gulliver, George & Ann: 35, 36, 262
Guy, Andrew: 144

Half Moon, King Street, Melcombe Regis: 1, 93, 120-122, 127, 131, 232
Hambro, Charles: 25
Hamlin, Mrs: 37, 78
Hancock, John: 144
Hanks, Helen: 244
Hann, Thomas & Sarah: 126
Harding, Charles & Edith: 5
Hardy, Clifford 229
Hardy, Edward & Percy: 96

Hardy, John: 105
Hardy, Richard & Jane: 93-95, 99
Hardy, William: 213, 236
Hargreaves, George: 27
Hart, William Mattias & Mary: 164, 166, 172
Hartnell, James: 200
Harvell, George: 242
Harvey, policeman: 57, 195
Hatchard, Mary: 23
Hatton, James: 21, 196, 232
Hawkins, John Otter: 66
Hawkins, Philip: 175
Hawkins, Richard: 31-32
Haylock, Lieut John Mozart: 152
Haylor, Mary: 97
Hayman, Henry (Harry) & Mary: 38, 97, 98, 105, 107
Head, police constable: 256
Hedges, George & Mary: 173, 174
Hemmings, Charles: 21
Hendy, James Richardson: 120
Henning, Edmund: 141
Henning, J: 112
Herbert, Graham: 76
Hewlett, George & Elizabeth: 1
Hewlett, Thomas: 99
Hibbs, Jeremiah: 24, 86, 94, 249
Hide, Joshua: 116, 135
Hide, Thomas: 20
High West Street Tavern, High Street West, Weymouth: 66, 123- 124
Hill, William & James: 40, 161
Hillier, Ruben: 82
Hine, Ann: 144
Hines, Alfred & William: 98, 107, 110, 111, 216
Hiscocks, Charles: 118
Hitt, sisters: 95
Hodder, William & Elizabeth: 186
Hodger, George: 88
Hole, Thomas: 70
Holland, Charles: 216-217
Holloway, Alfred John: 147
Holloway, James & Eleanor: 152
Holt, Walter: 173, 225, 226
Honeyborne, George: 222
Honeyborne, Levi & Ann: 61, 243
Honnor, Beatrice: 161
Honywood, Lady: 114

Hope Tavern, Hope Street, Weymouth: 124-126
Hoskins, John Hearn: 206-207
Hounsell, George: 203
Hounsell, Joseph & Emma: 40, 176
Howard, Joseph: 175
Howard, Thomas: 155
Hughes, Charles & Agnes: 236
Hugo, Baptiste: 140
Hunt, Arthur Richard: 82
Hunter, Thomas & Mary Ann: 124
Hurdle, William: 185

Ireland, Jane & Benjamin: 88, 185
Iveney, William: 116

James, Edmund: 244
Jeanes, John & Harriet: 26, 27, 162
Jefferies, John: 1, 3
Jefferies, Mary: 3
Jenkins, Simon: 35
Jersey Hotel, St Thomas Street, Melcombe Regis: 126-128, 136
Johnson, Captain WH: 140
Johnstone, Sir Frederick: 25, 51, 136, 175, 185
Jolliffe, Charles: 226
Jolliffe, Robert & Alice: 85, 86
Jolliffe, William: 146
Jolly Sailor, see Friendship Inn.
Jones, Charles: 117, 140
Jones, John & Charlotte: 187
Jordan, Richard: 11

Keeley, Ellen: 110, 234
Keeley, Joseph: 111, 122, 232
Keeley, Thomas: 110
Kellaway, Thomas: 122, 232
Kenton, Elizabeth: 197
Kerridge, Benjamin: 108
Kerridge, Hannah: 108
Kerridge, James: 110
King, Leslie: 71
King, William & Susan: 251
King's Arms, Trinity Road, Weymouth: 129-130
King's Head Hotel, Maiden Street, Melcombe Regis: 21, 133-136
King's Head Inn, East Street, Melcombe Regis: 130-133, 144, 247, 248

INDEX

Kingdon, Billy: 96
Kirby, James & Cecilia: 240
Kirkaldie, William & Alice: 76
Knaresborough, John: 108, 172
Knight, Frederick: 128
Knight, Mrs: 121
Knight, Robert: 133

Laker, RS: 82
Lamb & Flag, Lower Bond Street, Melcombe Regis: 136-138
Lambourne, Charles: 58, 122, 256
Lane, Edward: 56
Lane, John: 65
Lang, Henry & Martha: 136, 238
Langford, Edward & Elizabeth: 158
Langrish, Joseph: 105
Larkham, Benjamin Case: 184
Lawrence, Albert & Ada: 19
Le Warne, Thomas Prist: 58, 187, 213
LeCoq, Peter: 105
Legg, Alfred: 85
Lewis, Nathanial: 129
Lidbury, Police Superintendent: 3, 13, 16, 45, 162, 168, 185
Loats, John: 67
Lodder, William: 171
London Hotel, Upper Bond Street, Melcombe Regis: 127, 138-141
Long, William: 146
Longman, John: 33
Longman, Thomas: 152
Loveday, Sydney: 128
Lovelace, William: 57, 229
Loveridge, Robert: 219, 256-257
Lucas, Sidney Charles: 221
Luce, Dennis: 150
Luce, JB: 141
Luce, Thomas Dorney: 134, 248
Luce's Hotel, see Victoria Hotel, Melcombe Regis.
Luckham, Quartermaster RH: 70
Lumley, William: 104

Mabb, William Russell & Elizabeth: 10
Mabb's Hotel, see Albion, Franchise Street, Weymouth.
Mabey, Joseph, John: 164, 173
Mace, Edward: 129
Mace, George: 261

Mackay, Corporal John: 21
MacMahon. police constable: 263
Maidment, Joseph: 209
Male, George: 144
Mann, Lieut Commander Fred: 59
Mansell, John: 108
Marine Hotel, Bank Buildings, Esplanade, Melcombe Regis: 118, 141-144
Market House Inn, St Edmund Street, Melcombe Regis: 144-146, 180
Market House Tavern, Maiden Street, Melcombe Regis: 110, 146-148
Martin, Edward: 71
Martin, Samuel: 108
Marwood, William: 39
Mason's Arms, St Alban's Row, Melcombe Regis: 148-151
Masters, Charles: 110, 147
Mathews, Thomas & Sarah: 51
Mathion, Jean: 106
Matthews, Cyril: 205
McBean, James: 147
McCabe, Luke & Eliza: 41, 42
McMahon, police constable: 182
Meade, Arthur Tom: 42
Meakin, Joe & Nina: 138
Meech, Mr: 49
Meech, police constable: 216
Merriman, Hugh: 98
Mico, Sir Samuel: 105, 107
Middleton, Albert: 58, 113, 114
Middleton, Lillian May: 114
Military Arms, Barrack Lane, Weymouth: 150-152, 152
Milledge, George & Grace: 61, 62
Mills, John: 31, 32
Milton Arms, St Alban's Row, Melcombe Regis: 11, 152-155, 251
Mitchell, John & Harriet: 238
Mitchell, police constable: 35, 100, 222
Mitchell, Thomas & Jane: 32
Moody, William: 169
Moore, Moses: 111
Moore, Samuel: 184
Moors, George & Sarah: 195
Morris, Inspector Charles: 12, 50
Morris, John & Mary: 66
Mouat, Mary: 71
Munden, George: 32
Murray, Francis: 216

Muston, Edward: 261

Nag's Head, New Street, Melcombe Regis: 155-158, 215
Neale, Alfred: 82, 204
Nelson Inn, North Quay, Weymouth: 156-158, 158
Netherbury Arms, see Belvedere.
New Arrival Inn, see Duke of Albany.
New Bridge Hotel, Little George Street, Melcombe Regis: 158-160, 225
New Cooper's Arms, Maiden Street, Melcombe Regis: 160-161
New Inn, High Street, Weymouth: 14, 27, 119, 156, 162-163
New Music Hall Tavern, St Nicholas Street, Melcombe Regis: 163-164
New Rooms Inn, Cove Row, Weymouth: 164-166, 170
Newbolt, Thomas: 176, 232
Newman, Edward & Jane: 201
Newman, J: 15
Newman, Sarah Ann: 163
Newman, Thomas: 101
Newman, Vincent: 139
Newton, Mary: 35
Nicholls, John: 144
Norris, William: 235
North, George: 262
Northam, Walter: 11
Northover, Charles: 179, 180
Nothe Inn, Barrack Lane, Weymouth: 66, 138, 166-169, 182, 232, 244
Nunn, Robert Joseph Bascombe: 198

Old Bridge Inn, see Bridge Inn.
Old Rooms Inn, Cove Row, Weymouth: 22, 108, 164, 169-173
Oliver, William & Jane: 76, 195, 196, 262
Onslow, John Williams: 67
Orange Bar, see Albion, St Thomas Street.
Orchard, Ambrose Charles: 77, 78, 230
Osmonde, Ernest: 18

Palmer, John: 147, 236
Palmer, Thomas: 56
Palmer, William: 73
Park Estate Inn, Lennox Street, Melcombe Regis: 173-175, 185
Park Hotel, Grange Road, Melcombe Regis: 175-177
Parker, George: 14, 162
Parker, Harriet, Edward: 12
Parker, Robert & Sophia: 180
Parker, Thomas: 35, 119
Parkman, George William: 110
Parkman, Robert: 36
Parsons, John: 15
Pashen, George Albert & Amy: 188
Paul, Walter George: 250
Pavey, Charles Lanning: 206
Payne, Charles: 160
Payne, William: 71
Pearse, George: 53
Penny, James: 254
Penny, Taver: 33, 130
Perks, John & Frances: 125
Petty, James: 96
Phillips, John & Elizabeth: 79
Phillips, John Drew & Charlotte: 255
Phoenix Hotel, Great George Street, Melcombe Regis: 78, 177-178
Pitman, Joseph: 238
Pitman, William: 178, 238
Plume of Feathers, Little George Street, Melcombe Regis: 178-180
Pollard, Mary: 102
Porters' Arms, St Mary Street, Melcombe Regis: 12, 15, 19, 144, 180-183, 188, 223, 232, 266, 239
Portland Arms, Maiden Street, Melcombe Regis: 88, 124, 145, 173, 183-185
Portland Railway Hotel, Commercial Road, Melcombe Regis: 82, 186-187, 206, 221
Pothecary, John & Mary: 116, 207
Pouney, Robert: 63
Powell, PC: 3
Prankard, James: 257
Prankard, John: 100, 258
Prankard, Samuel: 99
Preedy, Thomas & Eliza: 229
Pride, William: 244
Prince Albert/ Finns, Great Little George Street, Melcombe Regis: 58, 178, 180, 187-189
Prince of Wales Tavern, Park Street Melcombe Regis: 189-190, 197, 230
Prior, police constable: 206
Prodger, David & Elizabeth: 215
Pruden, William Robert: 58, 118

INDEX

Puckett, James: 120
Puckett, John: 141
Puckett, William: 150

Queen's Hotel, King Street, Melcombe Regis: 2, 3, 190-193

Rabjohns, Simon John & Ann: 76
Railway Dock Hotel, Rodwell Avenue, Weymouth: 53
Railway Hotel, Park Street, Melcombe Regis: 193-195
Railway Tavern, Commercial Road, Melcombe Regis see Clifton Hotel
Randall, William and Jemima: 120
Randbury, Jack: 105
Ranelagh Hotel, Ranelagh Road, Melcombe Regis: 56, 198-200, 253
Rashleigh, George: 14-15, 16
Rashleigh, William: 39
Read, George: 138
Read, Harriet: 53
Read, Harvey: 262
Red Lion, Hope Street, Weymouth: 200-201
Red, White & Blue. see Yacht Inn.
Rendall, Thomas: 244
Rest & Welcome, Boot Lane, Weymouth: 201-202
Rex, Charles: 36
Rex, Mark & Mary: 130
Rex, William & Sarah: 130
Reynolds & Heathorn, Brewers: 58, 235
Reynolds, Bill & Lil: 66
Reynolds, John: 31, 32
Reynolds, William: 91
Richardson, police constable: 146
Ricketts, Emmanuel & Hester: 76
Ricketts, Eric: 115, 138, 253, 264, 266
Riggs, Henry: 60
Rising Sun Inn, Prospect Place, Chapelhay, Weymouth: 198, 202-203
Robbins/Robens, John: 78
Roberts, Eli: 91
Roberts, James: 262
Roberts, Mathew Dix: 82, 186
Roberts, Matthew & Elizabeth: 160
Robinson, Edward: 175
Rodberd, John & Jane: 127
Rodway, Arthur John: 199, 202
Rodwell/Tavern Hotel, Rodwell Road, Weymouth 87, 204-205
Roe, Frank: 74, 133
Rogers, Alfred: 186
Rogers, William James & Elizabeth: 93, 95
Rogers, William Weston: 212
Roll, William: 136
Rolls, Richard: 88, 185
Roman, Nathaniel & Eliza: 68, 69
Roper, Henry John: 158
Rose & Crown, Crescent Street, Melcombe Regis: 169, 205-206
Rowe, J: 69
Rowe, Olive Winifred: 218
Royal Canteen, see Nothe Tavern.
Rupell, Job & Rachel: 235
Russell, George Harry: 25
Russell, Job: 187
Russell, Thomas: 23
Russell, William: 211
Ryall, George & Jane: 240

Sailors Home Inn, Chapelhay Street, Weymouth: 216-218
Sailors Return, St Nicholas Street, Melcombe Regis: 28, 32, 58, 96, 215, 218-220, 234, 250
Sampson, Catherine: 113
Samways, William: 235
Sandbrook, Laban: 155
Sansom, James & Sarah: 15
Sargeant, Job: 32
Saxon, Robert: 115
Scattergood, Mr: 98
Scott, Arthur: 159
Scott, George Pearce & Mary: 116
Scott, Samuel & Ann: 87
Scriven, Samuel: 247
Scriven, T: 242
Scudamore, Jane: 45-46
Seaford, George: 194
Sealey, William & Elizabeth: 216
Seaman, George & Sarah: 17, 18
Seeley, Alfred & Mary: 256
Sequah see Osmonde, Ernest.
Seward, George: 91
Sharpe, Alexander Miller: 163
Sheppard, James Lidford: 150, 169, 205
Sherry, David & Sarah: 262
Sherry, Thomas & Mary: 62, 150
Ship Inn, Maiden Street, Melcombe Regis:

215, 220-222
Shipwright's Arms, Salem Place, Weymouth: 222-224, 232: 239, 266
Short, Job & Charlotte: 101
Shrivell, Captain Harry: 58
Siddons, William: 164
Sims, Abia: 151
Skinner, Revd John: 135, 171
Sleep, William: 63
Sly, Edward & Fanny: 104
Sly, James & Harriet, 72
Sly, Solomon & Elizabeth: 93, 120, 121, 131-133, 214, 261
Sly, William & Betsy: 135, 183
Smedley, Frederick & Matilda: 4
Smetham, Edward: 62
Smith, Elizabeth & Joseph: 27
Smith, Frederick Shefton: 46
Smith, George: 74-75, 254
Somerset Hotel, King Street, Melcombe Regis: 57, 159, 224-225, 263
Soper, John: 136, 213
Spencer, Sarah: 97
Spicer, Stephen: 116
Spranklin, Sarah: 75, 85
Spring, Francis: 127, 128
Spring, John: 138
Sproule, Andrew: 108
Sprucer, Fanny: 39
Stacie's Hotel, see Royal Hotel.
Stag Inn, Lennox Street, Melcombe Regis: 225-227
Stagg, William: 56, 163, 173
Stains, James & Eliza: 102
Stanbury, Elizabeth: 69
Staneway, John & Edith: 66
Star & Garter Hotel, Crescent Street, Melcombe Regis: 147, 227-228
Star Inn, Hartford Terrace, Park Street, Melcombe Regis: 93, 187, 228-230
Steam Packet Inn, Custom House Quay, Melcombe Regis: 230-232
Sterling, Francis: 11
Stevens, Thomas: 173
Stickey, PS: 74
Stockting, Sydney Tivitoe: 254
Stokes, Sydney: 36, 37
Stone, Charles & Charlotte: 189
Stone, Dominic & Fanny: 69
Stone, Maria: 41

Stoodley, Samuel: 265
Stote, William & Harriet: 22, 23, 71, 72
Strachen, Hannah: 110
Strange, Henry & Victoria: 59, 169, 244, 259
Strickland, James: 39
Stroud, Margaret: 198
Styles, William: 246
Summerfield, Frank: 103
Summers, Felix: 89, 176
Sun Inn, King Street, Melcombe Regis: 23, 120, 122, 196, 220, 232-234
Sutton, Richard Joseph: 28
Swan Inn, St Thomas Street, Melcombe Regis: 234-235
Sweetman, Matt: 20
Sydenham, Colonel William: 29, 34
Sykes, Major: 55, 198
Symes, GP: 69
Symes, James: 118
Symonds, William, Alice & Annie: 8, 9

Talbot, Charles & Marianne: 39, 88-89, 185
Talbot, James: 105, 178
Talbot, Thomas: 39
Taylor, Frederick: 122
Taylor, George Henry: 190, 244
Taylor, James & Charlotte: 155, 251
Taylor, William Dunn & Margaret: 6, 8
Terminus, Queen Street, Melcombe Regis: 236-238
Thomas, John: 126
Thorne, William: 245
Three Tuns, Maiden Street, Melcombe Regis: 22, 238-240
Thunder, Jumpin' Jimmy: 86
Tivoli Gardens Inn, Franchise Street, Weymouth: 54, 240-242
Tizard, James: 120, 230
Tizard, John: 86, 87, 189
Tizard, William: 21
Tomkins, John & Mary: 245
Tomkins, William & Elizabeth: 63
Tompkins, Charles: 128
Tooth, John: 53
Tredrea, Richard William Morgan & Sarah: 239
Trevor, John & Gladys: 227
Tuggey, Richard & Sarah: 203
Turk's Head, East Street, Melcombe Regis:

INDEX

78, 230, 242-244, 259
Turnbull, George: 178

Underwood, James: 195
Union Arms Inn, St Leonard's Road, Weymouth: 244-247

Vallance, Thomas: 11, 89, 222
Vallance, William: 265
Vickery, Police Superintendent: 8, 27, 56, 120
Victor Emmanuel: 119
Victoria Hotel, Augusta Place, Esplanade, Melcombe Regis: 58, 69, 73, 94, 96, 155, 221, 224, 247-250
Victoria Tap, New Street Melcombe Regis: 22, 152, 251
Vinnicombe, Thomas Hodges & Lizzie: 212
Vosper, Daniel: 157
Voss, George & Mary: 118, 141
Voss, Matthew: 105

Wadsworth, George: 229
Wareham, James & Marina: 160
Wareham, Simon: 53
Warland, James & Annie: 160
Warry, Ann: 51
Warry, Mr: 15
Waterloo Stores, William Street, Melcombe Regis: 42, 252-254
Welcome Home, St Nicholas Street, Melcombe Regis: 42, 254-255
Wellington Arms, St Alban Street, Melcombe Regis: 219, 255-257
Wells, Alfred: 50
Wells, John & Elizabeth: 25
Weymouth Arms, High Street, Weymouth: 99, 156, 162, 257-259
Whaley, Albert: 144
Whetton, Catherine: 26
Whicker, William: 155, 184
White Hart High Street, Weymouth: 22, 77, 108, 131, 166, 173, 196, 226, 259-260
White Hart Tavern, Lower Bond Street, Melcombe Regis: 260-262
White Horse Hotel, St Mary Street, Melcombe Regis: 22, 50, 262-264
White, Ada: 58
White, Charles: 224
White, Edward & Louisa: 91
White, Hannah: 159
White, police constable: 33
White, Thomas: 5
White, Wadham & Hilda Elizabeth: 62
White, William: 102, 165, 166
Whitehorn, Martin & Christine: 257
Whittle, James & Hester: 4, 155
Whittle, Thomas: 155
Wildey, Jonathan: 21
Wilkins, John: 111
Wilkins, Sydney: 111
Wilkinson, Charlotte: 68
Williams, James: 23
Williams, John & Mary: 244
Williams, Richard Theophilus: 111
Williams, William: 56
Willis, Bob & Mary: 235
Willis, Hubert, Jane & Elizabeth: 33
Willis, Thomas: 136
Willoughby, Mr: 45, 46
Winsford, Mary: 63
Winsor, John: 53
Winzar, Henry: 124
Woodland, Harriet: 199
Woodland, James: 42
Woodridge, George & Emily: 82
Woods, Frederick: 154
Woodward, Frederick & Rose: 59
Woodward, Henry: 212
Wooton, Sergeant: 100
Wright, Walter: 3, 140
Wright, William: 3

Yacht Inn, Governor's Lane, Melcombe Regis: 19, 183, 232, 264-266
Yates, Joseph: 130
Yearsley, James & Elizabeth: 44, 46
Young, Benjamin: 71